AF662511

Dom Moraes (1938–2004), poet, novelist and columnist, is seen as a foundational figure in Indian English Literature. In 1958, at the age of twenty, he won the prestigious Hawthornden Prize for his first volume of verse, *A Beginning*, going on to publish more than thirty books of prose and poetry, several of which are regarded as modern classics. He was awarded the Sahitya Akademi Award for English in 1994 for his book of poems *Serendip*. He also wrote a large number of film scripts for BBC and ITV, covering various countries in Asia, Latin America and Africa.

Sarayu Srivatsa trained as an architect and city planner at the Madras and Tokyo universities. She was a professor of architecture at Bombay University, the editor of the *Indian Architect and Builder Review*, and has written extensively on the evolution and growth of cities. Her book *Where the Streets Lead*, published in 1997, won the JIIA Award.

Apart from *The Long Strider*, she also co-authored *Out of God's Oven* (shortlisted for the Kiriyama Prize) with Dom Moraes. Her first novel, *The Last Pretence*, was longlisted for the Man Asian Literary Prize, and upon its release in the UK (under the title *If You Look For Me, I am Not Here*), was also included on *The Guardian*'s Not the Booker Prize longlist. Her second novel, *Until Then*, was published in 2022.

Praise for *The Long Strider*

'Coryate's 5,000-mile journey is interesting enough...But it is really the relationship between Moraes and Srivatsa that takes this book to a higher plane...This book, ultimately, is as much a tribute to their indomitable relationship and spirit of literary adventure as it is to the man they set out to write about.'

—*India Today*

'Their [Dom and Sarayu's] individual flourishes, distinct yet in tandem, make...[*The Long Strider*] a noteworthy *jugalbandi* between a biographer and a diarist. And it earns for Coryate those five minutes of posthumous fame that this land denied him in his lifetime.'

—*The Tribune*

'Dom Moraes and Sarayu Srivatsa have written a book that is, at times, as eccentric and startling as the life story of Tom Coryate. *The Long Strider* is a lively, many-layered tale that turns out to be nearly as much about Dom as it is about its ostensible hero...This is an ambitious exercise, and on the whole they pull it off.'

—*Outlook*

The Long Strider *in* Jehangir's Hindustan

In the Footsteps *of the* Englishman Who Walked *from* England *to* India *in the* Year 1613

DOM MORAES
SARAYU SRIVATSA

SPEAKING TIGER

SPEAKING TIGER BOOKS LLP
125A, Ground Floor, Shahpur Jat,
Near Asiad Village, New Delhi - 110 049

First published in Viking by Penguin Books India 2003
This edition published by Speaking Tiger 2024

Copyright © Sarayu Srivatsa, Literary Executor of the Estate of Dom Moraes 2024

ISBN: 978-93-5447-527-6

10 9 8 7 6 5 4 3 2 1

The moral right of the author has been asserted.

Typeset in Sabon LT Std by Jojy Philip, New Delhi
Printed at Chaman Enterprises, New Delhi

No part of this publication may be reproduced, transmitted, or stored in a retrieval system, in any form or by any means, electronic, mechanical, photocopying, recording or otherwise, without the prior permission of the publisher.

This book is sold subject to the condition that it shall not, by way of trade or otherwise, be lent, resold, hired out, or otherwise circulated, without the publisher's prior consent, in any form of binding or cover other than that in which it is published.

This book is affectionately dedicated to the people of Odcombe

Contents

Preface

I have always had an obsessive desire since I first, as a schoolboy, read about Coryate half a century ago, to know much more about him and to write a book on him. I am very glad that with Sarayu as co-author I have fulfilled two of my last ambitions. I must also thank Juzer Mohammed Husein, researcher and friend, who travelled with us for much of the time.

Though facts exist on the life and exploits of Coryate, there are not many. Nevertheless, every part of the Coryate story as I have written it is based on Coryate's own writing, the memoirs of Roe and Terry, and anecdotes told about him. Allowing for imaginative reconstruction, it is the truest story that can be written about him. Only once have I deliberately strayed from the known facts. Juzer protested that on Coryate's last journey to Surat, Richard Steele and Thomas Herbert, brother of the poet George, escorted the dying traveller. For my own reasons, I have made his friend Edward Terry his only escort.

For essential information and advice, we consulted several scholars who despite the pressure on their time did their best for us and provided us with invaluable material. They have our gratitude.

During our travels, retracing Coryate's journeys in the subcontinent, we often asked ourselves whether the India Coryate encountered was much different from the India that exists today. An acceptance of the caste system and the horrible practice of sati certainly existed then, and were far more pervasive than they are today. Yet we would speculate that the people might have been better then. Today communalism and consumerism affect too much of the population. Coryate met many people, and though some were evil, most were not. This was an interesting idea to explore: a comparison between India then and India now; and it is part of the reason why the book has been written by two different authors about two different areas of history.

—*Dom Moraes*

1

Men, Women and Old Boots

That winter evening, he stood on the warped planks of a quay on the south side of the river. He could hear the heavy water slap and splash, and feel it swell underfoot, as the Thames answered the tide. It was well past six by now, pitch dark, and an arctic wind wailed from the west. He pulled his cloak closer and turned towards the Mermaid, one of the huddle of wooden houses behind him. Scanty fires burnt inside most of them. He smelt meat and fowl at roast, and felt acute hunger.

The ground was uneven and slippery with excrement and rubbish and glittered with the frost that had coated it. But he had always had sure feet. He was proud of how far he could walk, further than other men, and without difficulty where others faltered. The wind made its sound behind and around him, but as he came among the houses he began to hear another wailing, part of the wind and yet separate from it. It mystified him. Like a hound on a trace, he focused all his senses on this broken keening, trying to find its source.

He identified it now as singing, or, at least, as someone trying to sing. The icy wind shredded the words and dispersed them, skewed them this way and that, like the other sodden segments of winter rubbish it picked up and tossed away on its path inland. But still he held to his trace, curious about the singer, to whom he seemed to have come physically closer for he could now decipher some of the words being sung.

> *'O western wind, when wilt thou blow,*
> *Shaking the green leaf from the tree?*
> *O gentle death, when wilt thou come?*
> *For of this life I am weary ...'*

He knew the song, and it surprised him to hear it here. It was a Scots ballad and he could tell from the singer's voice that she was old and of Scots blood. But where she had hidden herself was beyond him. In the wilderness between the fire-lit houses, no human figure stood or moved. His insatiable curiosity made him search harder; once more all his senses were those of a hound work. More words came.

> *'When we rode down by Glasgow town,*
> *We were a comely sight to see ...*
> *My love was clad in the black velvet*
> *And I myself in cramasie.'*

He had been looking for a woman standing or sitting; it had not occurred to him that she might be lying down. She turned out to be what he had taken for a bundle of firewood, huddled in the lee of a house where no fire burned and which was probably empty. The wailed words rose from her sack-like shape and were squirted to him in intermittent spurts by the wind. He squatted beside her, even though she stank.

London itself always stank, even in winter, of putrid foodstuffs, human and animal waste, and unwashed people. The wind at this moment helped to carry the various effluvia away from him. But every stench in the city seemed to be have been concentrated in the gaunt, mare-like body of this woman, swaddled in filthy clothes: ancient residues of piss and puke, spunk, sweat, shit and tears. He did not turn his face away.

'Mistress,' he said, in all courtesy, 'I heard you crying out in distress. How may I help you? My name is Tom Coryate.'

Dimly, he discerned her face, very wrinkled, a face which he could not imagine as having ever been young. Her eyes flickered redly in the dark like the fairy lights on Exmoor, deeply feared by local farmers. She said in very thick Scots, 'I didna ask you what your name is. And I didna call for any man's aid, braw laddie. I were only singing for maself.'

For some reason, he replied in his own Somerset dialect, and said, 'Aye, mother, but tu me thu diddest sound baadly ailing.'

She turned her long, raddled face more fully towards his. He flinched from her breath. Her teeth were as broken and blackened as those of an ancient vixen. But he realized that she was trying to smile at him, and he tried to smile back.

'Ailing I am,' she said, 'and mair than ailing. I'm done, laddie. If ye crave sae much to gie me succour, take me across Thames water, up the top o' the great Tower the bitch Queen buildit, sae I can have a keek at Scotland this one last time.'

Coryate was already cold and hungry, and he now also felt very tired, because he hated to feel helpless. He rose from where he had knelt beside her, and looked down. As she leered up at him, he realized she was still trying to smile and this time the smile was so sardonic he resented it.

'I told you I would try and aid you, mistress,' he said in his court accent, 'but I can see no way.' It was true. He could not possibly take such a person into the Tower of London. He might give her money, but it would not help and in any case he had very little. He might call a priest, but it would take time, and his stomach rumbled for the comfort it would find at the Mermaid, now only twenty minutes of brisk strides away.

'Good luck,' he said, irritated by the situation he had created, and added in what seemed even to him a foolish way, 'But remember, you have my goodwill, and I am Tom Coryate.'

He walked away and heard her call after him, 'Ye didnae ask me whit ma name was, but no matter. Naebody will remember ye any more than they will me, master, once we're both deid.'

Sudden dread came to Coryate, and he quickened his strides towards the Mermaid. But she followed him in the darkness through which he fled her: for she was singing once more.

> *'O wherefore should I cleanse my face*
> *And wherefore should I cambe my hair?*
> *For my true love hath me forsook*
> *And swears he'll never love me mair ...*
> *I set my back against an oak,*
> *Thinking that it was a trusty tree ...*
> *But first it bent and syne it broke ...*
> *Sae my true love hath forsaken me.'*

The thin, woeful effort at song was lost for a minute in the wind and then renewed itself. It was now irritating him and making him guilty, and the words were singularly inappropriate for a woman so hideous and so old.

> *'But had I wist, before I kissed*
> *That love had been so hard to win,*
> *I had locked my heart in a case of gowd*

And pinned it up with a siller pin ...
And O, that my young babe were born
And set upon the nurse's knee
And I mysen were deid and gone
Wi' the green grass growin over me.'

When he entered the Mermaid, Coryate felt frightened and unclean, as though he had not simply talked to the dying Scots whore but had cohabited with her and caught the pox. A sense of contamination itched at him. But the long room, with its trestle tables and benches, was familiar. It smelt of smoke, hot food and beer. Fires belched and hissed in open hearths. Apart from the barmaids, everyone there was male, flushed with drink, not yet noisy. His mind settled down, comforted.

In the back part of the tavern, where the Mermaid Club members customarily collected, Ben Jonson sat alone. Coryate approached him nervously. One never knew what Master Ben's mood might be. Tonight he seemed unusually benevolent, slouched by the fire, a cup of warm sugared wine in his hand.

'Once more I behold our Somerset squire,' he said as Coryate sat down on the bench opposite, clutching a mug of sack like a charm against evil. 'How is the weather in the West Country? Do the wenches still have roses in their cheeks? Do they tumble on their backs and spread their thighs as easily once they did?'

Coryate did not like this kind of conversation. He sipped a little sack. It was the only liquor he liked, but he took it in moderation. He rinsed it around in his mouth for a while, as he preferred to do; the taste reminded him of the way oranges smelt. When Jonson had finished speaking, Coryate said,

'Master Ben, I know little about wenches, but one day you must travel with me to my village, Odcombe, near Yeovil.'

He leant forward across the table as though trying to climb across it into Jonson's mind. The old poet watched the face of his companion, which, as he named his village, became as uplifted and transformed as that of a biblical prophet who had watched God walk at night among olive trees.

'A good name for the fellow's village,' Jonson thought. 'He's an odd one himself. But, begod he bears study.' And looking now at Coryate across the drinking table, in the most revealing scrutiny any person can make of another unless it is across the table of coming torture, he saw that the man looked like one of those dolls created to be clownish. Children wreak mirthful but violent acts of inhumanity on such creatures.

A huge head, that of a homunculus, crowned it, covered with golden curls. A beard dangled like a last minute addition to its chin. The body was dwarfish and squat, with long simian arms. But the legs were long and strong, those that a Greek champion might have had when the races first started from under the shadow of Olympus centuries ago.

Coryate was saying, 'Odcombe, Master Ben! All you could want in the world is there. The purest air in the world, the sweetest water! The most splendid wool from our flocks! The most honest and worthy men and women!' He sounded as though he spoke of the Promised Land. 'Therefore I want my village to be remembered. And I will make it remembered.'

Jonson was already fairly drunk. 'Why not write about Odcombe, then, Sir Thomas? Eh, lad? If it is, as you say, the land of Canaan, then celebrate it. Last year you walked around Europe, and you wrote about it, aye, and your bare-bubbied whores in Venice. And you have a good serviceable style of prose.' His voice steadied, speaking of what he knew best. 'You can tell us in London what it is like in the West Country.'

Coryate spoke, and the fire that rose in the hearth behind him painted the walls with his grotesque shadow. 'Master Ben, I wish to write of places none of us know. It is to the Indies that I wish to go now. I have come to know there is a king there, the Great Mogul, and even now our East India Company waits to sail to his country and enter into trade with him.'

A barmaid, whose thick flaxen Saxon hair swirled round her shoulders, bent over the table to pour more liquor. Her blouse fell away to reveal large white breasts and nipples like bitten rosebuds. Jonson, slurping wine into his beard, leered openly. Coryate did not. Jonson noticed this as clearly as he did the barmaid's breasts. Coryate's eyes, blue and bulbous, were fixed on horizons that did not exist in this room.

'Beyond that country lies China,' he said, 'from which the silks come. After India, I shall go there. I shall be the first man to write of those places, Master Ben. It is by what I do there that Odcombe shall be remembered.' He took a sip of sack, rolling it round in his mouth in the irritating way he had.

Jonson's head was too full of liquor and Coryate's visions to function properly. Something else in him started to operate. He once had a friend, Will from Warwickshire, from whom he had taken years to recover and with whom he had drunk for years in this place, under the same roof, before the same fire. Whatever it was in Jonson that worked when he was drunk had worked with Will. He had sensed in Will a quality that set him aside from all the other men he had met. Now he smelt a similar quality in Coryate. He said, 'So you will sail to the Indies with the traders?'

Coryate said in a sardonic way, 'No. How can I? I have no fare and I do not want to travel with such men.'

'Then how will you go, Sir Thomas?'

'I shall walk,' said Coryate with conviction.

'You will walk to the Indies?' Jonson cried, and downed all his drink in one, beckoning to the prettiest and most bosomy barmaid he could see within call to fetch him another.

What he had got from Will in his youth, during his moments of perception, was that his friend was different from others. What he got from Tom Coryate now was the same, but Jonson's senses shuddered back from the other emanations from him, things he could not imagine, but that he felt would happen to this man: loneliness beyond belief, physical pain intertwined with it, and the stench of ultimate death.

On the other side of the table, Coryate had got up. 'I will walk to the Indies,' Coryate said. 'I shall write to you here from the Great Mogul's court. But for a while I am going down into Somerset. Master Ben, pray visit Odcombe one day.'

After Coryate had left, Jonson sat at his table for some time, shaking his bear-like head in a way he had not done since Will Shakespeare had left for Stratford to try and become a family man.

~

A month later Coryate came home to Odcombe. He travelled on foot, as was his habit, with the loose shambling countryman's stride that had made miles drop away behind him all his life. Winter had started to shed its chilly angularities and turn into spring. The combes had taken back the depth and clarity of colour that is peculiar to the English countryside, a colour as secret and vivid as the inside of an emerald. They were stained white here and there with herds of grazing sheep.

As he walked through these familiar places, where he had first been called the Long Strider, he continually sniffed the soft and fragrant air, as though it was a panacea to all pain and felt, as he rarely did, happy.

The boots that had carried him through Europe were now burst at the seams and had been often mended by the hands of Frenchmen and Italians. They were not as comfortable as they had once been and looking down at his feet in the roadside mud, Coryate formulated one of his great schemes, suddenly as he always did. He saw ahead of him the thatched houses and church of Odcombe, where his father had been vicar for many years. The rectory had been burnt down a little while ago, but all the other structures in the tiny village were as he remembered, built in the malleable pinkish-yellow stone quarried from Hamden Hill (locally known as Ham Hill) between Odcombe and Montacute.

The cottages seemed to glow in the afternoon sun, to contain and radiate light as Coryate thought the buildings must do in the holy city of Jerusalem. Only about two hundred people lived in Odcombe and it only possessed one inn. As the former vicar's son, Tom Coryate was well known to the villagers, and he was aware that they mostly considered him a little mad. It was not only that he had travelled on foot to strange, unheard of cities in distant countries. In his youth he had started a kind of crusade, marching the men of Odcombe against those of the nearest market town, Yeovil. The Odcombe forces had been heavily outnumbered and very severely thrashed.

Tom Coryate's madness, however, had been most clearly manifested when his father died. It had been in the middle of a bitter winter, with thick frost over the earth. Instead of burying George Coryate as any good Christian man should have done, his son had secreted the corpse in one of the caves under Ham Hill, and left it there for six weeks. He had forced the corpse, stiff with rigor and the bitter winter cold, into a coffin. He had taken the coffin, in a wheelbarrow, up to a low cave on the flank of Ham Hill. He had left the coffin there, strewn with sparse winter flowers, white candles flickering around it.

George's encoffined corpse had remained in the cave for six weeks, minimally sheltered from the black frost and a wind that shrieked like a devil outside. At the end of the time, as the worst of the winter wavered and withdrew, Tom took the coffin to Odcombe church for an orthodox funeral. The villagers had not known whether or not to attend this surely improper kind of ceremony. Eventually most did. George Coryate was now properly buried in the chancel.

When asked why he had done this, Coryate replied that he had waited for the arrival of someone worthy of burying his father in consecrated earth. Most Odcombe folk had thought this idea might be a form of sacrilege, but they had not been certain. They also respected Tom, because they had heard he had written a successful book and was a member of Prince Henry's court.

Now, as he came through his birthplace, the people he met, few as yet because they had mostly not come back from the fields, hailed him with surprise and a certain amount of pleasure. The parson who had succeeded his father hurried out of the new rectory with an invitation to come in and drink a pot of beer, but Coryate declined.

'Thank you kindly,' he said. 'But I lie with the Phelips family at Montacute for the next few days and I should reach them before nightfall. But I shall pass by on my way back, and send you word of the day and time. Then, if you would, please call our people to the market cross for I wish to tell them news of great import and to present our church with a gift it will treasure forever.'

The vicar nodded. He was somewhat bewildered, but he had never expected not to be by the younger Coryate. His eyes followed the dishevelled figure down the tilt of the slope out of Odcombe, till it disappeared into the mouth of one of the sunken lanes, headed towards Montacute, on the farther side of Ham Hill.

Coryate was at home in the deep lane. It was sealed in on either side by high slopes, as densely forested as some part of tropical Africa. In certain places, the trees on either side of him entwined their branches to create a canopy overhead. His nostrils filled with clear, very pure air, intermixed with the odour of wet leaves and earth, and the fungi that grew amidst the ferns. His sense of smell was aroused, and his ears responded to what, in this sunken tunnel through the forest, should have been the heart of stillness and silence. But Coryate could hear the multiple twitter of different birds, and could identify each one. The trees were alive with the dialects of insects, and from the fields beyond he heard sheep bleat.

In the dusk of this day, since he had come, he passed the mouth of the cave where, a decade ago, he had left his father's corpse. It had not decomposed at all in that arctic winter, but shrivelled into itself like one of the mummified pharaohs of whom he had read. As he swung out on to the unsheltered top of Ham Hill, a thin, very fine rain settled like dew on his hair and clothes. When he looked into the combe on his right, he could see the monolith of Montacute House, lavishly lit, with the smaller lights of the cottages sprinkled around it like fallen stars. As a boy he had walked the same way and seen it while it was being built, heard the hammers and saws at work on the golden stones and oaktrees that had gone into that mighty structure.

This place was part of him. It was here that he had first met the Phelips family, now his patrons. They had thought highly of his potential. They had sent him to Oxford, where he had failed; they had got him into Henry's court, where his position was no more than a buffoon's. Because of all this, he was now bedevilled by a fierce need for success. As he came down the hill to Montacute, the gradually strengthening wind and rain behind him drove him forward.

~

He was now in the great house, in a small private room, at a table. Ned Phelips sat at the head and carved venison and ducks. His wife, at the other end of the table, smiled benevolently at Coryate. The Phelipses had known him as a boy. Only three other guests were present. Two were young men whose names he had not caught: courtiers of no consequence. The third was a woman, who had been introduced as Anne, Countess of Harcourt; she was in some way related to his hosts, and Coryate could not take his eyes off her.

Certainly, she possessed remarkable beauty. Her long glossy black hair swirled round her bare shoulders. In her heart-shaped face her eyes were large and long-lashed, the evanescent colour of smoke. Her nose was delicately sculpted, her full lips moist, and her body could accurately be described as voluptuous. Her voice was low and musical, which, Coryate agreed with Master Shakespeare, was an excellent thing in woman. She also smelt most sweetly of vetiver.

Writing of his travels in Europe, he had wished to show his readers a sophistication he did not possess. He had made much of his encounter with topless courtesans in Venice. But the truth was that he had always been awkward with women and the Venetian whores had terrified him. His reaction to Lady Harcourt disquieted him even more. It contradicted most of the little he knew about himself.

Ned Phelips finished his dissection of the carcasses that lay before him. He offered Coryate his charming, crooked smile and said, 'Tom here can entertain us with his latest madcap scheme. He wants to travel to the Indies, he tells me, and on foot at that. There are broad seas to cross, but he thinks that like our saviour he can walk on water.' Laughter rippled round the table.

Coryate was annoyed, particularly since Anne Harcourt laughed as hard as the rest, her breasts shaking like globes of white gelatine in her lowcut dress. As often when annoyed, he resorted to bombast. 'Well, Ned, I know I must sail part of the way,' he retorted. 'But my journey is well planned. First, I will walk to Palestine to tread the paths trodden by our Lord. Then I will take ship across the Inland Sea and from the Asian side continue on foot to the Indies. I may not have money like you, yet have I strong legs and a stout heart.'

He glanced triumphantly at Anne, but she was laughing still. His breath caught angrily in his throat, but he calmed himself. 'I will write a great book on the Indies, better even than my *Crudities*. No man knows the people of that land. I will be the first to tell the world. I have studied Persian in preparation, for it is the language spoken at the court of the Great Mogul, Jehangir.'

This time Anne looked more impressed. She stopped laughing. Ned Phelips' equine face showed real concern. 'Such a trip might take years, Tom,' he said. 'How much money do you have?'

Coryate said confidently, 'I can raise, it may be, ten pounds.'

At this the Phelipses and the two young men burst into uncontrollable shouts of laughter. Anne Harcourt alone did not laugh. For the first time she looked directly into Coryate's face, and her own beautiful face showed pity and an astonished kind of admiration.

'I pray that you will reach the Indies, Master Coryate,' she said softly, 'and even more that you will come safely home to England.'

That night, when the rest of the house was asleep, Coryate, awake and lonely in the company of his multiple devils, heard a knock on his bedroom door. Anne Harcourt stood outside, clad in a long diaphanous nightgown. Through it he could see the purple peaks of her breasts, the deep cleanly etched navel, and the thick black nest of her pubic hair. With a rapid and lithe movement she made herself completely naked. He had never seen anyone so beautiful. She took him in her arms. 'This is to wish you Godspeed,' she said.

Until a chilly dawn they grappled amidst the sheets, cried out with ecstasy or some grief of a terrible nature, found and lost each other over and over. Coryate, until this night, had been virgin. After she left him, he lay half-asleep. He inhaled her fragrant body from the palms of his hands, savoured dregs of her saliva in his mouth. Over and over, he repeated to himself the brief syllable of her name.

They spent the next three nights together, and for three days Coryate walked her through the landscape he knew as well as he was coming to know her body, and they talked. He told her of his early days in Odcombe, his humiliations and failures at Oxford and the court, his great walk to Venice, and finally they talked about the mysterious Indies and the unknown Chinese Empire that he wanted to see. Though she did not speak to him about her own life, her mind became to him as beautiful and necessary to his life as her body, and as explicit in its needs.

On the fourth morning, he went down to the breakfast room alone, and found Ned Phelips there, eating bacon and bread. He had not seen his host for some time, and was surprised by the odd, quizzical way that Ned looked at him, and the false quality that was, for the first time, apparent behind his normal bonhomie.

'Ah, Thomas,' Ned said, 'have some of this very good bacon. Farmer Guy over by West Coker butchers a pig every month to ensure my supply all year.' Coryate helped himself. Ned continued, 'I have been trying to help you, writing to friends in the East India Company in London. The envoy the Company is sending to the Mogul's court is Sir Thomas Roe, a good man whom I know well. I will give you a letter for him if perchance you come upon him in the Indies, and he may then be of assistance to you there.'

He went over to the sideboard and, with finical care, cut himself a piece of Cheddar from a large round that lay on the sideboard. 'But,' he added, 'the friends I wrote to also said that trying to reach the Indies on foot and without any funds is a madman's enterprise. You will die on the way, they swear. Thomas, I speak to you as a mentor and a friend and I beg that you abandon this fool's caper. I know how much you crave stature and repute, but this is not the way. Do not look too high above you, or the sun will blind you.'

Humiliation and fury flooded Coryate. He listened with disgust to the sounds of Ned eating Cheddar, and through a final mouthful, say words that numbed his heart. 'I have noticed that you follow Mistress Harcourt like a mooncalf,' Ned said. 'Do not continue this. She is too far above you in rank and birth. You are but a poor parson's son, and she is a great lady. You are bedazzled by her, as by a sun.'

Coryate was now shaking all over. His face had turned white. Ned perhaps saw this, for he made a rough attempt at masculine amends. 'Besides, she is not the kind of woman you should know,' he said, and guffawed lewdly. 'She is well known in London by the smell of her cunt. Aye, she's a mare that a hundred men have mounted and ridden bareback while she neighs for more. I have done so myself.' But he was speaking to an empty chair.

Coryate blundered out of the room and ran across the smooth lawns into the open country beyond. His mouth worked wordlessly, and his beard was soaked in tears. He never wanted to speak to Ned or Anne while he still lived, nor to return to Montacute. But an hour's walk through the deep lanes to his mother's house in Odcombe, calmed and fortified him by the time he reached it. He asked the vicar to summon all the villagers to the market cross the next day.

~

The next morning was like warm aspic that enclosed Odcombe village. Sunlight was refracted through and from it. The glittering air had a damp herbal aroma. Coryate stood with the vicar on the platform at the market cross. Nearly three hundred people had collected around him—almost the entire population. They were flesh of the county, big-boned, their faces reddened by sun, wind, and a diet of mutton and cider. They spoke in the drawl and slur of Somerset, incomprehensible to people from other parts of England. Coryate understood this dialect for he had spoken in the same way until he had departed for Oxford. He also understood these large, slow, quiet, people; they were his own and would always be, however far his destiny took him away from them. He had known most of them and their families since his childhood and they knew him, though he had been away in 'furrin parts' so many years. Everyone in the crowd had already shaken his hand and called him by name. Even the smaller children had called him Master Tom.

These were good circumstances. It was good weather to leave what had been his home. That morning he had been to Odcombe church with the vicar, and looked at his father's tomb in the chancel, the same father who had taught him Greek and Latin, whose body he had shielded for six weeks in winter in the cave under Ham Hill.

He had a raw wound in his nerves, recently inflicted, which he knew, like Achilles, would never heal. He did not want to think of Anne, or any aspect of her. Had he thought it part of his fate, he could have walked back to Montacute and seen her. But his hurt told him not to. Her punishment would be his trip to the Indies.

The gathering was complete. He started to speak.

> 'You know I was a great walker as a lad. You know that I walked in far lands and that my walking brought fame to Odcombe. I desire to present the boots in which I walked to the vicar, to be displayed in our church here forever.'

He heard a rather uneasy stutter of applause as also of resistance. Boots to be displayed in a church, in front of the small pictures of virgins, saints, martyrdoms, and resurrections? The people of his home were doubtful.

But they accepted. They cheered as the vicar raised the burst and broken boots towards the sun, and Coryate accepted another version of false happiness. He was offered hospitality by the villagers, which he refused. But at the end of the day he found himself on Ham Hill, with the vicar, who had a handy flagon of sack.

He confronted the wind and his memories. Those now included the small wart on Anne's lower left shoulder, the birthmark just above her left lip and his talks with Jonson. These were his most precious possessions, and now he took a drink from the priest's bottle and resolved to throw every one of them away.

The vicar, who would never travel beyond Yeovil, looked in mild awe at the dwarfish man beside him and said timidly, 'Master Tom, shall I get a seat for you tomorrow on the coach for London?'

'No,' said Coryate. With his inborn sense of melodrama he twirled the curls of his beard and added, 'From tomorrow I shall walk with the wind.'

2

Diary One

April 1999–September 2000

Delhi–London–Odcombe

'Didi, sister, one rupee.' The scrawny beggar boy pulled at my arm as I stood by the iron pillar in the courtyard opposite the Qutub Minar. I shielded my eyes with one hand. The sun above was white with the heat of a Delhi afternoon in the heart of summer. He tugged harder at my arm. 'Five rupees pliss, didi. God will give you long arms to put around the iron pillar.' He did not say which God, which is rare in India. I turned to look at him. His eyes, yellow and wild as the clouds that contain one of the seasonal dust storms, seemed to mean what they said, but also to hold back, in place of rain, an irrepressible and cynical variety of laughter.

I gave him five one rupee coins. His eyes turned to lightbulbs, filled with sudden brilliance. 'You get good luck didi and your wishes come true,' he said and ran away. I watched as he crouched, small and wiry, nearby. He wedged four coins into the blistered earth, and catapulted the fifth, held firmly against his middle finger, for a carom strike.

Dom, dressed in an emerald green shirt, his silken white hair rinsed golden by the noon sun, came up behind me and inquired quietly, 'What was all that about?

I remarked, 'Did you know, if I put my arms around the pillar and my fingers were to touch then anything I wish for will come true?' He gave me a dubious look. I added, 'You should try. You have such long arms.' He raised an eyebrow. In defiance, I wrapped my arms around the pillar. Then I tried to get my fingers to meet around its circumference. They wouldn't. Dom didn't quite smile, but in the distance the beggar boy clapped.

'I'll wish anyway,' I said.

'Have you ever heard of Thomas Coryate?' Dom inquired, typically irrelevant.

'Who?'

'He was an extraordinary Englishman. I first read about him forty years ago in a book by an Italian traveller. Coryate surprised him by saying that the only piece of good architecture in India was this iron pillar.' Dom slapped the pillar with uncalled for familiarity, and added, 'Coryate told him that this was a Greek pillar. Because the style was Greek and it had Greek lettering on it. He said that the pillar was put here by Alexander.'

'How interesting,' I said, though I didn't think it was.

'Well, it was one of Coryate's mistakes. The lettering at the top of the thing is in Pali and the pillar was put up by the emperor Ashoka. Alexander never got as far as Delhi. Anyway, Coryate was a bit of a lunatic. He came here in the early seventeenth century, at the time of Jehangir and the East India Company, when Sir Thomas Roe was here. He walked to India from England. He died in Surat.'

His eyes had a lazy but unusually focused look; I attributed it to the glare of the sun. He ran his hand over the side of the pillar and muttered as though speaking to himself, 'I've always wanted to write a book about Coryate in India. He was a curious fellow.'

He did not say much more for the next two hours, until we were back in a city cafe, in which he was drinking beer and I was drinking tea. Then, looking intently at me, he said, 'Since we've just finished our book on India, would you like to collaborate a second time? We could do a book about this fellow Coryate, though it would need some hard work.'

'Me?' I laughed. I flexed my fingers and stretched my arms above my head. For some reason I felt this had turned out to be a good day. 'What did you say his name was?'

'Thomas Coryate. He came from Odcombe. That's near Yeovil in Somerset.'

A year and a half later, on a cold and rainy September morning in London, we took a taxi from our hotel to Waterloo Station to catch a train to Yeovil in Somerset.

~

I would have thought the English had got used to the rain. But the scene that confronted us at Waterloo Station proved otherwise. There were thousands of people, grim-faced, most of them sagging under soggy raincoats, others with sodden umbrellas clutched in their hands, clinging on to damp suitcases, twitchy children or long-suffering parents of either gender.

It had rained without a break for weeks. Rivers rushed vagrantly into the sea and onto everything else, and half the countryside was flooded. The mannerly English were not used to the unanticipated. And the day was just half begun.

I waited in front of the Upper Crust food shop. Two

suitcases in front of my feet formed a sizeable stronghold. I clutched in each hand, like some sort of ammunition, a ham baguette for Dom, and a Cheddar and rocket one for me. We had arrived at the station without breakfast. Our train was due at 9.45 a.m. It was past twelve and Dom, who had ventured an hour ago into the swarm of people to make enquiries about our train, had not returned. I stood rooted to the spot where he had instructed me to stand, baffled, tired, anxious and unavoidably angry; and in order to dissipate the annoyance bit by bit I started biting vigorously into the cheese baguette in my left hand. Just then, a plump man with a red shirt and complexion jostled me and I had bits of squashed cheddar on my face. Amidst the din, I heard my name mispronounced over the loudspeaker—*Sarah-you Sarah-you*. It was precisely at this moment that I saw Dom advancing angrily towards me through the crowd. He had been waiting for me at another Upper Crust outlet.

We struggled with our luggage to platform nine, towards the train, a defenseless giant centipede with people milling along it like ants. Dom asked an attendant whether the train was headed for Yeovil Junction. 'It's headed that way, man, is all I can say. You want to get anywhere at all, then just get on the motherfucker, or from all I see you are going to be stranded here for another day.' He pushed us into a carriage, then shut the door hard. The seats were all occupied. People stood in the corridors looking not only confused but with something like a twitch of terror in their throats. We found a vacant spot beside the toilet. I grabbed the newspaper stuck under Dom's armpit; spread it out on the floor, then sat down.

'What are you doing?' Dom muttered into his chin. 'That's today's paper; I've not yet read it.' People watched us, wearing expressions of lethargic interest; I didn't care, I was exhausted.

For want of something to do, I undid my shoelaces, peeled my shoes off, and rubbed my toes. Soon afterwards, as the train started to move, everyone else around us spread their raincoats/scarves/handkerchiefs/ magazines on the floor, and also sat down on them.

I tilted a suitcase onto the floor, coaxed Dom to sit down on it. He complied without too much unnecessary resistance. It was almost evening by the time the train pulled into Salisbury Station. It wouldn't go any further, we were firmly informed. We spilled out in a daze, disentangling our limbs, one by one. Three hours later, we boarded another train, bound for Yeovil Junction. It was dark when we got there, and pouring with rain.

Yeovil station had one deserted platform and old locomotives in the yard in front of it spoke of long forgotten times. There was no sound of nightbird or insect; no sound save the rain and the faint clicking of one loose metal plate against another. Besides us, only one young couple got off the train. We followed them, hauling our suitcases over a steep flight of steps to the road on the other side. The couple was met by an old man who led them to a car parked some way off under a solitary lamp post without a light. There were no taxis around. We stood in the rain under a sign that seemed to be a bus stop. It was cold and blustery, and dismally dark. One half of my umbrella wouldn't unfold and water dripped on my left shoulder already set awry by the heaviness of my handbag.

This was hardly the time for Dom, who had been infuriatingly withdrawn through the journey, to become loquacious, but he sniffed the Somerset air and did. He started a scholarly discourse about Thomas Coryate. I could see Coryate come up the dark road, atop an Indian elephant at the head of a huge caravan of horses, carriages, and nubile wenches dancing to Mogul tunes. Considering the events of the day, the weather, and the nature of my companion, I was not surprised that I had begun to hallucinate.

The old man we had seen on the platform stopped his car as he passed us and asked whether we needed a taxi. 'No taxis will come here,' he said, 'unless you phone for them. I'll call for one if you like, but do you know where you want to go?'

'Thorne village,' Dom replied. 'We're booked into a guesthouse there. Thank you very much indeed, sir, it's awfully kind of you.'

It was over half an hour before a taxi pulled up.

Mr Grimster was waiting at the gate of Thorne Cottage when we drove up. The taxi driver had called him on his earphone for directions. He picked up our suitcases easily in both his hands. He was a tall man, strong despite his age. 'I was getting worried,' he said to Dom, 'I thought you weren't coming. Did you have too much trouble?' Dom coughed and Mr Grimster said, 'You must be exhausted, I'll show you your rooms, and then you can come down for a nice cup of tea.

'I think I need a drink more,' Dom muttered to me as we climbed upstairs. 'Thank you, Mr Grimster,' he said to him, 'tea would be super.'

'Call me Bill,' he replied.

Over tea, a cup of which Dom let stand on the table, he told Bill about Thomas Coryate and our book and asked him to arrange a taxi to Odcombe next morning. I clasped my teacup like a talisman; I terribly wanted some dinner. Thorne Cottage had been advertised as a bed and breakfast place with a pub within walking distance that served good meals and excellent wine. I asked Bill where this pub was. He looked at his watch. 'They stop serving at nine,' he said, 'if you hurry, you might still get something hot to eat.' It was half past eight.

Pointing to the road, he said, 'walk to the end, and turn right, and do you see that light out there, that's the pub. If you walk fast you might make it in ten minutes.'

I pulled my coat tight around me as we walked to the end of the road. The rain had not stopped and the breeze that sheathed it was cold and damp. As I turned right, Dom pulled me back. He gazed at the faint, solitary, and very distant light, and said, 'That's not a ten-minute walk!' We stood quiet, side-by-side, looking up at the hooded sky. The slow constellations swayed in their ancient courses, far above our heads.

Dom pointed to the shadows outlined by light on falling rain, 'That looks like a ring of stones.' They appeared to me like coagulated dumplings of haystacks stricken by damp. 'Stonehenge isn't far from here,' he added, 'in fact we must have passed it on Salisbury plain. Everything in this part of the world is connected to Stonehenge in a sense. Some people call Somerset, Mummerset, as a joke of course. If two local people talk, they mumble and one can hardly understand them. But there is another reason; it is connected to mime, *mimer.* A long time ago, at equinoxes, solstices, the locals would wear masks and mime at fairs; they would dance. This land is connected to the rituals of the Druids. Have you ever heard of the Long Men?' He sculpted the darkness with his hand. 'They were figures made of stone on the hills, with enormous penises, ritualistic phallic figures. Most have gone.'

He seemed unaware of the weather, and my expressed desire for dinner.

A wizened man passed us. He wore a rat-coloured raincoat, which looked as if he had got wet in it, and it had shrunk on him. He sighed as he looked up at the dark sky. Rain dripped from his spectacles, onto his nose, then his lips. He said, 'Terrible night, isn't it?' Then he waved a shaky hand, and disappeared in the direction of the pub.

Dom said in a low voice, somehow roused and urgent, 'All the English myth and magic came from this region. Merlin the wizard was a Druid; he came from here. Also King Arthur. Coryate must have known all this. There was something about his mind ...'

The rain was falling harder and I could hear the wind howling in the trees. 'The other thing about Somerset,' Dom said, still oblivious to other people's needs, 'is that it has been a rather lawless place. The coast of Somerset and the West Coast of England have been linked to smuggling. The coast was open and the people here had relatives in France and Spain and they would deliver several crates of French brandy and yards of Spanish lace to their brothers and uncles here. There was a great demand for French brandy and Spanish lace in England those days. So you see,' his tone was gentle, 'why the people here have odd sounding names; they sound like French names, flattened out.' He gave me examples.

'Let's go back, Dom,' I said, taking him by the arm and leading him back to Thorne Cottage. An hour later, terribly hungry, and after Bill and his wife had retired, I raided the kitchen. Dom didn't attempt to stop me, though he made mild protests. 'It's all right, it's just a few slices of bread. They won't mind,' I comforted him, patting his hand as he stood beside me in the kitchen, still trying to remember the provenance of Somerset names.

I made some toast, coffee, I borrowed two slices of honey-roast ham from an expensive-looking packet, a few pieces of roast chicken from a plastic tub in the fridge, butter, cheese. I found my favourite blackcurrant preserve on a shelf above the toaster. Black olives. Also Tabasco. And from the fruit bowl I selected a banana and a large nectarine. After our meal, I rolled three five-pound notes into an empty glass on the table.

Dom dragged the glass towards him. 'Let them be, Dom, they're for the food we ate,' I slapped his hand. Dom pulled out his wallet and stuck a ten-pound note into the glass. 'I didn't mean *that*' he said, 'but why not see if there's any wine in the cupboard?'

~

I cannot sleep with the windows shut or the curtains drawn; I feel claustrophobic. I woke up early, therefore, furrowed under the duvet, the sun splashing on my face. I could hear Dom snoring in his room. I showered and went down for a cup of coffee. It was early, but Bill was already in the kitchen. He had put out the plates for breakfast, and kindly poured me my coffee. I asked him where I could get an audiocassette. I had brought a pocket recorder that I thought we might need. 'Try the shop down by the post office,' he said, 'I'm not sure they stock 'em. But in Yeovil you'll surely find a shop that does.'

I walked down the road. It was almost dry except for a few stray puddles near the edges. The air was crisp and smelled new; it was not a leftover-from-yesterday smell. But the plants, trees and hedges were limp and worn, after having been whipped by the ferocious rain and wind. The sun shone halfheartedly although it appeared as dry as parchment; and a tentative rainbow made half an arc across the sky. This, I could tell, translated into uncertain weather. I hurried past some houses and came to a small cottage. One room in it was the post office, and the other the store, which was small and stocked basic daily necessities.

The storekeeper, an old man with a grey beard, his face wrinkled and red as a pomegranate, showed no surprise when I asked for an audiocassette. I looked at his inscrutable face. Under shaggy brows, his grey eyes were half closed. He did not reply; he read the newspaper and waved a hand in the air in a steady curious sidewise motion like the tail of a cow chewing on hay. I asked him for a top-up card for my mobile phone. He waved a cow-hand once more, flipping a page of the newspaper. I needed to break a fifty-pound note, I hesitated wondering if he would oblige, and instead I asked him for a bar of Snickers. He shook his head impatiently, turning redder. He pointed to four bars of Cadbury chocolates in a shelf next to him. 'Only these now,' he mumbled.

'Thanks,' I said, 'but I don't want these. I don't like Cadbury's.' It was only then he looked up at me. He chuckled richly. Wiping his moustache he said, 'Neither do I.'

~

All the way to Odcombe, Dom, who was in excellent spirits, talked to the driver. 'Take us to the pub,' he said as we approached the old village.

'Pub!' I cried looking at my watch. 'It's five to eleven in the morning. You're not going to drink now?'

Dom laughed. 'Why not? I'd give anything to have a drink now. Last night there was no wine in the cupboard, remember?' He added seriously, 'A village pub is the best place to get information.'

The pub, The Mason's Arms, was a beautiful long cottage built in yellow sandstone and with a thatch roof. It was shut. 'It's not possible,' Dom pushed the door with both hands and then appealed to the taxi driver. 'How can it be closed at this time?' He took off his spectacles and lit a cigarette. 'Let's try another pub.'

'This is the only pub in Odcombe, mate,' the driver informed him.

'Only pub! How can it be the only pub? There can't be only one pub.'

The driver shrugged. 'The people here are changing, sir,' he replied dryly. 'The younger uns're more concerned about their health and work. They've no time to drink.'

I walked to the back of the pub, which seemed to me to be the house of the owners. I peeped through the glass door. A huge dog leapt at the glass, barking ferociously. A young lady appeared and held the dog down. She stepped out of the door. Dom ambled towards her. He asked her whether she had heard of Thomas Coryate. She frowned, tapped her lips with a finger, pouted. 'Sorry,' she said, 'don't know the name. Does he live here?'

'He did,' Dom said, 'four hundred years ago.'

'Maybe the vicar would know of him,' she said indifferently, leading us into the pub through the back door. She switched the lights on, opened a pair of windows.

'Is this the only pub in Odcombe?' Dom asked.

'Yes, it is,'

'What time do you open?'

'I'm sorry sir, I can't give you a drink now. The pub only opens in the evening,' she said in a firm business tone, 'and only three times a week. Everyone is so busy these days. No one comes to the pub anymore except a handful of old men who have nothing else to do. And so we're losing business. We may have to close down.'

She looked through the telephone book for the vicar's number. She dialled it; there was no answer. 'He doesn't seem to be there,' she said scribbling the number on a piece of paper, 'here, you could try again later.' She walked to the front door, opened it and stepped outside. We followed her. At the top of the road a fat old man was collecting garbage. 'Hey, John, do you know what the vicar is doing today?'

John said, 'No love. What do they want with him? They want to get married or something?' He laughed, his stomach jiggled.

'No, John, they want to know about a Thomas Coryate. Ever heard of him?'

John shook his head. 'Never heard of that one. Strange I know everyone in this village. Been collecting their garbage for years.' He shouted to the man cutting a hedge on the other side of the road, 'Hey, Peter, you know where the vicar might be today?'

Peter held up his clipping tool, 'I heard he'd gone to a funeral over by Montacute yesterday. But he should have got back by now.'

The young lady shrugged, 'I'm sorry I can't help you,' she muttered. 'Maybe if you came here in the evening, you could ask some of the older customers?' She closed the pub door firmly behind her.

'Let's get back to Yeovil,' Dom said to me, 'I saw a nice pub as we drove through this morning. The Mermaid, I think it's called. I must feed you some lunch. And,' he added with a grin, 'I could do with a large glass of red wine.'

As we drove off the driver suggested helpfully, 'Sir, if you're so desperate to find this Coryate bloke, why don't we just look him up in the phone book?'

At the Mermaid, Dom ordered his drink and I left my mobile number on the vicar's answering machine. Half an hour later just as my order of beer-batter fried fish and mushy peas was set before me, my mobile pealed. It was the vicar. I gave the phone to Dom. He talked, gulped his drink, gave me back my phone, ordered another drink, and rapidly sent it after the previous one. 'We've to go now,' he announced, 'to Odcombe church. The vicar says he can't see us but he says a woman will meet us there in twenty minutes.'

'What about my fish?'

Dom stared at the plate in front of me. 'Oh, poor fish. I'm sorry,' he said, 'I'll buy you another one later. Promise.'

~

The old church was like something out of a black and white postcard turned sepia, except for the white daisies and purple wild flowers along the drive; and the lady waiting for us at its gate was straight out of Enid Blyton. She was probably about fifty, rather short, pleasantly plump in a long squirrel-coloured coat; her wavy hair was cut in a sixties bob. She wore a dark blue pleated skirt and a white nylon blouse over it trimmed with what would have been utterly modish forty or fifty years ago—a profusion of lace on the collar and sleeves. Her lips were painted a bright pink, a very popular colour of the sixties, and resembled small tulip bulbs. When she talked she pronounced each word carefully, shaping each with her lips, pausing briefly at the finish of every sentence and looking up as though she was waiting for a black dot to drop out of the air and attach itself to the sentence, ending it. And each time this occurred she twirled her index finger in front of her.

She tapped her shoe on the ground and said, 'This is Higher Odcombe. And that,' she pointed to the hamlet downhill, 'built on the slopes of Ham Hill is Lower Odcombe. You'll find the village pub there.' She twirled a finger in the air.

'We were there this morning,' I said.

An indescribable sound rose from her throat, she said as if by pure reflex, 'Rubbish, you can't have been there; it is closed at that time of the day.' She added with a grunt. 'The village school closed down last year. It is being converted into a private home. You must have noticed that most houses are built of yellow stone. It's Ham stone from Ham Hill quarry not far from here. The church is built of the same stone.' She walked towards the church. 'The original church was eight hundred years old,' she said, 'it was rebuilt in the early fifteenth century and extended and modified later. However, the old materials were used as far as possible. The tower is of fifteenth century construction and as for those grotesques overlooking the court, the original masons used their own imagination when carving them, basing them on local characters.' Her tulip lips stretched into a taut smile, 'The villagers often speculate about whose ancestors they resemble.'

She took us inside the church and pointed to a wall. 'Can you see those shoes on the wall? These are carved out of Ham stone. When Coryate returned from his European trip he gave his boots to the church. They were hung on a hook in the northeast corner of the nave over there, and they remained there until 1702. But when the church was renovated, some worker must have thrown them away wondering what they were doing in the church in the first place. Therefore, the church members decided to carve Coryate's shoes permanently in stone.' She interlocked her fingers and held them against her skirt. Nodding her head she said, 'Thomas Coryate was the only great man born in Odcombe. Do you know he introduced the use of the fork into England? Also the parasol.'

Dom turned to the window next to him; he stroked the woodwork, fretted and old. 'I wonder if Coryate touched this,' he said to me and added, 'I can imagine the mad bugger wandering about here.'

The lady pointed to a stone plaque on the rear wall. On it was an inscription about a sum of three hundred and fifty pounds donated to India for a village affected by a drought in the 1970s. It was odd finding something like this here. She explained, 'The families of Odcombe felt they had to do something for the country in which Coryate was buried. So they collected some money and sent it. It wasn't much, but it was a gesture.' She sighed, 'It's a pity, not many in this village know about Thomas Coryate. We want everybody to know. Recently we had a lecture on Coryate in the church grounds.'

'What about the vicar, does he know much about ...' Dom asked.

'He's new,' the lady interrupted him. 'You must meet the old vicar. Archie Dean. He is deeply interested in Coryate. I have his number. I can call him now and ask him whether he will see you. I'm sure he'd be delighted to meet you. He's really old though.'

She made the call. 'He'll see you this evening,' she said. 'His home is not very far from here. He lives in West Coker now. But before you leave Odcombe, I think you should meet Reg Warr. I'll give you his number and address. He runs a walkers club. Coryate was a great walker you know.'

~

Dom said, 'Why not look for Reg Warr's house now? I don't think it's far from the church. We might fix an appointment for tomorrow.' I was hungry, I reminded him. 'Ah! The fish.

Once we've found his house we'll go back to the Mermaid,' Dom announced looking suddenly pleased, 'I must feed you properly, and I can have a bottle of wine.'

The taxi slowed down in front of a house. 'I think this is it,' I said as Dom stuck his head out of the window to read the number on the door. With the abruptness of an apparition, an elderly man appeared from behind a bush. 'Do you need any help?' He looked at the taxi driver, and then studied Dom with understandable curiosity.

'Good morning,' Dom said.

'Afternoon,' I corrected him remembering my uneaten fish. I said to the stranger, 'We were looking for Mr Reg Warr.'

'That's me. Yes?'

Some minutes later, we were in his drawing room sipping Earl Gray tea; I was snacking on jam biscuits. The room had all the accumulations that people usually gather over time: books, paintings, maps, pictures, framed photos of grown-up children, flowers, curios, a well worn rug, and old broken and mended commonplace things, timeless because they were mundane. Reg Warr talked about then-and-now Odcombe. 'Lots of things were different then. Things have changed now,' he said.

Before the fifties, Odcombe was an important village; it supplied water to large areas of Somerset. The local people were basically farmers and stone masons, or they were employed in the twine and sailcloth industries in Coker. The women made gloves and a gloving machine was a common feature in people's homes. The farmers didn't work on the land; they were involved mainly in dairy farming because their dairy products were cheaper than those from Denmark. But now they had converted their homes, sold their land or built on it. People were now mainly employed in the helicopter factory or worked in supermarkets. Most of the younger people had left Odcombe.

'Have you always lived here?' I asked.

Warr wiped his spectacles, carving time to think. Turning to me, he said, 'No, I was born in West Coker. I came to live in Odcombe in 1989. I remember I used to cycle to Odcombe as a boy. My father had told me about Coryate; he said that he had hung up his boots in the Odcombe church after he came back walking from Europe. He said they hung there for many years until someone stole them. But I think if they were hanging for a hundred years they would have fallen to pieces anyway.' He laughed, and then looking at his watch he said, 'I am afraid I have to leave now. I have to meet my wife in twenty minutes. Do come again.'

It was pouring now, the rain drumming on the car with hyphenated fingers. We drove quietly to West Coker. The taxi revved up a steep slope with a noise like a circular saw going into a weathered Burma teak log, which died into a splutter as the taxi stopped at the old vicar's house. Archie Dean was a tiny slender man. His cheeks were flushed as though he had enjoyed a couple of whiskeys while he awaited us. Sitting in his favourite chair by the fireside, his face lit up with pride as he talked about Thomas Coryate. We didn't stay very long; he told us his wife was sick and in bed, and he would soon have to take a bowl of soup to her. As we prepared to leave, he said he was happy we were writing a book on Coryate. In a voice that shook slightly, he asked us when the book would come out.

Dom explained that a book of this kind required sponsorship and financial support, and that the travel and writing would take up a lot of time. 'We can't start without funding.'

'I'm ninety-four,' the vicar smiled. 'I'd like to see the book. I hope you find the funds soon.'

We walked into the garden. One of the trees was so thick with flowers that the scent was overpowering. It was enormously quiet outside except for the splatter of rain on the roof tiles. We walked out of the gate and down the steep slope into a perpetual blue-green twilight. Our taxi was parked in a clearing under a tree. The driver was fast asleep. Just as he started the taxi, a knock sounded on my window and I saw a shadowy figure outside. I rolled down the glass. It was the vicar. His eyes were intense; he said eagerly, 'I just had an idea. I'll start a collection at the Odcombe church. We will collect money every Sunday; it won't be very much. There aren't many families left, you know. But on special days and during festivals we might collect a bit more. By the time you return next year I'm sure we could give you about two hundred pounds to help you write your book.'

3

Full Sail on Dry Land

Jonson was not an outstandingly difficult man, but he was an impatient one, particularly with other writers. He had crushed the confidence of many young literary pretenders with no more than a sentence or two, snarled sideways through the fringes of his greying beard. Yet he was genuinely troubled about Coryate, whom he respected; he had helped publish his book about the European trip and had praised it. Jonson knew that Coryate, who had few friends, considered him to be one of them. Equally, this strange Somerset man fascinated him. He had come to think of the Long Strider as a figure escaped from Greek tragedy.

When Coryate came back from Somerset and they met as usual at the Mermaid Club, Jonson was bewildered to find that his friend was suffering from heartbreak over a brief, wholly physical affair. Jonson was aware that amorous contact with women these days usually ended in an annoying and painful disease. Most of his friends had been poxed more than once. But their affliction had been of the body. Coryate's was in the mind.

Jonson had written magnificent and musical verse in the classical style about women. But like many men of the period, he knew very little about them. He had heard much about Anne Harcourt. In spite of his bear-like looks he had delicacy of spirit, and because of that he did not tell Coryate all he had heard.

But the fact that Coryate's too easily broken heart coincided with his insane idea of walking to India disturbed the poet very much. His orderly intellect made him impatient of the concept of love. He felt that he knew what women were like, also what they were meant for. So he summoned the bustiest of all the barmaids, put his hand up her skirt without reproof, and ordered a whole bottle of wine for himself and another of sack for Coryate, who was unused to such alcoholic excess.

When the barmaid returned with the bottles, the great poet turned to the dwarf by his side and stared at him, for once mystified and unwilling to admit it.

Then he lifted his cup and said, 'I have a sentence I say to other writers, honest Tom, when first I meet them, and though we are no strangers, I say it to you now: "Either amuse me or amaze me." You have done both in the past few years. But I wish now to ask you more directly than before. Few men have done this to me who are not very gifted or very mad. Which are you?'

Coryate turned his slightly bulbous eyes, the colour of the summer sky in his own county, on his companion. He shook his head in incomprehension. 'Why should I be mad?' he asked.

'Why, look at yourself, Tom. It is not thwarted love that makes you want to go on foot to the Indies, for you spoke of it to me before ever you met Mistress Harcourt. Why does any man wish to go on a journey that will lead him to his death? This venture will lead you to yours, certain as night follows day.'

'Not for certain,' Coryate said, 'I will see Odcombe once more.' Someone shouldered through the door behind them. The lolling flames of the candles on the table and the curled fires that purred in the hearth leapt up, changed shape, and illuminated his face briefly but in the precise detail of a Dutch master's drawing, before they settled down and became inanimate.

In this moment, Jonson saw Coryate's face more clearly than he had ever done before, and realized that a Dutch master might have used it as a model for the face of a martyr. It was an innocent and open face, naturally flushed like that of most west countrymen. But, strangely, the thick curly beard made it look younger and the wide eyes seemed to look towards some horror held in the future as though they eagerly anticipated it.

'Thomas,' said Jonson, 'pray don't tell me that you are doing this for your village's sake, for I do not think you are.'

'The boots in which I walked through Europe,' Coryate said, 'those I gave to the village church, which accepted them gratefully as a memento of me and there, above my father's tomb in the chancel, they hang today, and will do so forever.'

The poet seemed about to laugh, but stopped himself. He had ordered food for them both, and even when the barmaid bent over to serve them, his very intelligent eyes did not waver from Coryate's face, nor did his hand, as it would usually have done in such circumstances, mechanically slide into her blouse. He looked at his companion as though he had seen a miracle.

'You have written verses, Master Ben,' Coryate said, 'that will make you live forever, but I cannot do anything like that.'

'So,' Jonson said musingly, 'you choose to throw away the life you have to try and achieve the fame you want. It's a fool's choice, but what of it? Eat your victuals while the heat's in them, Master Tom, for there's a cold wind tonight from the west.'

An hour later, as they finished their meal, Coryate said, 'First I shall be in the Holy Land of Palestine, then I shall sail to the city of Aleppo, and from there I shall start on foot for the Indies. God willing, I will reach the Great Mogul's court within two years.' He might look unprepossessing, but his smile was that of a deformed angel. 'And I shall write from there, I swear.'

'Aleppo? Aleppo? I have heard of this place,' Jonson said. 'Will Shakespeare mentioned it in some play. But he was never there, nor have I been. You will be the first of us to see it.'

He leered round the room for some buxom young barmaid who would allow him to finger her freely because of who he was. Coryate said his farewells and, slightly unsteady from all the sack he had drunk, went out into Bread Street to find mild spring rain dripping from a dark sky. He thought of the old Scots whore he had met last winter. He need not have done so, but he felt personally guilty for the nature of her life and coming death.

He searched the wharves but could not find the tumbled bundle of singing rubble that had been her. She had been obliterated from the English rain as completely as he intended to be, though in a different way. He was sometimes a kind man and felt sorry for her, even though she had stunk so abominably.

~

Days later, he was gnawed by sudden panic, thinking of the hardships ahead. This was strange for him, for he was one of the few men in England with much experience of travel. The great wayfarers like Drake and Raleigh had plundered and looted as far away as the Americas for the ungrateful, redheaded, now dead Elizabeth, but they had been men of war, which Coryate was not. His travels were limited to Europe, a continent more or less at peace; and when he first crossed the Channel, as he had recorded in his *Crudities,* he proved such a sorry sailor that he had varnished the sides of the ship with his vomit.

Still, it was not the possibility of seasickness that caused him anxiety, but the sense of finality implicit, this time, in his departure. He was not very fond of London, with its stenches and its stews, but he knew it well and it represented something to him that he could not identify exactly. He realized, for all his recent protestations to Jonson, that he might not return to the city while he lived, that he might suffer much before he died. They were groundless chimeras, true, but real terror filled him. He had prepared himself for this trip as thoroughly as possible, but he knew that there was too little information on the Indies for him to have foreseen exactly what he should prepare for.

Coryate's temperament had always had a manic quality about it. He could be greatly cast down or greatly uplifted, and these moods might succeed each other within minutes. He knew that he had been talking about his intended trip to the Indies for the past year. If he did not start very soon, he feared that people would consider him more of a braggart and a fool than they already did. He had half-expected that Ned Phelips would subsidize his expenses. But after their last encounter, he did not want to approach Ned. His injured pride would not allow it.

However, his journey could not happen without a little

money at least, and he hardly had any at all. He was ashamed that he felt a slight sense of relief. He had recently though reluctantly started to agree with all the others who had warned him that this was a lunatic's enterprise. He was almost convinced that he should give it up. Much ridicule might follow but he had learnt to endure ridicule at Prince Henry's court, where he had made long bombastic orations to amuse the better born and earn his keep. After his walk to Venice and the publication of his book, he had become briefly famous. That time was over; now he must try to be humble.

He regretted this, since he had always had an excellent opinion of himself. But he told nobody of his indecision, and when his fellow courtiers sarcastically asked him when he would leave for the Indies, he would reply that there were still some arrangements to be made. He was not yet ready to be ridiculed.

Suddenly, in the middle of a sodden July, he received a letter from Ned Phelips. His mood of bitterness and depression lifted at once and turned into euphoria. The letter said that Phelips had always had Tom's interests at heart. He thought the trip to India a mad idea, but since his protege seemed bent on it, he had decided to help. He had made inquiries, and enclosed with the letter a draft that would cover the costs of a voyage to Constantinople. After this, his benefactor emphasized, Tom would be on his own.

All Coryate's doubts and dreads fled in a flash. He suddenly felt that God, as well as Phelips, was on his side. He chose to forget that Phelips's support was grudging and halfhearted, and that God's might be the same. He walked to the docks, and eventually found a ship's agent who told him that a tramp trader, the *Samaritan,* was supposed to leave in October for Constantinople. It would stop at a couple of

Greek islands on the way, to take on water and provisions. This was an added inducement to Coryate, who had a passion for ancient Greece.

He paid for his passage with Ned's money. The agent told him it would take about six months to reach Constantinople. For six months, then, his needs would be taken care of on board the *Samaritan*. Once she made landfall in Constantinople, he would have to pay his way. Coryate was ready to travel, and now he felt no apprehension, but a burning desire to start without more delay. In September he went down for the last time into Somerset to see his mother and to collect ten pounds from her.

~

After the death of her husband George, the rector of Odcombe, about five years earlier, the church authorities had provided Gertrude Coryate with a cottage quite near her former home in the rectory. It was a thatched wooden cottage like that of any other villager, but somewhat more spacious than most. She was comfortable there and the church supplied her with the necessities of life. Also, a relative had left the family some land, which she rented to a tenant farmer. She was not exactly poor, and she had several women friends in the village. Even with George dead and her son Tom usually miles away in London or overseas, she was seldom lonely, though she was often sad.

Gertrude had been pretty as a young maid, Somerset in blood and bone. Her father was a rich farmer, her family well known around Yeovil. But in the past, when George's friends from London came to visit him, she had embarrassed them, and him too, for they could hardly understand a word she said. So she ceased to speak. She felt they pitied her husband.

He could talk to them as they talked to him, as equals, and she couldn't.

He spoke to her in the Somerset dialect, in the slurred accents of the region. When Tom was born, he also grew up speaking two languages, one to his father and his father's friends, one to her and the local people. She felt separated from both of them, servant and cook where she should have been wife and mother. But George was kind to her, and little Tom loved her.

She had been frightened when he turned out to look as he did, with a grotesquely shaped head, like an inverted sugar loaf, too big for his small body. Even though he was the rector's son, the other village children laughed at him. Whenever he went out of the house, he came back crying. She tried to keep him at home, but he had the nature of a wanderer. He would walk alone for hours on end, even as a child. As he grew older, he found a protection against the taunts of his peers that was as effective as solitude. He developed and wielded a tongue as savage as a sword. His tormentors, astonished and wounded, shrank from it.

Yet he always remained her Tom, the small child who came to her for comfort in the end. But paradoxically, Gertrude, unlike other mothers, allowed herself to accept the differences between her and her son, first of language, then, after he returned from Oxford, of culture. She ceased to understand much of his speech and many of his actions, but she was afraid to query them for fear she would lose his love.

When Tom had left his father's corpse in the cave, she had wept and protested. He had maintained an unaccustomed silence, and had not listened. The entire village had protested at this heathen behaviour. Tom had made clumsy and unconvincing attempts to explain it to them. She had never understood it.

The episode had proved to the rest of the world that her son had a twisted nature and an iron will, like Richard the Third. She was perhaps alone in knowing the doubts and indecisions that swayed him. She had heard that in London he was considered a buffoon. This amazed her, for even as a child he had been uncommonly serious. She had scarcely heard him laugh aloud in all his life, except sometimes when he was with her.

But, hurtfully aware that away from her he spoke another language, lived another life, she became confused. The Tom she knew might be her private illusion. The Tom seen by the world might be the world's illusion. A hidden Tom must exist whom only he could know.

~

Coryate came over Hamden Hill and paused for a moment to look, as usual when he passed that way, into the cave where he had once hidden his father's corpse. Then he went on. He walked with smooth loose strides, his squat body relaxed, arms swinging. He breathed comfortably. So much travel on foot all his life had taught him the best way to walk. He was convinced of it. He savoured the smells of a Somerset autumn, or, better than that, an Odcombe autumn. Wild flowers of many colours were scattered at his feet. A slight, delicate chill in the early morning air sharpened their fragrances. Somewhere off in the woods, shrilly, a vixen barked. Roe deer grazed with the sheep.

He came to his mother's cottage and found her at the front door, talking quietly to her neighbour. 'Good day, Mistress Hallett,' he said, then turned to smile at Gertrude. Typically, she did not make any display of surprise or pleasure; indeed, the neighbour woman seemed much more excited. She kissed him on the cheek. Ever since his walk to Venice first made him famous, the villagers had accepted him, though they thought him slightly demented.

He was proud of his mother's reluctance to show emotion. He was also very glad to see her, as always. She got rid of Mistress Hallett with exquisite quickness, and led him inside the cottage. Only after she had shut the front door did she take him in her arms. 'Why did you not send me a message?' she asked. 'I was like to faint when I heard your voice of a sudden, and saw you standing there.'

'I thought to surprise you,' he said. 'I had to thank Ned Phelips for a favour, and I lay last night at Montacute.' They both spoke broad Somerset dialect, and nobody not of the county could have understood what they said. I am going away again,' Coryate told her.

She was not surprised. For what other reason would he require ten pounds from her? A bet with the linen draper Emblett in Yeovil had financed his trip to Europe but now, so far as she knew, he had no source of money beyond what he picked up at court and what he took from her. She did not grudge him any of it, though ten pounds was a large sum. But if he asked her for so much, he must have need of it.

'Where do you go this time?' she asked, a trifle timorous. When he returned from Europe she had asked him for details of his trip. He had gladly and lengthily described it to her (she was aware of his boastful streak) but she had never heard of any of the cities he had visited, nor most of the countries, and Tom had been irritated by this. She knew she was ignorant, but did not want her son to feel she was.

'I told you last time I was here, mother.' He would have

been annoyed had it not been for the fine weather outside and the familiar clean smell of the cottage: pomanders and fresh linen, and apples from the trees outside. 'I go to the Indies. But on the way I will visit the Holy Land. I will pray at the sepulchre of our saviour and bathe in the river Jordan. If I can, I will bring you back some relic from those holy places.' Knowing Tom, she doubted that he would, but she was pleased that he had thought of it. She smiled gratefully at him.

'But then,' Coryate said, 'I go to the lands of the Great Mogul, to the Indies. I will have audience of him, so he aid me travel to Tartary and China, as did the Italian Polo.' Since he had last met his mother, his plans had taken on a more grandiose shape and scale. 'In Tartary I will meet the Khan, in China the Emperor.' Gertrude's eyes had by now become glazed and wide. 'Then,' said her son airily, 'I will retrace my footsteps to Aleppo and make my way through Cairo in Egypt where once the Pharaohs ruled in splendour. From there I will enter the country of Ethiopia, the domains of the Prester John ...'

All these unknown names of places and honorifics horrified Gertrude. She now had only one question to ask, and she dreaded the answer.

'But, Tomalin,' she said, 'all this must be a goodly distance ...' Coryate interrupted her with violent affirmative nods of his misshapen head. 'By my accounting,' he said, 'the boots in the church carried me 1975 miles through Europe. On this trip, I estimate, my new pair will have to take me, at the least, 5000 miles.' Gertrude stared at him dumbly, but recovered sufficiently, in a while, to ask her question.

'And how many months will you be away?'

'Months?' her son guffawed through his beard. His stained

teeth showed. 'Months, mother? Remember the distances come to 5000 miles. It will be ten years before I come back, and more belike.'

Gertrude felt the floor shift, and spin like a cartwheel under her feet. Tom caught her by the arm before she fell. He stared with horror and disbelief at his mother, whose mouth opened and closed like that of a fish dragged from the river, conclusively removed from the single element that could sustain its life.

~

Coryate had been worried at first when his mother swooned in his arms. He had feared that she had some sickness; and there was no apothecary within miles. But when she came to, she was as steady as ever. She talked to him about normal village matters, the weather and the crops. She cooked him all the dishes that she knew he favoured. But she never asked him any more questions about his coming journey. He slightly resented this, for he felt she should take interest in his great venture. So he talked about it himself, but when he did, the glazed look came back to her eyes and she withdrew into silence.

In any case, he was out most of the time. He had come home as he had done immediately before he left for Europe, and for the same purpose. He wanted to rest his mind from the stresses of the city, and harden his body for the calls he would make upon it in the near future, as a Greek athlete might before he travelled to Olympia. He also wanted to test out his new boots, made to his finicky specifications by a shoemaker in Eastcheap. They were light, but of seasoned leather; and not too tight, for his feet would swell after a hard day. They were not handsome, but why should they be?

Their only work was to walk and they would see even harder use than the pair now in the church.

Coryate did not know exactly what kind of country he would have to traverse once he had left Aleppo. Few other travellers had taken this route to the Indies. But by various methods—notably by coaxing cash from the young and malleable Prince Henry—he had contrived to acquire some maps. They partially covered the areas through which he would have to walk. By studying these and perusing scraps of information left by previous travellers, he formed some idea of the hazards that lay ahead. The terrain he would face was not consistent in its physical features. He would have to negotiate wetlands and deserts and ford rivers, notably the Tigris. For much of his walk he would be in very high and perilous mountains, especially in the final stages, for he would have to come down to the Great Moghul's country through the Himalayas. Coryate took note of all this.

Somerset had no deserts, but it had rivers, wetlands, and, if not exactly mountains, a few steep hills. Moreover, it had open Country, and that provided most of what he needed. He set himself to cover twenty miles a day. He walked in different directions every time. It irritated him that the landscape was so familiar to him, but he could hardly change it. He climbed hills and waded rivers, and most of all he walked. It was usually dark, and he would be tired, when he got home.

Gertrude always waited up for him with hot food. Coryate, having eaten it, liked to sit at her feet, his head in her lap. She would run her fingers through his coarse curly hair as she had done all his life. At such times he regretted his coming departure. It sometimes also occurred to him that he should spend more time with her.

~

Few people encountered Coryate as he walked, but unless they knew him as Master Tom from Odcombe, they were seriously alarmed. Apart from his peculiar appearance, he constantly muttered to himself as he moved with an easy stride over the fields. Often his eyes were tightly shut as his lips worked, and his face was screwed up in intense concentration. If those who passed him by deciphered the sounds he made, their alarm increased, for the sounds made no sense to them.

Coryate had devised a method to defeat the boredom of incessant locomotion. He was surefooted and when on smooth and predictable terrain he would close his eyes and recite Greek or Latin poetry aloud to himself. He found that this soothed him and made his feet move to a rhythm. If the ground underfoot was unfriendly, he would continue to mutter to himself, but with his eyes open.

But occasionally, the mellifluous rumbles in his throat ceased. He glanced around him. All this landscape had associations. These were the fields he had walked through three years ago, troubled and alone. He had come back from Europe and written the *Crudities*. They had caused him much trouble. His style, baroque and elaborately facetious, came to him naturally, but many people found it unreadable.

He knew this was why no bookseller would print his work. But he knew also that in the *Crudities* he had done something new and unique. Embedded in the verbose and flamboyant prose was an amazing amount of close, detailed observation. It described the oddities and splendours of the places he had visited in Europe as no other book had done before, and he was happily aware of what he had achieved.

In the rough, tussocked fields of his country in winter he had found the solution to his troubles. He had gone back to London and consulted two friends, Master Ben and the dark-avised sensualist, Master John Donne, members of the Mermaid Club. They had caused more than sixty poets to write verses on the *Crudities,* mostly derisive, and they had also composed some. A furore ensued. All these verses were attached to the text, as a kind of preface, and a bookseller had seen the possibilities and agreed to print it. At the last minute, Coryate added his father's Latin verses to the book. The volume had come to more than 800 pages but still sold very well. Coryate became famous.

He smiled crookedly to himself as he recollected that coup. The book that followed it, *The Crambe,* had not been a success. *Crambe* meant cabbage cooked twice over. The book had been a rehash of the first volume and most people had found it flavourless. No matter. The book to be written on his coming travels would be a marvel to all the world, and now he could hardly wait to start.

~

He knew a little about the habits of ships. They could sail weeks later than they were supposed to, or earlier; they were unpredictable. Certainly if the *Samaritan* had cause to sail earlier than expected, the shipmaster would not wait for him. As things stood, she was supposed to put to sea in mid-October. But at the end of September Coryate, nervous, announced to his mother that he must leave next day.

Gertrude received this news with wry stoicism. There was little to pack. When Coryate went to Europe all he had taken with him was an extra shirt. The journey on which he now embarked was longer and more complex. This time he took more clothing, and a blanket, for winter was on its way and he would have no money to spend buying clothes on his travels. He furnished himself also with as much ink powder and paper as he could conveniently carry and a supply of quills, cut and uncut. Gertrude packed all this into a small, compact bundle. She made him a parcel of victuals to eat on the road.

That night, Coryate sat at the foot of her low chair, his head in her lap. She ran her fingers through his hair. She did not want to upset or annoy him in their last few hours together, but after a while she could not bear the silence. 'Tomalin,' she said, 'my son, why are you not like other men? Why do you not behave like other sons?'

'If I am not like other men,' Coryate replied sleepily, 'you should be proud, mother. And I am not like other sons only because I cherish you more than most sons do their mothers.' Silence fell between them once more. Coryate felt her tears falling on his face, though she made no sound. He shut his eyes so as not to see hers.

'And yet you would leave me here with no news of you for ten years?' Gertrude could not stop herself now. 'First you leave your father's corpse unburied for months on Ham Hill, then you leave your mother here, as good as in her grave, and tell her that in ten years you *may* return? Aye, you're very different from other men. Why do you make this crazed venture to lands no Englishman has seen? Why should *you* want to see them?' She now wept without any reserve, her last dignity abandoned. Coryate stared at her, appalled.

She saw the expression on his face. Sniffing loudly, because it was physically impossible not to, she wiped away her tears and blew her nose. Then she rose to her feet, pulling the tatters of lost pride around her. 'Enough,' she said. 'We must both to bed. You have an early start to make. And I do not want you to remember me like this.'

At dawn the next day, she stood at her door and watched Coryate walk away eastward towards Yeovil. At first he went slowly, and often turned back to wave, but then, as he found the rhythm of his stride, he walked faster. Where the Yeovil road dipped into distance, he seemed to remember a last duty, stopped a last time, and turned to wave.

Then he strode downhill. She could not see him any more. She went back inside the cottage and pushed the door shut.

~

At London docks on 16 October 1612, Thomas Coryate, carrying a small bundle of possessions wrapped in sackcloth, boarded the trading vessel *Samaritan,* bound eastward towards Constantinople.

4

Diary Two

October 2000–June 2002

Odcombe–Mumbai–London

As the taxi trundled downhill, we left the vicar waving to us, a large umbrella held up in one hand. Darkness flapped like crow's wings around him.

'Wasn't it thoughtful of the vicar to offer us two hundred pounds,' I said to Dom. 'Imagine starting a Sunday collection in the Odcombe church for our book.'

In the week after our meeting with the vicar, we had seen all that there was to be seen in Odcombe and talked to a small number of people who had something to tell us about Coryate, which wasn't very much. At the end of each day, we made notes in our book and soon found that the entries were being replicated.

'We better get back to London soon,' Dom said as we improvized some sort of dinner at Thorne Cottage. The rain raged that night.

But the next day the rain clouds had been dispersed by a wind so cold that it shivered within itself. For the first time in days, glass windowpanes around the village glittered and flashed as they reflected the aberrant sun. Dom was eager to start our daily trip to Odcombe. We drove to the St Peter and St Paul's church on the hill and once more he prowled around it, inside and outside, examining everything with the intensity of a researcher looking for relics of an ancient civilization.

As I stood looking up at the church, the soundless wing of a bird brushed my shoulder. I couldn't identify what it was, not knowing English birds, but it glided up towards the belltower. The bells that hung there were unpolished and seemed very old. The bird perched beside them. *Ghooot ghooot,* it cried, its head raised to the sky.

I entered the church through a side door left open. Daylight shone opaquely through the Victorian stained glass windows of the nave and north transept depicting Jesus Christ and the twelve apostles. The Enid Blytonesque woman who had first opened the church for us had told me that the windows had been taken from St Anne's Church in Hewish, long redundant. They were fitted in the 1980s, she said, in place of the austere Victorian windows that had been there until then.

She had advised me to take note of the window at the northeast corner of the chancel. Archie Dean and his wife had donated it to the church when he retired in 1991 after thirty years as rector. As I stood in the chancel, I realized that the bones of Coryate's father, George, were somewhere under my feet. Goosebumps ran down my spine.

I approached the altar. Icicles of light splintered in through the cross in the centre of the window, encircled by glass in a circle of burning red. The Blytonesque woman had decoded the design for me. 'The red is for Fire. The blue around it is the Holy Ghost; the green is for Growing Things, and above it shining, is the Light of Life.' I sat down on a bench looking up at the light; then I heard Dom calling me.

'The outside of the church must be as Coryate saw it,' he mumbled abstractedly, 'but there've been a hell of a lot of changes inside. I don't know why they can't leave old churches alone. That goes for everything old, people as well.'

On our way back to Yeovil, Bob, the taxi driver who had been driving us around for several days, told Dom that he had looked up the telephone directory and there was not a single entry under the surname Coryate. But he had been able to track down a descendant of Coryate's sister who lived in another village not far away from Yeovil. He offered to drive us to her house.

'Not today, no,' Dom said. 'But thanks a million, Bob.' He looked at the piece of paper that Bob had given him; his eyes were impassive as he folded it carefully and put it into his wallet. 'What's this lady's name?' I asked urgently. But Dom only turned towards the window, and lit a cigarette.

We got off at the Somerset County Library. Dom paid the fare to which he added a generous tip. Then, as Bob drove away, he ground his cigarette out on the pavement with the heel of his shoe and laughed.

'What is it?' I asked.

'Bob's a sweetheart,' he said as we walked into the library. 'But this wouldn't have been any use and, besides, Coryate never had a sister.'

The librarian was a small and wizened man. His eyes were watchful and icy blue, and his face a vigorous red, bony and clean-shaven. He wore a yellowed white shirt and a dark blue suit. He muttered to himself constantly, but was helpful. He shambled down the aisles of shelves, one hand behind his back, pointing out the books to Dom with the other.

They talked about Coryate, which filled them both with obvious pleasure. As though they were a duo of conspirators, the librarian led Dom to a glass cupboard in a room, opened it with a key from a large bunch and let him look at some very rare books.

Later we walked to the Mermaid. While Dom drank his quota of wine, I filled myself with enough hot food for the rest of the day; somehow the cold made me uneasy. Bolstered with one or two bottles of wine, a plastic corkscrew, and parcelled pies and savoury puffs from a takeaway for dinner, we returned to Thorne Cottage. By nightfall we had finished the wine, but the food was soggy and limp; we raided the kitchen for bread, butter and eggs. I selected a pink crystal wineglass from the shelf, and put it on the table with some money in it. The routine was set. The wineglass was to remain on the table, a hieroglyph comprehended by Bill and his wife, until the day we left.

But I remember that night, his face radiant from the aromatic glow of the candle, highlights in his eyes as though they were painted on the irises, the sound of rain drumming on the windowpane, Dom sang in a soft broken voice, out of sheer high spirits, I suppose:

> *'I set my back against an oak,*
> *Thinking that it was a trusty tree ...*
> *But first it bent and syne it broke ...*
> *Sae my true love hath forsaken me.'*

~

Bill let me use his computer to key in the notes I had made in the library. 'The printer's no good,' he said. 'But there're some business centres in Yeovil who'll print for you.'

I located a cyber cafe in the alley behind the New Look store not too far from Burger King. The young fellow who owned it was friendly. He was dressed in a military green pullover and brown cargo pants with deep pockets. He wore rings on each of the fingers of his left hand, and one eyebrow was completely shaven. In its place was an arc of steel studs.

I asked him, in the course of our conversation, and as he showed me how to operate his computer, if he had heard of Coryate; he hadn't. He seemed interested in the story and to my astonishment offered me a 50 per cent discount on the use of the printer and reduced my log-in fee.

'Just pay for an hour,' he said his hands stuffed benevolently into his pockets, 'and use the net for as long as you want. It doesn't happen every day; two people coming all the way from India to write about a dead Somerset man.'

I ran into Bob at the taxi rank. He waved cheerfully to me as I got into the taxi in front of his. 'Did you find Thomas' relative?' he shouted as I drove away. 'I'll look for your book in Smith's when it's out. Good luck to you both.'

On our last evening at Thorne Cottage, Bill gloomily told us they were sorry: they had been invited out to dinner and couldn't spend the evening with us. 'There's some salmon pie in the oven and a tomato-and-olive salad in the fridge. Do please help yourselves,' his wife said as they left.

Dom had bought a bottle of expensive wine. We settled down to our feast of salad and pie in the dining room. I lit the rectangular candle, which had steadily consumed its own shape. Dom ceremoniously put the wine bottle on the table and twisted the plastic corkscrew into the cork; it promptly broke. I searched for a metal corkscrew but couldn't find one. I tried a screwdriver, then strove to split the cork with a knife.

It was no use. The evening wilted away. I stood the bottle between the candle and the pink crystal wineglass, unopened, undrunk, its dark red contents reflecting the candle's flame. Dom looked forlorn; to make him feel better I said earnestly, 'If you want a drink we could walk to the pub.' My suggestion immediately made him feel worse.

The next morning, we drove to the church. Curiously, the flowerbeds along the driveway seemed more colourful in this dismal weather. Then we drove further up the road to look for the caves in one of which Coryate had stored his father's corpse. The mouths of the caves were sealed with heavy undergrowth. 'Growth seems very quick here,' Dom observed. 'Almost tropical. No, that's a silly thing to say. But this place is really addictive, and the people are marvellous.'

As we walked to the car, he said, 'I wonder why Thomas ever left here, particularly to go to bloody India.'

At Thorne Cottage, we found a note Bill had left for us on the dining table. 'Sorry to have missed you this morning. We've had to go to Yeovil suddenly. Please leave your address in Mumbai. We hope to see you here next year. Good luck with your book. Have a drink before you leave.'

In the middle of the table was our bottle of wine, open, the broken corkscrew next to it, and another wine glass that matched the pink crystal one in which I had left banknotes last night. The notes were still untouched. Dom put the money on the table, with a scribble of thanks and good wishes to Bill and his wife, and poured the wine. 'It's not as good as I thought,' he said sourly, 'but it was thoughtful of Bill, don't you think?' The sun was out when we left.

~

The next day in London we combed secondhand bookshops for a copy of Michael Strachan's book on Coryate. The day after that we went to the British Library; they said we needed a temporary membership card. 'We can't issue one without a recommendation letter,' the woman behind the desk told Dom.

'We can ask Christopher MacLehose for the letter,' Dom said as we walked into the street. 'In any case we ought to meet him. I'd like to know what he thinks of the Coryate idea.' MacLehose, the owner of the Harvill Press, was a friend of Dom's.

Dom had a call next morning from a bookseller who had been able to locate a book we needed. He rushed off, asking me to meet him directly at the Harvill Press where we were to meet Christopher MacLehose. Over lunch, Dom and he talked about many things but never about the Coryate book.

When he had finished his coffee, Christopher folded the paper napkin in front of him. 'Tell me about this curious fellow from Somerset,' he said. Dom told him. Dom asked him for a letter of recommendation for the British Library, and more urgently where we could find funding for the book. 'And Christopher, we're going to be broke rather soon; do you know of a cheap place to stay in London?'

MacLehose made notes on the napkin. He looked up when he had finished, said, 'Let me tell you what I can do. I'll write you the letter for the British Library. The other thing I can do is to talk to someone at London House. It's not very far from the British Museum; it's a dormitory of sorts for research scholars. I need to get three people to recommend you two for this. Now, regarding the funding,' he said folding the napkin into a tiny square and putting it into his pocket, 'why don't you write me an outline of the book when you return to India. I can't promise anything, but I'll see what I can do.'

The letter of recommendation for the British Library arrived the next day by courier. We got our passes without too much trouble and started our research. While we looked at ancient books, Dom with deep and unrequited love, and I with some reservations about the dust they had collected, we lived first in a cheap hotel and then in London House.

This was a hostel for senior students and rather austere, but I wasn't bothered by that. What bothered me, and I think Dom too, though he never said so, was that it was full of young people who reflexively moved away from us, as if the aging process was a transmissible disease. When I grumbled, Dom inquired unsympathetically, 'How do you think old Thomas would have felt in India?'

Once we had finished our work in the British Library, fifty pounds between us and with Dom running a low temperature, we left for Mumbai.

~

'We'll follow Coryate's route from Afghanistan to Pakistan and into India, then all the way to Surat and his tomb,' Dom explained. 'But you'd better not come with me to Afghanistan,' he added. 'If we can get a visa for you then possibly you can join me in Pakistan. Although I don't think it'll be easy.'

We would need big money for a trip like this, I realized, and, therefore, more than one organization to support us. We wrote out a lengthy and detailed synopsis, and sent copies out to several sponsors. We sent a copy to MacLehose. A year passed rapidly but we had found no one to back the project; and MacLehose never replied.

'This book's never going to be written,' Dom declared sadly one evening. It was a grey, overcast day in December. 'Poor Thomas Coryate. Apart from Archie Dean, who's a Somerset man, nobody's willing to help us.' Dom looked despondent; his head hung low and he stared vacantly at his palms lying limp in his lap. 'Two hundred pounds, the vicar said he would collect for us. At least he showed willingness.'

It is hard to imagine now how each event was choreographed to happen. We fixed a date after which, we told ourselves, we would stop looking for sponsors. I packed away all the notes and other material we had collected on Coryate in England. I worked on an idea for another book we could write together. Not because we would have something to do, more to assuage Dom's misery. I left him early one evening with a rough outline for the book. He was running a low temperature and didn't appear too well. 'I think I'll go to bed early,' he said. Night was about to fall, a pinkish blue.

Next morning he called early. 'Do you think you can come here by ten?'

'Why so early? Are you OK?'

'There's a man coming here at ten ... I want you to talk to him.'

'Who?'

'A chap called Mukul Patel. He says he manufactures men's shirts. His shop's on Old Ice Factory Road, not far from that block of flats that belonged to my mother. This Mukul chap came to my flat late last night with an offer to buy the entire block of flats,' Dom said. 'He wants me to sign some papers this morning. Can you come?'

Two weeks later the transfer of the property took place in a dilapidated courtroom. Mukul Patel, a plump sleek man in a shiny polyester safari suit and a saffron kumkum dot on his forehead, came out with Dom. He was smiling. He bowed to Dom and made a namaskar that was not reciprocated. Instead, Dom glared at him and marched over to the taxi in which I waited.

We got into the taxi. 'That frightful fellow,' Dom snarled as he got in. 'He only paid me half of what we'd agreed on. He told the judge that the building was on the verge of collapse and he would have to spend a lot of money to repair it. This is entirely correct, I agree, but why did he want to buy it in the first place? Then he told the judge that I had no documents for the property. Which of course,' he added pensively, 'is unfortunately true.'

The taxi sped through the afternoon crowd. Despite ending up half as wealthy as he could have been, Dom hummed a tune. 'This is for Tom Coryate,' he declared, patting the briefcase in his lap. It wasn't much, still he laughed in sheer pleasure. 'If he was alive, he'd never have believed it, that a Gujarati swindler from Surat, a shirt manufacturer from Old Ice Factory Road, made it possible for us to write a book about him.' Dom continued to pat the briefcase with both thumbs. 'This money's only enough for a small part of our travels for the book. We'll have to find sponsors for the rest of it. But let's start again. You haven't thrown away all the notes we made on Coryate have you?'

It seems to me now like a curious lesson from the plot of providence that operates unaided but with irony. I wasn't prepared for the most awful event possible. Neither was Dom.

It happened some weeks later: one evening as we returned after an encouraging meeting with a sponsor, Dom remarked that a mosquito had bitten him on his neck, and it had swollen. Two days later the swelling had grown into a lump the size of an orange. The doctor suggested that Dom get some tests done. They confirmed the most brutal fact we had ever faced. Dom had cancer.

He had some time, the doctor told Dom candidly, but not very much, unless he agreed to undergo radiation. Dom refused any form of treatment. 'I don't have a lot to do,' he said without undue excitement, 'I want to go to London for one last time. I want to be able to finish writing the Coryate book. And if there is some time left after that, I want to work on my collected poems. Tell me how I can stay around long enough to do those things.' He laughed, but his eyes were moist as he said to me, 'What I need immediately is to get as pissed as is humanly possible.' He did.

It was a sheer number of things, friends and acquaintances, and goodwill accumulated over years that helped us locate sponsors without further delay. The lack of time and the urgency of his condition, the shock and despair, and more notably the huge pretence of normalcy between us seemed to make our arrangements work. Two weeks after surgery had removed the tumour from his neck, Dom and I were in London.

It was early June, and summer, but it was cold. It rained nearly every day. We may have been sad, but, unquestionably, we were also glad.

~

As soon as we reached London, Dom called up Reg Warr. A few days later, we boarded the train to Yeovil Junction. We didn't expect Reg at the station; but he was there, welcoming us like old friends. He had booked us in a resort hotel in West Coker. On the way to the hotel he told us that Archie Dean was expecting us at 4 p.m. We dumped our luggage at the hotel, then went to a nearby pub for lunch. When it was time, Reg drove us to the vicar's house.

Dom asked him about Archie Dean. 'The last time we met him he was remarkably fit for his age, but his wife, we couldn't meet her, she was unwell. How is she?'

Reg cleared his throat. 'Oh, you don't know then. She was driving home from work later than usual. As she turned into the main road, her car hit a truck. She died on the spot.'

'I am so sorry,' Dom said. 'It must have been terrible for the vicar. How does he manage by himself?'

'His daughter lives in West Coker, not far away from him. She comes every day. You'll meet her.'

The vicar was in the front garden as we drove up Chur Lane. He looked older, pale and slightly shrunk. His grey hair was combed neatly. He walked with difficulty into the living room, one hand against his back. Four large sofas were arranged in a semi-circle around the television set. He sank into the one near the wall with extra cushions, and carefully settled himself on them. 'I slipped and fell, and I've sprained my back,' he explained.

I looked at the ancient map on the wall and up at the large, almost black, uncut wooden beam running across the room. Outside the window, a large bush was studded with red roses. Incense burned in the fireplace. The vicar asked abruptly, 'I suppose you want to collect local information. Have you heard the story of the Odcombe church bell?'

The church, he told us, had five bells. But the cage was for six. A local builder agreed to restore the church if his name was engraved on the sixth bell. So a group of people went from village to village, with a recording of the sounds of the five bells, and a tuning fork. They had to find a bell that matched the sound of the other five. They found a suitable one in a church in Raddington. The church was being used only by four people, three of them were school children. And the tower wasn't safe. So they bought the bell for a hundred pounds, and hung it in the Odcombe belfry.'

Dom looked puzzled. The vicar shifted in his chair and his face crumpled in pain. He smiled feebly, and told us some more rather pointless tales, his voice frail and almost inaudible. His chin dropped steadily into his neck. Dom looked at his watch, 'I think we must leave now.'

'Don't tell me that!' The vicar sat up in his chair. 'I think I can hear my daughter in the kitchen. She's getting tea ready. You must have some.'

'Would you like to see my garden while we wait for tea?' he asked me. He got up from his sofa with difficulty. 'Come along,' he said flicking a hand in the air. 'Follow me, all of you.' He led us through the dining room, through the back door into the garden that tumbled downward towards the road. His face lit up as he pointed out each flower and tree. As we walked back to the house, I could hear the sound of cutlery and china from the kitchen. I could smell melted cheese, smoked-something and cake that was freshly baked. Shortly, the daughter was at the back door calling us in; she was large with a pleasant face. We followed her into the dining room.

We sat at a long wooden table, the vicar at its head. Along the length of the table plates were arranged: sandwiches, cheese toasts, tarts, three types of cakes, cookies and pastries. If this was high tea in West Coker, what were lunch and dinner like?

Dom unfurled his napkin. The vicar turned to him, 'I assume you are a practising Christian?' Dom held the napkin against his mouth, mumbled incomprehensibly into it.

'I see,' said the vicar. 'And you Sarahyou?'

'She's not Christian,' Dom replied hastily.

'That leaves you, Reg.' The vicar turned to him. 'Will you say grace?'

Reg joined his hands and with his head bowed he thanked the Lord. It was an elaborate grace that he made up as he went on. Finally he said, 'Bless them, Lord, the two who have come from afar and are here with us today. Bless them on their quest for Thomas Coryate, once of this parish.'

The vicar offered Dom a plate of sandwiches. 'I hope you will finish the book soon,' he said; he had made a similar remark on his last trip. 'I am almost ninety-six and you must realize I haven't much time left.'

Dom said, so quietly only I heard him, 'Neither have I.'

~

It was not the sound of the rain that woke me. Rain in Somerset falls gently as though on hammocks of clouds: soft and tentative. I was used to the torrid, noisy rain of the tropics. It was the distant cry of a bird. *Ghooot ghooot,* as if a deep masonry well was wedged in its throat.

The window of my room was slightly open and the breeze was cool and crisp. Outside the window, the orange blossom tree, flushed with flowers, smelled sweetly of simmered scent. The day was already bright, not with harsh yellow light but one that was softer, whiter, pearl-coloured; and the sky was a brilliant blue even after the rain, festooned with slightly moist clouds like laundry hung out to dry.

I looked at my watch; it was only a quarter to six. Would it be all right for me to walk through the village, a stranger in a strange place? Dom, who was in the adjoining room, I was certain was fast asleep and would not stir for another two hours. I plucked the pair of jeans from the chair where I had dropped them the previous night and dressed in a terrific hurry. Pulling my coat firmly around me I walked up the meandering road towards the fields, following the cry of the bird. *Ghooot ghooot.*

I walked past cottages with slated roofs, and walls built uniformly of the local yellow Ham stone and hung with thick helmets of flowering vines, which cast scalloped shadows. Enormous roses grew in their pocket-handkerchief size gardens that spilled onto the road in a cunningly well-planned tangle of wild flowers. Unable to resist, I bent over a lemon yellow rose as large as a saucer; its sweet scent filled my nostrils.

As I turned my head, I noticed an old man a few yards away watching me; he smiled, waved a hand. 'Good morning to you,' he said, 'I see that you like flowers.' He looked at the rose near my nose, then smiled once more, 'Very nice day indeed, but,' he held up his umbrella, 'if I were you I would be prepared for it to rain soon.' I mumbled a greeting, a meek thank you, waved a reluctant hand in the air, then crossed the road, and walked away.

I startled a pigeon on the pavement. With a flurry of wings the pigeon perched itself on top of a lamp post. It was a large, plump, light-skinned bird, grey-white, but in comparison to its size it made rather polite murmuring sounds. Rooks, very black and with vast wings, flew quietly overhead and sparrows twittered on the grass. As I turned the corner I saw a huge dog, almost chinless, its eyes covered with straggly hair. I froze in my tracks. A young bearded man, similarly scruffy came up behind the dog. His coat was worn out. I gaped suspiciously at him. 'Good morning,' he said holding the dog's collar. I crossed to the other side of the road. 'Enjoy your walk,' he called out as I hurried up the road.

A car full of people momentarily separated him from me. 'Good morning,' two women waved out to me as the car sped away. 'Good morning,' I muttered, surprised; they didn't even know me.

I walked to the top of the hill and stepped into what appeared to me a gigantic inverted bowl of green acres. Further away, I could see the road twist and transform into a shallow trough edged with high earth banks and tall reeds almost ten feet high on both sides. Not far from where I stood I saw a large snail-coloured bird in the field—its neck stretched out to the fullest extent, its head lifted up to the sky, its throat gulping convulsively, it gave a yawping cry: *Ghooot ghooot ...*

A sudden wet breeze blew my hair into a tangle, the sun was bun-warm, and the dew had made spitlines on the grass. On an impulse, I removed my shoes and socks; picking them up in each hand I ran down the grassy hill. Bits of grass like minuscule blades pricked my feet. A snail crunched. A twig snapped. It started to rain. I ran towards a tree, tall, its trunk thick as a Greek column. I pressed my cheek against its bark. It had a sweet pungent smell, a combination of cinnamon and wild jasmine. I was glad to be here. I had seen Coryate's country as it was today. I thought about Dom, imminent pain choking him, and remembered the day when I had hugged the Ashoka Pillar and he had told me about Thomas Coryate. So much had happened since then. I pressed my body to the tree trunk, wrapped my arms around it. My fingers didn't quite meet.

~

We returned to London a week later. Dom met his friends one by one. He didn't know if he would see them again.

Their meetings were gentle and dignified. Only Christopher MacLehose proved to be elusive. We fixed to meet three times; each time his secretary called up to cancel the appointment. Christopher was in Amsterdam; he was expected to arrive by the morning flight and we had a definite date for lunch. But the flight was late by five hours.

It was our last day in London. Dom left a message on Christopher's voicemail asking him to join us for a drink at a pub close to where we stayed. We were surprised to see him towering at the door against the light. The bar was noisy so Christopher walked us to another; it was crowded, so he led us to yet another. We walked to six bars but could find none that weren't noisy and packed. Dom was breathless and terribly tired. 'You don't mind skipping the drink?' Christopher said to him as he walked us into the park by the Serpentine. A sign told visitors not to feed the pelicans.

The sun had sunk and the sky was cellophane blue. I left them sitting on a bench. Christopher didn't know that Dom was ill and I knew Dom wanted to say goodbye to him. Not far away, a dishevelled man fastidiously selected bits of food from the garbage bin, and beyond him I saw five birds shoot up from the river in a perfect circle against the sky.

5

Oasis in the Desert

Books had fascinated Tom Coryate even as a small boy. The first ones he had ever seen were those in his father's study, a room that the rector habitually locked when he was not in it. George Coryate prized his small library, which contained a few rare volumes, some from his Oxford days. He was afraid that Tom might, by childish mishap, deface them; even more, that Gertrude might dust them.

But one day he decided to show Tom his books. The boy, at seven, had attained the age of reason and the rector was pleased by the respect he showed the musty volumes stacked around the walls. Tom had to stand on a stool to reach the higher shelves. At first George supervised his small son's behaviour with the books. Reassured that they would be safe, he allowed the boy the freedom of his library.

But Tom first had to ask his father to unlock it. The rector would then lock him in, until he called to be let out. Gertrude often muttered about her exclusion from the premises. She asked her husband what books he had that he did not want her to see, and why he should allow an innocent boy access to them. But it was not for some months after he died that she violated his posthumous privacy, weeping.

She had found no book she could have objected to, and hadn't expected that she would. But the desolate study had become a shrine to Tom. He remembered how it had looked when his father was alive, when the bookshelves and desk had dwarfed him and the dusty volumes were beyond count; how it had smelt: of books, his father's armpits and beard, and errant scents of whatever season it was.

From those books, seen before childhood abandoned him, what Tom best remembered were the pictures, especially one. It showed a gaunt naked Christ, bleeding profusely and nailed to a cross. Thunderheads massed in the sky above him. Yellow stone hills, like Ham Hill, surrounded him, stained with purple flowers. Nearby, from habitations made of the same malleable stone, hooded heads peered.

One evening, George Coryate had found his young son, home early from one of his long walks, studying the picture as though he needed to memorize it. The rector said, 'That is a portrayal of our Lord Jesus as he died to save humankind.' Tom said impatiently, 'I know. But where was it?' His father said, 'Jerusalem', and the boy replied, 'I'll walk in that same place, once I'm a grown man.'

Gertrude often quoted this story to relatives and friends, as proof of her son's precocity and piety. But George said, 'What the boy told me does not show that he will turn saint. His wish is not to walk where our Lord did. He needs strange places because it is in his nature. If he comes where no other Christian has been, no God will guide him, but only what he believes in, and maybe that will be best.'

~

The gyre-like whorls of the trail upward unwound without end, but gradually, higher up in the hills, the air became free of dust, and cooler. Simeon, who shambled like an ape beside him on the narrow path, announced, 'Soon now we will see God's city!'

Coryate's skin was blistered crimson, his blonde beard verminous and discoloured with dust. But his complexion was still recognizable as that of a white man, a Christian. Simeon, a pilgrim from Syria and a follower of the Asiatic Church, had accompanied him since they first accidentally met at Joppa. He saw the white man as a brother in the faith; mostly a floundering and noisy nuisance, but still a species of Christian and, therefore, a brother.

They hitched their packs up on eroded shoulders to lurch round a turn in the road. Simeon cried out and raised his hands, for on the hillside now visible, ahead, strewn with yellow rocks, was a collection of ramshackle huts and low houses built of those rocks. From the picture he had seen in the Odcombe rectory, Coryate recognized the city of Jerusalem.

But little more remained to be recognized from the picture, or other representations Coryate had seen of the holy city. An Islamic town, governed by Turks, had replaced it, and the muezzins issued reminders for prayers from the minarets five times a day. Their prolonged ululations, punctuated by phlegmy glottal stops, offended Coryate's ear as well as his religious beliefs.

The Romans, in a previous millenium, had pulled down the monolithic Jewish temple and most of the monuments. The great stones were strewn about the hillsides; some used for Muslim tombs in a graveyard at the foot of the hill. But Coryate remembered the purple wild flowers on the slopes from the picture. They reassured him. He was in Jerusalem.

The town was full of pilgrims from many places, also of those whose natural prey they had become. Though not a sceptical man, Coryate had realized long ago that tricksters and holy places had an affinity for each other. But when Simeon suggested that they visit an Arab tattoo expert to decorate their wrists with indelible images of the Holy Land, Coryate agreed without question. The process was tedious and painful and he spent precious pennies on it.

They lodged free in one of the pilgrim shelters. Most days they ate Arab bread with falafel (fried chickpeas): an economical and filling diet that greatly appealed to Coryate. He was lucky in his companion. Simeon was a petty trader in Damascus, with only the most basic physical needs. He knew how to live cheaply. He also taught Coryate much more than the rudimentary Arabic he had so far got out of books.

Simeon had been a trader all his life. Until this trip he had considered himself knowledgeable about other men, even himself. His experience assured him that in the end all men were motivated by needs and, therefore, by money; but his experience was of no use to him when it came to Coryate. Simeon was squat, bulky, anthropoid, with long arms that swung loosely as he walked. Coryate, his eyes full of urchin pleasure, often made malevolent puns in English that matched the Syrian's name to his looks. Simeon did not understand these remarks, but he watched the other man closely, and laughed whenever he did.

Coryate laughed often, for no reason visible to his companion; a high, braying sound that, even in a densely packed souk, turned heads towards him. He also talked incessantly, sometimes to himself. At these times the lids of his bulbous eyes seemed to nictitate like a bird's, and the words he muttered were neither English nor Arabic, but had a rich, resonant and ancient sound that awed Simeon.

But when the two men were alone, they spoke Arabic. Coryate had learned enough to carry on a conversation. It was in this way that Simeon heard why the Englishman had come so far from home. He wanted to travel through desert and mountains to India. Simeon had met other traders with the same desire, but however rich they were, the distances and expenses involved had finally put them off; the profits might be too small to justify the investment.

But Coryate was not at all interested in trade. Simeon dolefully recited, like black beads on a rosary, a list of the hardships strung out along the road to India. The giaour, Coryate, listened carefully, unaffected. People had no fear, perhaps, when they had no money. This notion came to Simeon suddenly, and troubled him. He questioned himself.

At first he had thought Coryate might be mad. If so he was, by the customs of all Arabs, a protected person. But now Simeon did not think him mad. Mad people did not do what Coryate did. At evening, he squatted on the stone floor of the shelter. A kindled wick floated in a bowl of oil beside him. He placed a wooden board across his lap and spread sheets of paper upon it. For hours he covered sheet after sheet with a loose, scrawled script, unknown to Simeon. Afterwards he yawned, stretched and snored.

He was trying, he said when Simeon asked, to describe what he had seen during the day. This sounded fatuous, for they had seen nothing unusual. But Coryate was always looking at houses, at trees, at rocks, as though he had never before seen any. He watched people go about their daily tasks as though they were angels, not ordinary Arabs. He was not afflicted by madness, Simeon decided, but by a kind of sanity nobody else would understand, and because of this was more vulnerable than other men.

It was to protect Coryate that Simeon walked with him into Galilee. Bandits abounded in the area. Afterwards, he reflected that they would hardly have bothered to rob a dwarf in soiled Arab clothes. But in the end he was glad he had come. By Kinnereth lake, Coryate became uplifted, joyful as a child. He stared at the low blue hills around, from which a shrouded sun came daily to walk on the water. He examined the local fishermen's shacks and coracles as though they were made of some precious material. He defaced many sheets of paper with his scribbles.

When they returned to Jerusalem, Coryate took leave of Simeon. He needed to take ship to Aleppo. The trader was staying behind, and was regretful when they parted. A bond had been welded between them and Coryate trusted him as few others did.

He had entrusted Simeon with a parcel of papers to be delivered in Damascus to any English traveller on his way home, but only if Simeon thought the man reliable. The traveller was to deliver them to an address in London. Simeon was reluctant at first to accept this responsibility, but Coryate insisted.

Then the merchant found a small caravan that would take his friend to Smyrna. Coryate did not seem to feel regrets when they parted, but, rather, appeared to be gleeful at the prospect of new travel. As he embraced Simeon, his loose sleeves slipped back to reveal the complicated black crusader insignia that had been branded on his wrists in Jerusalem.

'It was you persuaded me to command these,' he said. 'I thank you. They will be with me while I live. Whenever I set eyes on them I shall remember you. Though,' he added sourly, 'they came too costly.' He shuffled away to be lost in caravan dust.

~

Coryate's world underwent changes, sometimes every day. He had climbed the frozen path across Mount Van, a path sometimes little wider than a ledge, and slithery with snow. He had waded the Tigris, though in that season the water only came up to his calf. He had been forced to wait four months in Aleppo before he found a caravan large enough to be safe for the long trip to India. But his situation was, by its own nature, unsafe. He had learned from his experience in Europe and had taken care, from the time he entered Asia, to conceal his meagre money in different parts of his apparel and possessions.

In Aleppo, he had not only survived insufferable heat, but also the attentions of blowflies and of thieves. The Turks and Armenians hated one another, but were as one in their desire to plunder strangers. A burly Turk soldier, a Spahi, took seventy shillings from him by force; Armenian tricksters cozened him of ten more. Thereby, he lost nearly half the money he had, with not half his journey yet done. This filled him with fear that soon none would be left for his survival.

Meanwhile, the great caravan he was with, a travelling town, its boundaries demarcated by armed outriders, passed the grim black fortress of Diarbekir and entered the true desert. The caravan contained more than 5000 mules, camels and people. A giant cloud of scuffed sand rose around it, and charted its slow progress for the carrion birds that hovered over, in a sky leached of colour by the sun.

Coryate's whole world had shrivelled into sand. The wind roared and flung it about. Sometimes it swirled round his body and clothed him in fire. Often it came at him from the front so that he had to wade against it like a scalding tide. He had taken to native dress early on in this trip. Though his heavy robes and headcloth were encrusted with sand, and held it in their folds, they shielded him from the heat better than western clothes did. But grit sealed and seared his nostrils and eyes; the never-ending wind deafened him.

As the colossal mass of beasts and men moved on, it made its own muffled sounds of suffering. The wind keened around it like a mourner, or uttered wild, convulsive shrieks, but mostly roared in a dull monotone. Coryate, his head tightly wrapped and lowered, butted his way onward. Now and then his body collided with that of another man, or an animal's wet, furry flank, but such contacts did not reassure, they only emphasized its own isolation.

Towards nightfall, gongs and drums were beaten, a trumpet brayed and the long eddy of movement slowed to a trickle and stopped. The drivers settled their animals for the night. Those camp followers who, like Coryate, had no animals made themselves feel useful. They built up fires of dry camel turds and spread their blankets by the reluctant flames. A slow, bone-deep chill would come with the darkness.

Soon other men joined the firemakers. Most of the company travelled in parties, and most of these had food to cook and conversations to renew with their fellows. Only a few solitary wayfarers like Coryate, too poor to buy food that needed to be cooked, sat alone. Coryate had made a few attempts to talk to other men during the night halts, but was usually rebuffed. He chewed his dry provender—Arab bread, dates and preboiled chickpeas—on his own.

But he did not feel sorry for himself, nor seem to encourage pity. While the Muslims, led by a mullah, prostrated themselves and prayed, he kept busy, scribbling by the light of the banked fire. Then he wrapped himself in his blanket and lay down.

The camp, even in the dark hours, never slept. Camels grumbled, mules snorted, ropes creaked. Above all, Coryate could hear the steady pullulation of human snores. Also many unhappy men were up all night with dysentery. Their groans came to him on the chilly air, and the other sounds they made. By dawn the camp would smell like a latrine.

But Coryate watched the desert. It fascinated him always. The wind never ceased to sculpt it. The rounded dunes would disappear in a flurry of sand, then suddenly be rebuilt in a different place, either as more dunes or as long, exquisitely exact, parallel ridges, or shapes that seemed part of mysterious, elaborate architectural constructs, old as the world.

At night, when the moon shone on it, the normally lion-coloured sand took on the utterly pure whiteness and texture of Christmas snow in Odcombe. But the stars were not English: they glittered in millions over Coryate's head, and sometimes one or the other slipped from its place and fell towards earth, leaving a shining trail behind it, even in that absence of air. Whenever he saw this, awe filled him, and later his sleep was childlike, till broken by the drums at dawn.

~

An oasis known to all travellers stood in the heart of the desert. Densely leafed palm trees threw shadows down around a pool of water that was at most times of the year fragrant and cool. Today, an observer overhead would have imagined that a gaudy ornamental garden had sprouted in the oasis. In it, rows of small flowers formed a symmetrical circle around a colossal central blossom, mauve as a cross-bred rose. Inordinate numbers of insects seemed to swarm around it.

From ground level, the observer would have seen that the insects were in reality liveried servants and the flowers were tents. The mauve tent, larger than the rest, overlooked the pool. Outside it a young woman, consciously beautiful, stood by a table. Her slender hands arranged dried flowers in a vase. She glanced down at the pool. She knew how desirable a picture she made, her hands full of flowers, even dried ones, and regretted it was not warmly reflected by male eyes, but only by an unresponsive mirror of water.

From the tent behind her she heard Robert call, 'Make speed, milady. The caravan should be here soon, and our guest with it.' Things had moved at speed since, that morning, a messenger had come from another large caravan, this one approaching the oasis from Aleppo. This meant the Shirleys would have to make room for it and move on this very day.

It was no great matter. They were well furnished with comforts and money, however rough the trip ahead might be. They had a sufficiency of body servants, including a personal maid, and also of fighting men. But the messenger had brought a missive in English, sent by a traveller who was with the caravan from Aleppo. He had been told they were English; he greatly desired to meet them.

The letter had been scrawled on poor paper, in extraordinary and flowery language. Ordinarily, Robert would have thrown it away; but on reading it a second time his eyes narrowed, and he said, 'Coryate? Coryate? Meseems we have two books with us, written by this same fellow. We got them in Portugal, and they were all the rage in London then. Aye, Coryate. I have heard he has influence in Prince Henry's court. We must butter him up, Tessie, and cosset him as we can. One day in London we may stand in need of some service from this fellow.'

Robert Shirley always used people; it brought him rewards as a rule. He was one of many Englishmen of the time who lived by his wits. He had intelligence and a presence; he called himself Sir Robert, and his beautiful Circassian wife, picked up on his travels, had proved an asset as Lady Teresa. They were on their way back to the imperial court of Persia, for the emperor Shah Abbas was Sir Robert's master at the moment. They had come from Jehangir's court, where they had been well received. Shirley hoped to become very rich after his peregrinations in the east.

'We shall have to move out of this place after we have entertained him,' he now told Teresa. 'You have ordered the food and drink? Now dress to please him; aye, curtsey to this Coryate, let him ogle your bubbies to his heart's content, but no more. We have not the time. Make haste, Tessie, make ready.'

A cloud of dust out in the desert proclaimed the arrival of the new caravan, but it was still a great way off. The servants struck all the tents except the Shirleys' own, and loaded up. Most of Shirley's caravan was ready to move by the time Coryate's arrived, but his brobdinagian mauve tent still stood in the oasis and Shirley made it clear that he would not budge until he had entertained his countryman.

The leaders of Coryate's caravan grumbled and scowled at him, but he could see that they were impressed by his friendship with this obviously powerful English lord who served the Shah and was bound for his court. His stature had increased immeasurably, which delighted him. They neared the oasis walls. Then those in front of the caravan cried out, amazed. Some gestured to drive away evil.

For outside the walls, like guardians, stood two beasts of stupendous size and unnatural shape. Each was as large as a two-storied house. Their hides, the colour of slate, ridged and leathery, hung loose on their enormous frames. They twitched ears like giant grey leaves with ragged edges, to fan away the flies. Long tubes hung down from their faces, and these were not only prehensile but also very flexible.

The creatures used them to scoop up hay from the heaps that lay before them, and then convey it to their gaping pink maws. Their legs, thick as tree trunks, were chained. They rolled from side to side in their fetters like ships at anchor, and uttered pitiable moans. One raised its long frontal tube and emitted a loud cry. Many travellers wailed in dread, and angered one of the men who stood near Coryate. 'Cowards!' he shouted to the fearful crowd, 'imbeciles, those are no more than beasts of burden. I have seen them before, in the Mogul country.'

Coryate was never afraid, but invariably curious. He had read about these beasts, called elephants. He now walked forward, away from the caravan, till he stood before them. They seemed in constant motion, rolled from foot to foot, shook and flapped their great ears and swayed their trunks. He studied the face above him, which had a melancholy look. 'Well, well, poor fellow,' he said, 'you mean Tom Coryate no harm.' He rubbed his hand upon the animal's leg, like hot treebark. Then he turned unhurriedly away.

A tremendous shout went up from the caravan behind him. Coryate knew that from now on he would be taken notice of by his fellow travellers and treated well. He pondered for a moment on whether he should deliver an extempore oration in Arabic on the shameful nature of cowardice. Just as he had decided he would, someone touched his arm. It was a black flunkey, but very splendidly liveried, and he spoke in English, surprisingly with a Venetian accent.

'Be pleased to follow me, Messire,' he said. 'My lord awaits you.' Coryate bowed stiffly and followed him. He smelt of pomade. Coryate surveyed himself, wondered how much and of what he smelt, and wished he had anticipated such encounters. He regretted his attire, but had never, in all his careful preparations, thought to carry any change of clothes.

~

The Shirleys' enormous tent had been divided into compartments furnished as rooms. Each room had its purpose; the largest one was reserved to receive company. It was furnished in the eastern manner, but in the most palatial style. Persian carpets covered the mud floor. Around the walls of the tent were rectangular mattresses covered in brilliant embroidered cloths, and strewn with pillows and bolsters. Low brass tables decorated with inlay work stood by each. Everything was in symmetry except Shirley, dressed like a British diplomat.

He was enthroned in a high-backed wooden chair in the centre of the floor. Lady Shirley, coiled like a cat, occupied a brocaded stool at his feet. She wore a lowcut blue velvet dress. The tops of her breasts, also velvety but round and very white reminded Coryate of Anne Harcourt's. He gaped, overwhelmed.

Shirley would also have gaped, if his education had allowed him to, at his strange and filthy guest. He could smell Coryate from some way off, and judged that his hair and body were infested by small vermin. He was also a dwarf. For a rare moment he was deprived of coherent words. So was his wife. Her face showed consternation; amusement also.

Coryate had prepared a speech, in which he thanked God for having ordained that English people should meet in such a wilderness. He had hastily but carefully memorized it, so that it would seem to be spoken extempore. But the unaccustomed splendour around him, and the tops of Lady Teresa's breasts, had made him forget it completely. Total silence fell.

It was broken when the black manservant offered the guest tea. Coryate held up his bowl to be filled. Then Shirley, who had had time to recover his aplomb, said in his rich, melodious voice, 'Greetings, Master Coryate. You are Master Coryate, are you not, he that travelled in Europe and wrote books, courtier to Prince Harry—Master Thomas Coryate?'

He awaited the answer anxiously and was relieved when it came. This man did not look like his idea of a courtier or a man of letters; but appearances could deceive, and these were curious days. 'Good sir,' he continued, 'it is a fortunate chance that fetches you so far to meet your sincerest admirers. For we so greatly value your books that we have carried them through all our travels, aye, from Europe to this desert where now we sit in amity.'

Teresa took two bound volumes from her lap, and rising gracefully from her stool, brought them to Coryate. When she bent to hand them over, he nearly fainted; but the familiar look and feel of the books restored him. He was filled with a wild pride and happiness as he turned the pages. 'Truly this is a marvel,' he said. 'It touches me in the heart.'

'How often your words have comforted us,' sighed Lady Teresa, 'in our hardships; for though you see us prosper now, we have had many. We are grateful to you, Master Coryate.' Shirley, listening, nodded and made English sounds of affirmation.

Coryate looked down at the two fat volumes, touched them tenderly, even kissed them. He groped in his mind for certain remarks made to him by Jonson, when deep in wine. 'In some ways,' he announced at last, 'an author's books are like unto his children. When he ages they are his succour; but when he first sends them forth into this world, he trusts they may serve others, or comfort them. Now I hear from your own lips that my books have done this for you. Aye, aye, truly this is a marvel.'

He felt he should offer his hosts some recompense for their kindness, and thanked them the best way he could. He read several passages aloud to them, from the *Crudities* and even from *The Crambe*. They were good listeners, and were completely silent, except for occasional hurriedly stifled coughs.

When he paused for breath, Lady Shirley interrupted him abruptly, but with a delightful giggle, 'Master Thomas, this day you have given us much provender for the mind. But the body must have solace also. Our repast is ready, and we must leave this camp soon. We had best make haste and eat.'

It was said with a pretty firmness that pleased Coryate. Somewhat reluctantly, he gave her back the books. 'I trust my small reading pleased you,' he said, fumbling for words in his emotion, 'and I thank you. I have said that to an author his books are like his children. You were kind to mine and treated them well. You have kept them with such care, it is as if no human hand had ever turned these pages.'

His gratitude seemed to embarrass the Shirleys.

~

Lunch was served to them where they sat. Sir Robert remained in his chair. A high table was placed in front of it for his convenience. So he dominated the room and the conversation, as he wanted to do. He needed to find out more about this fellow Coryate. The books Coryate had read from seemed pompous rubbish; Sir Robert had seldom been so bored and Teresa had had to try hard to keep awake.

But the man *was* famous, in his way, because he had written those books, and he *was* the courtier Coryate, supposedly an intimate of Prince Henry's. Shirley had known for years that the best way to make another man tell you his thoughts was to reveal your own. Coryate proved to be very interested in India, which Shirley had but recently left. If Coryate wanted to listen, Shirley could talk; then later perhaps Coryate would talk too. Shirley wanted to discover what his mission in India was.

So he rumbled on mellifluously as the meal went on about the Emperor Jehangir. Salim was his real name, and his friends called him that. Salim had problems along his borders, Shirley said. Few people realized that large parts of the country lay outside his empire and that there were other rulers there. For some years now India had been peaceful, but Salim had to be constantly on the move to ensure it remained so. So also his son, the crown prince Khushru. Coryate would certainly meet him at court.

Shirley, as an emissary from Persia, had seen much at the Mogul court. When he described its ceremonies, its pageantry, Coryate's eyes shone and he listened with the expectant eyes of a child. Shirley told him of the great gifts Jehangir had given him; also the gifts he had sent through him to Shah Abbas in Persia. 'Those two elephants outside,' Shirley said, 'those are for me to convey to Shah Abbas; also those brutes there.' He pointed to a dark corner and Coryate, curious always, went to look.

Three hobbled antelope stood there, piles of excrement and hay around their delicate hooves. They were like no other deer Coryate had seen: black, with white bellies and spiral horns. Their eyes were huge and longlashed, like women's eyes, and looked sad. Their coats were dull and they did not react when Coryate very gently caressed them.

'Salim sent two pairs,' Shirley said. 'One of the does perished in the passes. I fear the rest will follow. My men say that coming from their country has broken their hearts.' He laughed. 'Salim hunts them with leopards that run like the wind. It is a spectacle you must see, like our foxhunts, but more colourful. The entertainments in India are very fine.'

He added, 'On the way back, come to Shah Abbas's court. I will tell him about the books you have written. He's fond of learned men. It may be you will find out how generous he can be. He will be specially interested when he hears you come from Henry's court.' The glint of a grin showed through his beard. Shirley had decided that his time had come. 'Now, brother Thomas, since we have become friends, tell me why Henry sends you to India.'

'He has not sent me to India,' Coryate said, surprised, 'I go there thinking to write another book, such as no man has written before. I would seek assistance from this Emperor, Jehangir or Salim, to walk on to Tartary and the land of China, and to write of those places also. I have left the Prince's service, Sir Robert. I travel alone and as you perceive by my state, without money. I had ten pounds with me when I left England. Half of that was stolen from me in Aleppo. Prince Henry has not sent me to India. Were he to send any man, it would not be me.'

Shirley looked at him without expression. From her stool at his feet, Teresa stared at Coryate with huge sloelike eyes, sad as the antelopes' eyes, and as far as they were from home. Coryate rose to his feet and faced Shirley, suddenly guilty and ashamed, though he did not know why he should be. When Shirley spoke at last, it was in a flat tone. 'I wish you well,' he said, 'because I was once like you.' He took Coryate's hand, said a laconic 'Godspeed,' and disappeared into the interior of the tent. Teresa had also disappeared, though he had not seen her leave.

The antelopes stirred listlessly in their corner. Coryate stood irresolute, then saw the black Venetian at his side. 'Messire departs?' He turned to follow, and then Teresa came out of the shadows towards him. She pushed a small linen purse into his palm. It chinked. His fingers, through the cloth, felt the cold shape of coins. 'It is only a little money,' she said. 'Forty shillings. But it may help you.'

Coryate looked down at the tops of her breasts, and looked away. He walked after the black servant with the long easy stride that always surprised people in a dwarf. He passed the two elephants and the oasis walls. His shoes swished through the sand as he returned to his own caravan. He had worn out seven pairs of shoes in the last few months; the specially made boots had not lasted. When they came to the next town, he would buy another pair, a good pair, since he now had enough money.

6

Diary Three

July 2002
London–Mumbai

The sky had deepened its colour; it was true turquoise now. Clouds drifted past and obscured the flight of the circling birds. A cold breeze blew from the river. I hunched up, and wrapped my arms around myself like a refugee. 'You must be cold,' I heard MacLehose say, 'here, this should keep you warm.' I took the jacket he held out to me, pulled it over my shoulders; I stood and watched the river and its swans. As though ears had grown on the back of my head, I caught snatches of conversation from behind me.

'Yes, you were saying, Dom,' MacLehose said, 'you'll go back to India and follow Coryate's route there. I was wondering if it wouldn't be a good idea to come at it from the other end. Why not look up the records of the Mogul emperors? See if they have anything to say about our man.'

The garbage picker ambled past me, leaving behind him a scent trail of rancid rum. I walked back to the bench and sat down beside Dom, who lit another cigarette; his eyes drooped with tiredness. 'That's a good idea, Christopher,' he said.

MacLehose hauled his long torso from the bench. 'I've told my babies I'll be home early.' He grabbed Dom's hand in both of his. 'Good luck for your book, my dear chap, and take care of yourself. You shouldn't be smoking but I suppose you know that already.'

I held out a parcel. 'This is for you Christopher,' I said.

'For little me?' Christopher said. 'What is it?'

'A woollen scarf. It will keep you warm in winter.'

'Thank you,' he said. 'Are you sure you wouldn't want to keep that jacket on? You look terribly cold.' I had forgotten about it until he asked. It was well worn, warm and soft; comforting, but it must have travelled with Christopher for a long time. I returned it to its proper owner.

Next day, we left the orderly parks and thoroughfares of London behind us, flying home.

~

It was raining when we came back to Mumbai. The sky was blotched with clouds, an ominous tent overhead. In the jagged-light of street lamps I could see the outlines of buildings, water wound round them in endless swirls, like a saree. Then with a slap of thunder the night seemed to deepen although it was already three in the morning.

'I hope it keeps raining,' the taxi driver said; he put his hand out of the window and collected the rain in the cup of his palm. He splashed his face with it, and then honking assertively, he manoeuvred us out of the airport and into the ammonia-laced atmosphere of the city.

We passed unlit shanties made of cardboard and plastic huddled on one side of the road. Drunken men with work-numb muscles lay as though dead in their sleep. An unclad child wandered amidst them, wailing, rubbing its dribbling nose. The driver braked suddenly as a man darted across our path. He barked after him, 'Hey, you mother fucker. Did you get only my taxi to die under?' He muttered to himself, 'These sister fuckers from villages. They think their ancestors own the road.' His tone was angry but his eyes seemed resigned to fact. 'So many people now in the city,' the driver said, 'and no rain. All because of corruption.'

'Corruption?' Dom was awake enough to sound amused.

'Then what?' His nostrils flared. He adjusted the rearview mirror, looked at Dom in it. 'These corrupt politicians make so much money. Then go to the gods to pray for their sins. The gods are fed up. This is *kalyug,* sahib, the worst time of the world. War, earthquake, floods, drought, riots, what-all; train-crash, plane-crash, building-crash, even stock-exchange crash, *chi-chi-chi*.' He shot past a skewed traffic signal flashing amber light on a heap of garbage near it.

'I come from a village in Gujarat,' the driver said. 'Near the town of Morvi, it is. The earth also shook there, you know. In our village we have temples for cow goddess. We pray to all the cows in our village. But now people have stopped. They have sold their cows. They do road construction work. Railways work. And like me, they drive taxis in Mumbai. This time I go back to my village the temple pundit told me, earthquake happen in our village because we have stopped cow worship.' He turned and looked back at us. 'The gods are so angry, they stop the rain.'

'Oh dear! Not an entirely thrilling situation to come back to is it?' Dom muttered. I sat back and closed my eyes. 'Why didn't Coryate walk to somewhere sensible?'

~

Our immediate task was to locate scholars who knew seventeenth century India well, particularly British and Mogul history, and English history of the same period. 'It shouldn't be difficult,' Dom said. 'There are good professors in the old universities. What will be difficult is to find a researcher.'

'I'm sure we'll find a dedicated history graduate,' I said.

'It's not just his capabilities I'm worried about,' Dom said. 'We must be able to get along with him. Because,' Dom explained sardonically, 'he and we will have to spend a lot of time together. Imagine,' he added laughing, 'if I don't like the way he eats.' It was one of the problems that burdened him; he could not bear the noises people made as they ate.

The next morning, on a whim, and because we had to start somewhere, Dom called up Ayaz Memon, a friend and the editor of a newspaper. He had, not long ago, produced a book, which would have needed extensive research. 'I can give you lots of names. But I'll have to look up their contact numbers.' Ayaz said. 'Why don't we meet for lunch? I'll give them to you then. Say about half past one. Harbour Bar.'

Over wine and pan-fried noodles, Dom told him about the book. 'I have the right person for this,' Ayaz said, 'he's an odd fellow, but rather meticulous.' He seemed to hesitate. 'Do you mind,' he looked at me then paused, 'if he is a Muslim?' Then looking at Dom he hastily continued, 'Of course such matters would not matter to you. His name is Juzer. He prays five times a day. He is very diligent on keeping fasts. He talks endlessly. Otherwise he is good.'

'Juser,' I repeated.

'Juzer.' Ayaz said as he passed me a slip of paper. 'There are two more names on this list. But I suggest you try Juzer out first.' He signalled for the bill.

'Wasn't that an odd thing for Ayaz to say?' I remarked as we drove back to the suburbs. 'Did he think we might not want to hire this fellow because he is a Muslim?'

Dom gave me a quick look, then looking ahead, said, 'I think he thought *you* as a Hindu might not want to.'

It started to rain. The gods were not so angry after all.

~

I had tried getting Juzer for days but he never seemed to be at home. Each day I called his mother said, 'But he's gone to market.' *Market*? What did she mean by that, I wondered. I got him on the line early one morning. I explained about the book and briefly what we wanted. I told him I would like to meet him soon. He said he was too busy to meet for another week, maybe more. 'I have too much work on my hands,' he said. I assumed he was playing hard to get so he could charge more. So typically Indian, I thought. Even before I had met him I had begun to dislike him. After some thought, he added, 'Can you meet me at Crawford Market today?'

'*Market*?' To conceal my surprise I added hastily, 'What sort of time?' We fixed a time.

'But I don't know you.'

I understood what he meant. 'I am wearing a white kurta,' I said, 'over jeans.' I added, 'I'm not tall.'

'Same-same,' he said. 'White kurta, but mine is grey pants. I am carrying a red plastic shopping bag. I am tall.'

At the appointed time, I stood next to a stone fountain designed by Lockwood Kipling, Rudyard Kipling's father. Someone had coloured it like an exotic bird: green-yellow-pink. There was no water in the fountain. Cane baskets, jute sacks, broken old wooden crates and cardboard cartons lay messily around it. Surrounding it were fruit stalls gaily decorated with silver and gold festoons and tinsel lamps. I was early and got into a conversation with a fruit seller.

His name was Raju Mane. His fruit stall belonged to his grandfather and contained a variety of fruits including Chinese grapes, Californian plums, New Zealand apples and Kiwi fruit from Indonesia. Raju handed me his card. Venkatesh Fruitwalla.

'Venkatesh is a south Indian name,' I pointed out, 'but you are, I presume, a Maharashtrian.'

'So what. Venkatesh is a god's name,' he retorted possessively, 'anyone can keep a god's name. He is common. My family goes every year to the Venkateshwara temple in Tirupati. We offer money to the god. He makes us rich.'

A man came up behind me. He said over my shoulder to the fruit seller, 'Achha, do you know why people go to give money to god Venkatesh?'

Raju looked at him suspiciously. 'You want to buy something or not?' His tone was irritable. I turned around. The young man in a white kurta was thin and not very tall. His long beard was straggly; on his head he wore an embroidered skullcap. 'Good afternoon, madam,' he said to me. 'If you want to buy fruits you should go to the Byculla market. They're cheaper there. These people here hike prices up like anything. Thirty per cent even.' He held up a hand at Raju to halt his protest. 'Ask me about markets, I know what you get best where.' He waved his hand at me, 'Come let's go. By the way,' he grinned, 'I am Juzer.'

I followed him to Lobo stores where he handed a list to the shopkeeper who read aloud from it to a boy who took provisions from the shelf. Noodles—fifty packets, pasta—thirty, twelve bottles of tomato sauce, six bottles vinegar, ten kilos rice ... The goods were packed into two large cartons.

'Okay, boss, I'll collect these in twenty minutes,' he told the shopkeeper.

Young boys with large cane baskets followed me begging to let them carry my purchases. Juzer admonished them with a raised finger. 'Madam is not here to shop. Understand. Now scoot, all of you.' He laughed heartily. 'These buggers are scared of me,' he said stroking his beard. 'Last week only I had been to Ajmer. Little boys there were terrified of me. They thought I was Osama bin Laden.'

We crossed the road to Badshah. It was a small restaurant, old with a new air-conditioned section tucked into a mezzanine floor, curtained and dark. It was, as in several other oldish restaurants in the city, meant for juvenile lovers and adulterous couples. We sat below near the stairs. I studied the menu. It served a variety of milkshakes, falooda and soda ice cream pupp. 'What is pupp?' I asked.

'That American stuff,' Juzer said wrinkling his nose, 'Archie Comics favourite thing. Ha-ha-ha,' he laughed; his whole body shook. 'Ice cream soda pop,' he said. 'Don't have that American derivation. I know exactly what you should have.' He ordered two Badshahi faloodas. 'This shop is too famous for falooda,' he said. 'You have had before?'

'Maybe. I don't remember.'

'But,' he raised a hand and smiled, 'I am certain you are not knowing its history.' I smiled. 'Falooda is a Persian milkshake,' he said. 'Did you know, Emperor Akbar was too fond of cold drinks?' Now he was trying to show off his knowledge of Mogul history, I thought. 'He got ice in jute bags from the Himalayas.'

'Would the ice not have melted on the way?'

'No. No. No. Jute keeps ice very cold.' He gave me a meaningful look. 'Jehangir introduced falooda in India, probably. I can easily find out if you want. I think you're interested in Jehangir, no?'

Our falooda arrived in tall glasses; it contained milk, ice cream, red syrup and glutinous round seeds, which appeared to me like a hundred fish eyeballs.

'What is your full name?' I asked him as he dunked the scoop of ice cream with a teaspoon, then holding it down he slurped the milk and syrup clutching his beard with one hand.

'Juzer. J-U-Z-E-R. Z not S. Juzer Mundrawala. My family is from the village Mundra in Kutch. But even if I am dying I will not use that surname. See, there was some problem in my family. But I can't tell you why, so don't ask.'

'No, I won't ask.'

'I use my father's name only. Juzer Mohammed Husain. Mohammed with a double "m" and one "e", and the Husain only with one "s".' There was a gleam in his eye. 'Do you know what Juzer means?'

My mouth was full of ice cream. I shook my head. 'Juzer is a heavenly gazelle. It is supposed to have magnetic powers. It is not beautiful and all that. But it can mesmerize anyone with a glance.' He looked, earnestly at me.

'Tell me about your work,' I said. 'What sort of research work do you do?'

'Insha allah,' he raised his hands. 'I must not tell lies. I am not a researcher.'

I looked up from my falooda. I wiped one or two fisheyes that had stuck to my lips. 'You're not?'

'I am really an accountant. I worked in an auditor's office.' He stroked his beard, twirled it around his finger. 'I am a Bohri Muslim and our religion does not permit us to earn interest on savings. I asked my priest, is it okay if

I calculate other people's money? He advised me to change my profession, become a journalist. So I joined college again and studied communications. I got a job with Zee TV as a researcher. I asked my priest if it was all right to research for an entertainment channel. He was not very pleased, so I joined a newspaper as their political researcher. Still my priest was not happy. "Politics is bad", he said. But my boss was very happy with me.' He clicked his fingers. 'My work is very good. I can find out anything like this, like this,' he clicked his fingers several times, 'in no time. Yes, I can do your work very easily in three-four months.' He looked at his watch. 'Shit, I've to pick up all that crap from Lobo shop.'

I was curious so I felt compelled to ask, though I didn't want to hurt his feelings. 'That's a lot of groceries you ordered. Your family must have enormous appetites.'

He giggled. 'You're trying to joke,' he said. 'Actually I eat very little. I don't have time to eat breakfast, I go very early to market. Sometimes I forget to eat lunch even.' It showed on his body. He was extremely wiry.

It turned out that Juzer ran a catering business in Tardeo.

I tried to imagine Dom's expression when I told him this. But I thought he would like Juzer, as I had started to. He might be a researcher or a caterer, but he was an original.

'My sister and brother-in-law started the catering business.' Juzer said. 'It struck me that it was the best job for me to do. It is good to feed people. My priest agreed. So I quit the newspaper job. I joined my sister's business. There are some very intricate things about this line that only I can manage,' he said proudly, 'particularly the money part. I am basically an accountant, no? So I make sure we get proper money. Now I want to expand the business, and then I can concentrate on research only.'

'So you cater for parties and marriages?'

'Even that. But we mainly supply lunch to bank employees and a few other offices. We feed about six hundred people daily. I have six cooks. My chief cook, Mahendra, he is from Bihar. Although he looks Nepali, like this,' he pulled the corners of his eyes with his fingers. 'You just give him a spoonful of some dish, he will swirl it on his tongue then reproduce it exactly. He not only makes French food taste exactly like French but he also pronounces the food names like the French.'

We walked out of the restaurant into the afternoon traffic. The falooda felt cool in my stomach. Juzer asked, 'What does Mr Dom like to eat? I will bring him something when I come to meet the boss. I am looking forward to working on this project with him.'

'He is very fond of Bohri food,' I said warming to his offer, 'especially mutton.'

'Bohri? But we make all kinds of good foods. Mughlai, French, Italian, Mexican, Chinese, Thai, pizzas, hamburgers. I will bring him Mahendra's Saturday Special.'

'What is it?'

'Mexican mutton steak.'

~

He turned up the next evening on Dom's doorstep. 'This is for you, sir,' he extended a small parcel of aluminium foil as Dom held the door open. 'My chief cook has upset his tummy, so I could not manage to bring the Mexican mutton steak. This is Afghani chicken.' He stood there in a gleaming skullcap wearing a benevolent smile like a ruby arc. 'My name is Juzer Mohammed Husain.'

Dom took the parcel from him, muttered a thank you,

invited him in. He took off his shoes at the door, waved a cursory hand at me, then squatted on a cushion close to Dom's feet. He pulled out a note pad from the red plastic shopping bag. 'I've done some work, Mr Dom,' he started in utter seriousness, 'I have listed all the books in the libraries in the city on Core-yia-ti. I've also listed out some of the books by the English and Moguls in that same period.' He showed Dom the list.

'This is very good.' Dom's eyes filled with warm appreciation. 'You mean you did this all in a day?' He raised the parcel that he still held in his hand. 'Thank you for the Afghani chicken. It was very thoughtful of you. I like Afghani chicken very much.' He put the parcel down on the table. 'Now let's have another look at your list.'

Juzer gave the list to Dom. He smiled, 'So madam doesn't even know. She thinks you like mutton. Bohri mutton. That's too rich and spicy for you I knew. I can tell what people will like from their name only. And now I've seen your face, sir, I *know* what you'd like. A dish that is refined and delicate. That's why I got this Afghan chicken.'

I couldn't believe that I was hearing this. I laughed. 'So you can read his face?'

'Yes-yes. I am a very good face-reader. When I was in the library I ...'

Dom interrupted him, 'That reminds me, can you look up something else for me, Juzer.' He scribbled on a piece of paper. 'These are the countries that Coryate passed through before he reached India. Do you think you can locate some books with pictures of these places? I want Sarayu to see the sort of landscapes Coryate came through, the absolute contrast from the landscapes of Somerset he was used to, before he ventured into a madhouse like India.'

Juzer cast me a glance that I could not decipher. 'No problem, boss,' he said, 'we will show her such landscapes. She will know then.' He smiled condescendingly at me. 'Why don't you meet me tomorrow morning at the Iranian Culture Centre. Ten o'clock.'

It was a hot morning. The rains, as the taxi driver had predicted, had once again deserted the region. I waited on the pavement outside the Centre next to a pile of garbage. I covered my nose with my palm. The heat made the stink diffuse like vapour into the air. It was three-quarters past ten and Juzer had still not arrived. The stink worsened. I sheltered my eyes with my bag, looked up towards the main door. I saw him then, rushing out of the door. 'It's all done, it's all done,' he grinned and waved some pages at me. 'I've taken Xeroxes of landscapes. Separate copies for you also. Let's go. I want to show them to boss. I have everything he asked for.' He hailed a taxi. 'To Bandra,' he said but told the driver to go through Chor Bazaar, the thieves' market.

'Chor Bazaar?' I asked. 'Why?'

'Don't mind? I've just five minutes work there. I have to get mutton biryani. Then we'll go straight to Mr Dom.'

'I'm sorry but Dom doesn't like biryani. It's too rich and spicy.'

'That I know already. No-no, it's not for him at all. A friend of the family is getting engaged this evening. He wants to serve special biryani. I have all this additional work, so I couldn't get it ready. And Mahendra is still with upset tummy. There is a very good biryani shop in Chor Bazaar.'

The narrow lanes were choked with cars, bicycles and handcarts. The old buildings were cloaked with hundreds of signs, many of them in Urdu script. Here and there tall, robust goats were tethered to posts. 'When you see these buggers,'

Juzer indicated them, 'you know you are in a Bohri Muslim area.' He slapped the front seat, 'Boss, stop here.' He asked the taxi driver to wait in the lane.

We walked through an alley full of shacks with stolen and second-hand car parts. In front of each shop a board displayed stolen marques of imported cars. We turned into another lane with all sorts of fans, and further on, shops with a variety of old lamps. I stopped to look at a large suspended Dutch lampshade. 'Can you wait one minute,' Juzer put up a finger; he stepped into a tiny shop not more than three feet wide. I watched him as he tried on a number of skullcaps; he bought one with gold embroidery. 'This is my favourite *feta* shop,' he said, 'I always buy my caps here. I have one fully in gold. It looks very nice on me.'

We turned the corner into lane full of savoury and sweet shops. 'Two minutes,' he held up two fingers and darted quickly across the lane, like a fleeing genie. I noticed a wisp of his kurta, and then he had disappeared into a shop. White kurtas hung on its doorway; they swayed like dancing ghosts in the breeze. He ran back clutching a plastic bag. 'That's my tailor. All my white kurtas, he stitches. I am going to wear this tonight for my friend's engagement.'

I walked into the next shop. It stocked all sorts of compasses: small round ones in brass and large machines in glass boxes. I picked one. 'This must be very old.'

'All this is new, madam,' Juzer whispered. 'They are only made to look old. If you want to buy compasses I'll take you to my friend's shop. He has original.'

'I wonder if Coryate used a compass to walk to India,' I said as we left. 'Did he have a clock or a watch?'

'No clocks then,' Juzer said, then pointed to the shop opposite. 'Suleman Sweet Mart is famous for aflatoon.'

'What?'

'You've not had? It's a very Persian sweet.' He rushed into the shop. 'Boss, two small boxes,' he placed his order. 'One for you and one for boss Dom,' he said to me. 'Thank you,' I said. 'Dom has a sweet tooth.'

'I know.'

'What does it mean? Aflatoon.'

'It's a Persian word.' He called out to the old man, probably the shop owner, asking him what aflatoon meant. The old man shook his head. Juzer slapped his forehead dramatically, 'Arre, arre, baba, then why do you sell aflatoon if you don't know what it means?'

I heard the old man mutter to his staff, 'What kind of a nut is he. Comes to buy sweets and asks for Persian words.'

Juzer hurried down the street. Suddenly he halted in the middle of a lane looking up at a dilapidated two-storey building. He looked momentarily crestfallen. He told me why. The building would have been bequeathed to him but it did not happen; it was sold. 'I would have started a restaurant here,' he added sadly, 'that would have served the best biryani.' He left me waiting there facing his fractured dream as he ran into a gap between buildings to a shop at the rear to place the order for biryani.

All this had taken us more than half an hour. The taxi driver would be fuming, I remarked when Juzer returned. 'He'll wait,' Juzer said smugly, 'we still have to pay him.' He laughed. 'The driver is an old Muslim. He will offer namaz while he is waiting for us. That will keep the bugger calm.' He started to hurry down the road. 'I have to buy a *rida,* a gown worn by Bohri Muslim women, for my mother. She wants to wear it this evening. It will take only two minutes.' We walked into Bhendi Bazaar. At a corner shop Juzer bought a rida, pistachio green with yellow and pink roses embroidered on it. He got a thirty per cent discount.

As we stepped out of the shop, Juzer pointed to a young man at the end of the road. 'That one is a bridegroom. I can tell. He is wearing the white kurta and coat; also the *sehra* on his head.' He put a hand to his forehead as if something was troubling him. 'I wonder why he is running like that. And alone. There should have been a procession. Also the mosque is right here. Why is this bugger going the wrong way?

'Come with me, I'll show you our tomb,' Juzer said suddenly. 'It has the Koran written on its wall in gold and it had the world's third largest chandelier.'

He walked me around the corner. Thousands of people were in the street. Juzer stood perplexed once more, his hand pressed to his forehead. The men were dressed in white, and the women in colourful ridas. Conversation buzzed like an audiotape running at high speed. Juzer let out a yell over the din. A young man turned, smiled when he recognized Juzer. He was short, dark, with a straggly beard like an appendix on his cherubic face. He had on a white coat over a white kurta with gold-plated ruby buttons. 'This is Shabbir Mister,' Juzer said. An animated conversation started between them.

'It's a community marriage,' Juzer said to me. 'I knew it when I saw that fellow down the street. I think over two hundred grooms will marry today.'

Shabbir explained, 'It is an eighty-five-year-old tradition and the Bohri community pays for those who can't afford marriages. The Syedna will bless them himself. Now even rich families get their children married like this.'

Juzer giggled, 'Even I was married here.'

I looked at him. I would have never believed he was married. I told him as much.

'Why?' He asked. 'You think no girl will marry me?' He laughed as I mumbled incoherently. He pointed to the street ahead, 'I remember that day so vividly; we, the bridegrooms dressed in white, with sehras on our head came on horses nicely decorated. Our families and friends followed us. We assembled in the mosque ...'

'Is it possible,' I asked, 'for me to see the ceremony?' Juzer frowned. He spoke to Shabbir Mister in conspiratorial tones; then Juzer rushed me to a shop where he bought a pair of white socks. After seeking the shopkeeper's permission he led me to the rear of the shop, a storing place behind a bedsheet hung like a curtain. He held out the rida he had bought for his mother. 'Here wear this, and the socks. You will have to take out your shoes at the door.' He led me back to the mosque. 'Just look down and walk and don't say anything.' At the entrance to the mosque, Shabbir handed me over to a lady organizer who, he explained, would take me to the upper galleries meant for brides.

'What about you Juzer?' I asked.

'I can't come in dressed like this,' he replied. 'I should be dressed in white.' Then his face brightened. He took out a notepad and pen from his bag and walked through the door with me. 'I'll tell them I'm a journalist.'

The galleries were packed with women in colourful ridas. Some of them were heavily made up and wore a lot of gold jewellery. I sat between two such women. We looked at the hall below lined with men in white. The Syedna sat at one end of the hall. He started a prayer. The woman next to me said in Gujarati, 'One of the grooms, it seems, has come all the way from Dubai.' She asked me, 'Can you see yours from here? Is he handsome?' As instructed, I remained silent and looked chastely down at my white socks.

After the prayers were over the grooms went up to the Syedna in batches of ten. Each of them kissed his right knee and right hand; he blessed them individually. After everyone had had their turn, the Syedna called upon them to adhere to the tenets of marriage as laid down in Islam and prayed for Allah's blessings.

'Now they will all have a nice big lunch,' Juzer said when we were outside. 'But rich and spicy, not for boss.' 'What about that groom we saw earlier on,' I said, 'the one who was running down the road?'

Juzer said, 'I think he changed his mind about marrying.'

~

For the next two weeks, it rained almost everyday. The streets were flooded; the lakes were full. The trains moved slowly and late. Juzer disappeared from Mumbai. I left several messages for him at his house. He had gone to Kutch is all that his mother told me. She couldn't say when he would return. We had sketched out our travel plans. Dom was anxious to start the book. 'Forget Juzer. We better go ourselves,' he said irritably, 'we can't wait for him now.'

Juzer turned up late next evening at Dom's house. He looked tired. He squatted on the floor, and without uttering a word, he took two boxes from his bag and put them on the table. He looked at them as though he was saying a prayer in his mind. 'These are special sweetmeats from Bhavnagar,' he said, 'they are made of pure milk and saffron.'

Dom looked quizzically at him, 'You shouldn't have bothered about these, though it's very kind. But we have a lot of work to do. Where have you been all this time?'

Juzer looked down at his toes. I'm sorry, sir,' he said. 'But,' he whispered, 'my wife got a baby girl.'

'Oh!' Dom began to clean his glasses.

'That's great news,' I said.

Juzer stayed till late that night. We discussed our travel plans. We were sorry, we said, that he wouldn't be able to fly with us, because we couldn't afford it. He looked at us; his lips pursed together, he said, 'You both are going to Delhi first, then to Agra. I will reach Agra on the morning of the eleventh. I'll be there before you arrive.'

I said, 'What about your wife, your child? Aren't you required here?'

His face grew solemn and firm. 'No matter.'

After Juzer left, Dom said, 'He's really got involved with our work. When he sat there with that fervent look on his face, I swear he actually looked a bit like Bin Laden.'

So the team for the Coryate book was formed: an elderly and unpredictable poet, a researcher who was also a caterer and, as Christopher would have said, little me.

7

In Search of an Emperor

Coryate's slightly precarious status in the caravan stabilized somewhat after his companions had witnessed his encounter with the Shirleys. They had initially written him off in their minds as one of the least of the camp followers, undoubtedly a foreigner, but too penniless and mad to be profitably helped, and, therefore, perhaps best avoided. But a revelation had come to them in the desert. They had seen with their own eyes that he had affluent friends who were connected to the Shah. Now they paid more attention to him. Those beside him on the trail would listen patiently to his tales of travel, though they were told in broken Urdu, and were even otherwise incomprehensible. When they got fresh food supplies, which was not often, they let him have some.

He was pleased by their offerings; even more so by their attention. It was in his nature to exaggerate events, not only to others but also in his imagination. He had convinced himself that the Shirleys, monuments of Olympian benignity, had delighted in his company and had promised him preferment in the Persian court. He recounted this version of their tryst to anyone who would listen. Most of his listeners believed it, for they had seen parts of it happen. But very few believed any of his descriptions of London or Venice.

Very slowly, the caravan climbed into a country of stony hills, for which none of his companions had a name. Occasionally, they came upon fortified villages built of the same stone. Coryate saw no women at all in this country. But the men were lean and predatory. They wore ragged clothes, but carried yards of steel about their persons. Each man was his own armoury, but in spite of the burden he bore, loped quickly, certain of foot, through the rocks and the high places. Now and then, usually in the dawn hour before the caravan moved on, tall, wolf-like chiefs would come down the slopes to the encampment. The caravan leaders would talk to the chiefs, and plead eloquently with their hands, but presently they would part with pouches of money.

While these rites of passage were transacted, some of the wild men would wander through the camp. At these times the few women travellers hid where they could. The men stood about in little clusters and did not know where to look. The tribesmen's yellow eyes, which resembled those of hawks, roved over their faces, but did not seem to see them as men, only as potential corpses. Once Coryate, though his companions tried to prevent him, addressed a warrior in Farsi. The man spat at his feet. Coryate, undeterred, tried once more. A ripple of shock spread through the others, and they fell back, away from him, as the warrior spat like a gunshot in his face. He did not protest, but stood in the morning sunlight and wiped the warm slime from his cheek. Overhead, a white skein of cranes unravelled in the sky.

~

When the caravan moved on, Coryate had fallen into a sombre silence, unusual in him. It lasted for days. When he started to speak once more, he asked his companions when they would leave these hills. 'Soon, now,' the others comforted him. 'Soon we will reach the Mogul's country.' As they dawdled on, the cliffs became steeper. But fewer of the wild men were seen, and those mostly glimpsed were in the distance. One day, the caravan leaders announced that the Indian border was close. Next afternoon Coryate began dimly to discern on a mountainside ahead, glimmering in the heat haze and dust so that they seemed seen through water, the ochre and white houses of a citadel.

A horseman rode out towards them from the numinous town. He wore a yellow uniform, and though shadowed by the turban above it, his face seemed civilized. Behind him, in ordered formation, came a small body of other men, on foot, but uniformed like their leader. The trader who walked beside Coryate, Mustapha, uncovered his carious teeth in a smile. 'Praise Allah, those are the soldiers of the Great Mogul,' he said, 'and now at last we are safe, for we have come to his country.'

The gigantic body of the caravan, under its miles-wide tent of dust, slowed from what was already a crawl and halted. All through it, devout men prostrated themselves in thanks. Mustapha was one of them. Coryate looked down at him, skeletally spread on the dusty stones, and tried to feel elation, for after all these months and miles, he had achieved his ambition. All he could feel was tiredness, but he thought he should make some worthy and memorable gesture. He bent, prised up a handful of dry earth, and reverently pressed it to his lips. Those around stared at him in alarm and surprise. In the country of the Great Mogul, it was not considered seemly to eat dirt.

~

Once he had crossed the frontier at Kandahar, and come down into the foothills, the exhaustion drained out of Coryate and was immediately replaced by elation. He knew the processes of his mind and body, and was not surprised. He thought of the people at home, who had once derided him. By now, he was certain, they would have received and read the writings he had entrusted to Simeon. It was time he sent word to announce his arrival in India. It would be great news in London, he was assured, and would spread through the city like fire through hay. It might be that Anne Harcourt would hear of it.

The caravan straggled onward, its route demarcated by the *shekinah* or column of dust above it. It frequently passed other caravans on their way to the mountains. Though they were not yet out of the foothills, the road was well made and wide. There were villages beside it, surrounded by mud walls; also fields that stunted farmers scratched at with wooden ploughs. They grew cereal crops of poor quality, from what Coryate could see: the earth was cluttered with stones and, under a strong sun, particles of mica flashed in the dry riverbeds.

But the women were handsome, and seemed of a different race from the males. They plaited their long hair, and bound coloured strips of cloth around their brows. Their hair had the coarse texture of mares' manes and was often light brown or auburn. They wore drab long-sleeved waistcoats and full skirts. Coryate's companions whispered lewdly in his ears whenever they passed these women, who carried great bales of grass upon their heads and swayed their hips as they walked. 'They have a terrible lust for men,' said the camp followers. 'Each of them needs six or seven young husbands to satisfy her.'

This appeared to be true. The villages hereabouts consisted of small stone houses, each isolated in a mud-walled compound. A woman dominated each household, as Coryate observed; the men had subservient attitudes towards her and behaved less like husbands than domestic servants. When she summoned one of them to her bed, Coryate was told, he left his shoes outside the door, so that the other husbands knew that she was occupied. These details fascinated him, and he put them down in the notes he never ceased to make.

He was making them one night, by a smoky fire, when he had an unexpected visitor. A caravan bound for the north had encamped down the road, and Coryate could see its multiple fires as well as those of his own people. In the countryside around, he could see other pinprick fires from scattered villages. After the months of endured solitude in the desert and the mountains, he felt himself once more to be in the world of men, and this contented him, freed him of fears.

A long shadow interposed itself between him and the firelight, and Coryate looked up at an Englishman. 'Richard Steele,' this man said, in a London slur that caught suddenly at Coryate's heart. 'I go north, and they told me there was an Englishman here, going south. So I come to pay my respects, with a bottle of the best to make sure I'm welcome.' He was small, sharp-nosed, reddish, his tailcoat and breeches stained and defiled, but Coryate in his filthy Arab dress stank no less. Steele fished a squat bottle and two clay cups from his coat pocket, uncorked, poured. 'My friend Jack snores sound,' he informed Coryate, 'or he'd have come too, to drink with another Englishman.'

Coryate told Steele his name, hoping it would produce an effect. He was disappointed when it didn't. He told Steele he had written a book on Europe, and had now come to the Indies to write another. The other man remained unimpressed. But the warmth of the fire drew them closer. They pledged each other's health in raw rum. Coryate choked and sputtered, and Steele laughed. 'Got out of the way of it, I reckon, out in the wilds,' he said. 'Nay, but you'll find this in plenty further south. This, and sticky cunt, and heavy coin: there's plenty of all three for him as keeps his wits about him, like I does. I know this country.'

Steele had actually come to see whether the new arrival would be of any use to him. Within a very few minutes he was convinced that there was no advantage to be had from this ridiculous homunculus. Coryate might have been a courtier to Prince Henry, but almost certainly of lowly rank. Steele had never heard him spoken of. He had half a mind to waste no further time and depart. But the fire and the rum calmed his mood, and something childlike and innocent in the way Coryate hung on his words, eyes wide, lips parted, appealed to him. So he poured more rum and told Coryate about his life and India.

His stories fascinated Coryate. Men like Steele were outside his experience. Steele was one of those petty criminals who had come to abound in London: amoral, but with unsatisfied ambitions because the British islands were so small and offered him few opportunities.

Then the great wayfarers who rode the oceans for Elizabeth brought home treasures beyond price from countries whose existence had never before been known. The new lands discovered, the new prospects of profit that opened up, had made enormous venalities possible to small men. The heroes loomed up like colossi into English history, but dozens of minor adventurers sprouted like toadstools in their shadows. These men lived by their wits and had few scruples about what they did. The East India Company found them useful in the newly found lands in Asia, though they were seldom to be trusted.

'Aye, now Jack Mildenhall,' Steele droned on. 'He's fly. The Directors sent him to the Indies two or three years since, with a great load of goods for trade. But Jack, he never crossed Persia. The goods that he had, he sold in Ispahan, and then he ran for it. The Directors sent me after him—*me,* a thief-taker! I caught up with him in the end, but not to arrest him. Nay, we became partners. We found our way into India, into the very court of the Mogul. I have had speech with him. Such splendour you never saw as in his court, nor so much wealth as in that land, and of that they are ready to be cozened. I go now into Persia with my mate Jack Crowder, and we will gather much coin if we can work the trade between Jehangir and Shah Abbas.'

Coryate tried to understand this rigmarole, and could not. But he inquired in innocence, 'Perchance my friends in Persia, the Shirleys, are known to you? I last came upon them on the road to Ispahan, and they hold me in so high esteem that Sir Robert vowed he would get me preferment from the Persian king. She, too, was generous to me.'

Steele, wiping his matted beard, cackled contemptuously. 'The Shirleys? Pah! "Sir Robert!" Where got he that title? Perhaps from the Sultan of All Jakes? Shirley cozens the Shah as his brother Anthony did before him, but it will not last. Nor should you believe any oath of the Shirleys, for they are only made to be broken. As for that Circassian strumpet he calls his wife, she has been generous to more men than there are pebbles on the seashore. But in that at least you have had good fortune. I would not mind a taste of her generosity myself.'

He slurped rum, and his shoulders shook with lewd merriment. Coryate turned toward him, bewildered. He had suffered from illusions all his life, and several had been shattered. So he was prepared to accept what his strange new acquaintance was saying, especially since he spoke with such scornful authority. But Coryate's heart, as it thudded against his ribs, felt like a frozen bird trying to break free.

'If you would come to the Mogul,' Steele said, now apparently recovered from his epileptic fit of laughter, and as serious as he could ever be, 'in this season you are most like to find him in Ajmer town. He will lie there for some months. I hear also that Thomas Roe will come from London to direct the Company here, so he will come to Ajmer as well, and you may meet him at the court. But there are more English in India now, Thomas of Odcombe, than ever there were before. You should be wary of them all. Put not thy trust in ponces.'

Suddenly, perhaps because he was aware of his listener's innocence, he became truly serious. 'I know what I speak of, for I am one myself. Most of us are become so, who have voyaged here only for the sake of cunt and coin. The rest are wittols, who do not even have the sense to stray wild. The Mussulmans have some wit, though Jehangir and the rest drink like fishes. As for the natives, they are to be pitied by any man who has pity in him, which I have not. If you have, Master Coryate, you will suffer in this country. A few live in luxury and sloth, the others like beasts of the field. Elephants, rats, monkeys, serpents and demons, these are the gods of the blacks.'

The bottle was nearly empty. As Steele started to rise, a little unsteadily, Coryate came to a sudden decision and said,

'Master Steele, I have papers that I must have delivered in London. When you are arrived in Persia, since you know so many there, can you manage this matter for me?' It was a fervent plea, made from the heart, and Steele felt an urgent need to demonstrate his power and his kindness.

'Give them to me,' he said. 'I'll see the matter settled.'

At dawn next day, as the caravans lined up on the road prepared to leave, Steele and his companion, Crowder, sat at a fire, drinking hot toddy. Steele held a parcel in his hands. It was bulky, but seemed to weigh little, and it rustled as he tossed it into the flames. Then it flared up and became visible as a mass of curled and blackened paper that crumbled as it burned. 'What thing is that?' asked Crowder curiously.

'Nothing,' Steele said. He finished his toddy and spat into the fire. 'Only some useless shite that a poor fool entrusted to my care.'

~

The Indus, when he saw it first, took Coryate by surprise and filled him with awe. Never in his life had he conceived that so mighty a torrent could exist. He estimated it to be at least twice as wide as the Thames. On the farther side of this stupendous body of water, human figures, trees and houses were dwindled to minute dimensions, like a child's toys. The river had come from the Himalayan peaks, snow-fed. The transparent blue water had not yet been muddied by the dust of the plains. Whorls and eddies on the surface told of treacherous currents; here and there rocky reefs showed their teeth, and isolated islands rose. On either shore, caravans awaited their turn to cross.

It took two days for Coryate's caravan to ford the Indus. The goods, some of the pack animals, and most of the people, were ferried across on huge wooden rafts that travelled partly under sail but were mainly driven by oarsmen. The camels and their drivers waded over through the muddy shallows. Coryate seemed to recall that the Greek conqueror Alexander and his army had crossed this wide, wild water. He pictured how the sun would have glittered on the river, the Greek arms and helmets, and the face of Alexander, truly a dreamer's face.

He was now anxious, eager to move on, impatient to reach Ajmer and the court of the Great Mogul. The caravan would reach its destination at a place called Agra and he would have to go onwards alone. But he looked forward to that, for he had felt kenneled, travelling with such a multitude, and needed freedom to feel the earth respond to his heels once more. The caravan leaders assured him that Ajmer was close to Agra and that, by the benevolence of Jehangir, the roads had been made smooth for the wayfarer, and the footpads who had once frequented them had all been imprisoned or beheaded.

But they warned him also that it was still many days' travel to Agra and that they would have to pass through many more towns and cities to reach it: Multan, Lahore, and the old capital, Delhi. In Multan, a hot and noisome place, Coryate was enraged by a further, unforeseen delay, forced upon them by the governor of the town. His coffers were empty. He had recently passed a law that no travellers could leave Multan until they had stayed at least ten days, and spent some money there. Coryate had no money to spend, and so became more resentful; also, Multan was wholly Muslim in its ways.

It was, therefore, the first time since they had left Persia that he was forced to endure the braying of the muezzins from their minarets, five times daily, or to watch while everyone around him prostrated themselves on their bellies and prayed. This had, of course, also happened in the caravan at certain fixed hours during the day. But he had not minded, since at that time he and the worshippers were comrades in travel. He minded now; he minded very much, so much that he forgot he was in a country ruled by Muslims, where the religion was Islam. Perhaps, in his frustration, he did not care.

But he had also, by now, made some observations about Jehangir's country and its people, many of which perplexed him. He was a born observer. Very clearly, and in complex detail, his mind recorded whatever his eyes absorbed. What was not immediately visible to him passed him by. In the caravan he had met Indians who were not Muslims: a smaller race, darker, who chanted in muffled worship, from time to time, over small lamps and stone statuettes that they carried with them. The Muslims called these people Hindus. They were secretive and shy, and kept themselves aloof from the Muslims. Coryate had imagined the country of the Great Mogul to have been Muslim always. He could not understand the status of these others.

But since the caravan had come down from the mountains, he had seen many more people of this separate race. They dressed differently from the Muslims. Their language was not exactly the same. The country was littered with their places of worship. Small shrines by the road held statues in stone or plaster, male, female, androgynous, garlanded with festering flowers. In Multan, there were temples where the Hindus went, and in these, grotesque gods stood, some like beasts, some like unnaturally virile men and some like voluptuous females. These idols were adorned with flowers and coloured powders, and served by priests with shaven heads and white robes. The stench of incense and decayed flowers filled the temples and in the background he heard bells and the sounds of hidden, almost secretive music.

Surely then, Coryate thought, this was a slave race, allowed by its masters to practise its own forms of worship unhindered. He had heard that the Muslims were fanatics who persecuted other religions. But in Persia and now in India he had seen tolerance.

On the first day in Multan, he found a cheap teashop, with a bench at which he could write. His months with the caravan had enabled him to converse with the people around him sufficiently for him to understand and be understood. This made him more confident. He also felt relieved of a huge burden now that he knew Steele would somehow despatch his messages to England. Steele was a worldly man. He had his methods.

Lost in reverie, he was abruptly aware that someone had moved in beside him, and had nudged him to the edge of the bench he considered his. He turned his head abruptly and met sloeblack eyes in the globose and hairless face of a eunuch. Its yellow tongue licked thick, painted lips. '*Salaam aleikoum,*' said his new companion. '*Buon giorno, padrone.*' He continued in heavily accented Italian, 'For seven years I was the captive of the giaour, honourably taken in battle. For five of them I was body servant to a merchant in Venetia. There I learnt this language, which is perhaps yours, for I think under the blisters and dirt you are a white man.' He scrutinized Coryate with interest. 'This is a country I know, padrone, and I can help you, if I so wish, for not everyone helped me in yours, as you can perhaps see.'

'I hail from England,' said Coryate sternly, 'with no mongrel taint of Italy in my blood. I am Thomas Coryate, late of Prince Henry's court, and my birthplace is Odcombe, in the county of Somerset.' The fat man seemed to laugh as he listened. 'My name is Maqbool,' he said. 'In Venice, they called me Marco. So you are English. Many come here from those cold, wet, little islands now, and most are rogues.'

Coryate let this pass, partly because he had come to believe it to be true. 'So what do you seek here?' asked Marco. 'Coin, no doubt, like all the others. I take it you are with the caravan newly come to Multan, and will ride with it to Agra. I take it also that you crave audience with our Emperor and have it in mind that he will make you rich beyond belief.' He snickered. 'You have been spared speech. We know what it is you want. You should think of me as your friend.'

'I have not come for coin.' Coryate was affronted. 'I have come for knowledge. I have come to find out what your country is like, and afterwards I shall write what I discover in a book that all the world will read.'

Marco scrutinized him closely. 'It is true,' he said, 'that no honest man who was not also a fool would trouble to write a book, and you look more fool than rogue. Therefore, you may be honest. Perhaps I shall believe you, but first, let me tell you this is not my country. Let us go to a better place and talk. Let us talk in Farsi, padrone. It is less humiliating for me than to use this language I spoke as a slave.'

~

They elbowed their way down a narrow lane and came to what Coryate supposed to be the equivalent of a London chophouse. This occupied a long, narrow room; along each wall were cotton mattresses and bolsters, on which the customers lounged, with low wooden tables in front of each seat. At the farthest end of the room was the kitchen; fires blazed there, incandescent as rubies of the first water.

Half-naked cooks attended to each fire. Diamonds of sweat flashed from their faces and bodies. They plunged ladles in and out of great iron vats full of rice, scented with precious saffron and dyed yellow with turmeric. Chunks of mutton, chicken and dried fruit wallowed amidst the mixture. Other cooks, like conjurors, twirled kebabs on red-hot skewers, or tweezed ovals of unleavened bread from low clay ovens. 'Do not worry, Englishman,' said Marco, and smirked lasciviously amongst the expensive smells, but without apparently evil intent. 'I am no man's catamite now. I own this place.'

A waiter came and stared uncertainly at Coryate in his rags, but Marco issued brisk orders and he went away reassured and returned with bowls of herbal tea. 'Now,' said Marco, 'I will tell you about this country to which you have come, which may be Jehangir's, but is not mine. He drank mouthfuls of tea noisily, gargling each in his gullet before he swallowed it. 'My country lies across the Ice Mountains that you came over, and if Jehangir told the truth, it is also his.'

The waiter, head bowed, servile, brought them piled ovals of bread and pieces of grilled meat. Marco ripped at them like a ravenous beast, and Coryate found himself doing the same. Mutton grease soaked his beard; sticky slivers of food lodged themselves uncomfortably in the many cavities that his teeth had acquired on his travels. But he gnawed and tore at his food as Marco did and as, it occurred to him at random, the Mongol hordes must have done, who were perhaps Marco's not too remote ancestors. 'When the Arabs cut off my balls,' Marco explained, 'they did not destroy *all* my appetites. I like to eat, as you see, friend Tommaso. Afterwards, we shall talk.'

At the end of the meal, lolling amidst the bolsters, nibbling the red *loukoum*, a Turkish delicacy, for which he had first acquired a taste in Turkey, Coryate felt grateful to his host.

He had not eaten so well or felt so contented with life since after the dinner at Montacute when he had first touched Anne Harcourt's breasts.

'Tommaso,' said Marco, 'all our people came from a place where every summer the melons were swollen and ripe, firm to the hand and sweet to the lips.' Coryate started slightly. Someone had once told him the people of the Indies could read minds. But he recovered his composure. 'There we had cold air from the snows, and we lived well and bred the fat, lazy sons we wanted.' He took Coryate's hand in his and pressed it in a friendly fashion. 'But we knew about the country of idolators to the south, which could be squeezed like a rotten fruit. Here once a people lived, who built cities.

'They had a religion also, which divided them. Some were kings and warriors, and men that could think and write. They traded with Chin, with the blacks of the southern ocean, aye, even with the Hellenes and with Rome before the Caesars fell. And yet within themselves they were divided.'

Coryate tried to withdraw his hand from Marco's, but it was too firmly held, though Marco's hand was slippery with sweat. 'The people I see,' Coryate said, 'those who are smaller and darker and who worship beasts in their temples, you mean this is their country? You mean that you, the Great Mogul, his people, all of you are foreigners here?' Marco breathed loukoum and halitosis into his face.

'In this country,' Marco whispered, running his fat spatulate fingers up Coryate's arm, 'all are foreigners, except the heathens who first lived in the forests. Some of us who have come after have built temples and some have built mosques. But, Tommaso, you whites will be the next conquerors. This land is so rotten it will fall at a finger's touch. There is putrefaction in its air. Where our mosques were, your people will build churches. And then, believe me, those will fall also. Afterwards there will be much death.'

It was dark. The restaurant was empty except for the waiters. Marco brought his face closer to Coryate's. 'In this country,' he said, 'you should trust no other man.'

~

The day that Coryate's caravan was due to leave for Lahore, he stood in tattered Indian clothes outside a mosque. For days he had listened to the screams of the priests from the minarets and he was angry. The anger built up blacker because, before he could deliver the speech he had written in English and then transcribed into phonetic Farsi, he had to wait till the horde of muezzins, perched in minarets above Multan, had finished their cacophonous noon sermons.

As soon as their caterwauls had ceased, he stepped forward. There were not many people about at this hour, in the full heat of the day; but that did not matter. So a few pious men, staunch in their faith, were there to hear him. He flapped his arms like a stork about to launch itself into flight, and shouted as loudly as he could. He abused Islam and Mohammed, its prophet, the beloved of Allah, the lord of all Muslims, in words as blatant and shameless as it had been possible for him to unearth from the crevices of all the eastern languages he knew.

His face, already blistered by the sun, became purple with a species of passion. The sweat coursed down it like tears into his dishevelled yellow beard. 'I am like our Lord on Calvary,' he thought, as he saw a crowd of turbans and robes collect around him, and watched how the black eyes and beard-infected mouths slowly widened, first in stupefaction, then slowly into amazed comprehension.

'I might be crucified like my Lord,' he thought. 'Yet before they do that, they should know who I am.' And he shouted, more violently because the sun had swelled his eyes, 'I am Coryate, the Long Strider! I am from Odcombe, the most beautiful place in the world. And I have written two books which contain more wisdom than all your Koran.'

Marco came out of the crowd and seized his elbow. 'Enough!' he hissed. 'Enough, Tommaso. Are you a madman to stand in the noon sun and cry out thus? These people think you are, otherwise your throat would be cut by now. Come back to your caravan, where you will be safe.'

~

Lahore was a city of gardens and libraries, scholars in skullcaps, and veiled women. Glimpsed sometimes by accident, those pearl pale, oval faces, huge eyes underlined with kohl, full lips reddened, embossed themselves upon Coryate's retentive memory. In the days that the caravan lay there, like a beached seamonster, he became calmer. Beyond Lahore was the most beautiful thoroughfare he had ever seen, more like a Roman avenue than an Indian road, well paved and lined with trees. It was so wide that the cumbersome caravans easily passed each other upon it, and Mogul troops guarded it.

On its grassy verges many people walked: Hindus in saffron robes, beads round their throats; Muslims in white with rosaries clenched in their fists. These were pilgrims, but there were also many showmen. They led chained black bears from the mountains, who would dance if they were whipped, or caparisoned monkeys. These, like the humans who ploughed the fields on either side of the road, did what they were told to do without need of the lash; mostly they imitated what people did. The camels and elephants Coryate saw were no longer a source of amazement to him. He accepted them as beasts of burden, what asses and horses were in Somerset.

They crossed a vast plain, blistered and red as Coryate's own face. Mustapha, who often walked by him, told him that they would soon come to Delhi, where the old Hindu kings had ruled. He spoke often of Timur, who had conquered this city. Slowly, Coryate realized that he meant Tamerlane, about whose exploits his acquaintance from the Mermaid, Master Kit Marlowe, had written a play. 'The Hindus of Delhi would not surrender,' Mustapha said. 'Timur-i-Leng, the lame one, killed 30,000 Hindus in the villages, and piled up their heads in a pyramid outside the city. Imagine, giaour, so many bloodstained heads!'

'And what happened then?' Coryate asked, childlike.

'Ah, they opened the gates. Timur entered, and cut off the heads of 30,000 more unbelievers. That made another fine pyramid inside the city, to match the one on the plain outside. But all were kafirs, so it mattered little.' He added carefully, 'Koryati, we in this caravan do not mind that you are a kafir. Your people fight well, not like Hindus.'

The caravan bypassed Delhi, because there was nothing there but ruins and a few surviving tombs and shrines. But in the brittle sand, Coryate's sandals, now terrifyingly torn, kicked up axeheads and rusted swords, blood baked into their blades. Some were made of flint. People had been battling over this useless territory for centuries.

Occasionally, the camels' tired pads uncovered human bones in the desert. Once an unannounced skull smiled up at Coryate from the dust. 'Alas, poor Yorick!' He seemed to recall this line, and Burbage, perhaps, at swagger on a stage, with a paper skull in his hands. But all his memories of England were dying. He felt this ferocious and foreign sun work upon his body and turn his skin into leather. Once there had been full English breasts like white doves bent over him, the good odours of beer and captured Spanish wine, welcome warmth, or under Odcombe roofs, the fragrant apple smell of scrumpy with cloves in it.

'Too many men have died in Delhi,' Mustapha said beside him. 'It is a place of bad omen, fated only for dry bones. Soon we shall reach Agra. There we shall see the red stone fort of Akbar, and the Jamuna river with its ships upon it, so many that you can cross dryshod from deck to deck, and the shops bursting with goods, and the musk-and-honey-scented whores of Agra, the pumpkin-breasted whores!'

8

Diary Four

August 2002

Mumbai–Delhi–Aligarh

We had last seen Juzer when he had arrived at Dom's doorstep with a box of sweets from Bhavnagar, wearing the guilty smile of a new father. He had been given tasks to complete before Dom and I left for Delhi. 'I want to know the exact month that Coryate was in Agra,' Dom told him. Besides this, he wanted to know the route Coryate would have taken and details of what the city had looked like then.

Some evenings later, Juzer dropped in at Dom's house, resplendent in a white embroidered kurta with gold buttons. He took off his shoes at the door, put down the bulky plastic bag he held in his hand, and assumed a Christ-like posture, his arms spread out, his expression benevolent. He looked untainted. His face was polished. His beard was shampooed. Had he been older I would have presumed he had dyed it to its present lustrous black.

'I'm coming straight from my mosque.' His lips widened

into a chaste smile. He paraded himself not unlike a little girl in a new birthday dress. 'This is *libas-e-anwar*, it's like a traditional outfit.' He turned to me. 'Don't you like it? It makes me look so dignified.'

From the plastic bag, Juzer retrieved a white cotton coat. 'This is the *saaya*.' He slipped his arms into the long sleeves. It was no different from a doctor's coat, only cut in a flare and longer; it reached below his calves. 'Just see how different this makes me look now.'

Dom made subtle gestures to me, indicative of his need to change the topic. I sat down, began to leaf through some papers on the table. With a jump, Juzer descended on the cushion on the floor opposite me.

Dom looked at him intensely. 'Speaking of Muslim clothes, Coryate would have noticed that the Hindus dressed differently from the Muslims in this country. He would have also noticed that their languages were not exactly the same. And I wonder how he reacted to the various Hindu gods and goddesses, and the way they were worshipped. After all the Church of England has rather quiet services. I think he may have seen the Hindus, at least initially, as a slave race, allowed by the Moguls to practise its own forms of worship.' He paused before he said, 'How would he have found out the truth?' Juzer shook his head. 'Anyone he talked to would have told him. And he was a talkative bugger. Now, Agra.'

Handing over photocopies from his bag Juzer smiled prosperously in the face of Dom's patient scepticism. 'Are you knowing about *neel*, sir?'

'Neel?'

'Neel means blue. Neel is indigo. The best quality of indigo was available in Agra in Coryate's time.' He considered the air around him like a scholar. 'Many European traders set up factories and trading houses here, there and everywhere. They all exported indigo.'

'Just this neel?' Dom said encouraging him to stick to the topic.

'No-no. Bengal and Bihar supplied silk, then from the east there was cotton, foodgrains, sugar, ghee. Then musk came from Bhutan, saffron, shawls and walnut from Kashmir, also diamonds and spices from Golconda in the south. All goods passed through Agra. A large quantity of goods was sold in the bazaars of Agra itself, especially spices, and the rest was exported by the European traders.'

Juzer offered with glee, 'These European traders had a hard time really.' He laughed, a bubble of spit sputtered at the corner of his lips. 'See, the rich Hindu bania buggers in Agra had big wholesale shops. The European traders tried to sell goods bought from different places in India to them. But these cunning banias had their own Hindu and Muslim agents who informed them about prices. So they demanded low prices from the European traders. Or they didn't buy for a long time. The European traders were forced to sell to them at any price.' A look of horrid fascination crossed his face. 'These European buggers never realized that the banias were even better than them at calculation.' His shoulders shook with laughter.

'I have worked out some dates, sir,' he said to Dom. 'I think it is very probable that Coryati spent a lot of time in Agra. Richard Steele was leaving Multan when Coryati proceeded to it from Kandahar. They would have met about fifty kilometres outside Multan around 29 May 1615. Coryati would have proceeded via Lahore to Agra. Assuming that he had spent ten days in Multan, seven days to walk to Lahore, two days in Lahore, and twenty days to walk to Agra, and presuming that he walked twenty-five to thirty miles a day, Coryati would have been in Agra about 29 June. Or early July.'

'And the route?' Dom leaned forward to grab the packet of cigarettes on the table. Despite the doctors' instructions and his own disgruntled attempts at not smoking, he was easily tempted when something got him excited.

Juzer said, 'There were two important land routes at that time. The northern route running between Peshawar and Sonargaon in Bengal, and an eastern route leading to Gujarat. Later a new route was developed running parallel to the River Jamuna. Along this route, pack animals and carts were easy to get for transportation of goods. People travelled in cushioned carriages. Coryati could have come in a cart or carriage. There were also other minor routes. All of them led to Agra. There was a lot of economic activity and all types of craftsmen and professionals came to the town. Carpets were produced there. There was textile production, printing, dyeing, gold and silver work, lace weaving, metal work, stone work, mining, quarrying and all that.' Juzer leant over and patted the pile of photocopied sheets he had given me. 'It's all there.'

Glancing at his watch, he became restless. He looked up at the fan as it spun unsteadily, chopping the hot air, and then looked down at his feet. He shook his head muttering to himself. With the agility of a grasshopper, he jumped up. 'I'm such a stupid bugger,' he said sticking a foot out. 'These socks are not right.' They were muddy green in colour.

Dom smiled, but one eyebrow arched up like a closed bracket. 'They look fine to me.'

'They should be white,' Juzer spread his arms. 'Then from the top of my cap to the soles of my toes I would look dignified.'

~

Delhi was smouldering in the heat. The breeze whined demandingly from the desert. It swished the trees and whipped up dust collected in heaps. Waves of hot air rose from the tarred surface shaping illusions of wetness on the roads. Now and then, clouds loomed over with a promise of rain. But it did not rain. The air, hot and sticky, adhered to our flesh like another layer of skin.

We had hired a vehicle for our journey from Delhi. Joginder Singh, the driver, reported an hour late. He was a lean and strong man, handsome in a hilly way. He belonged to one of the hill towns of the Himalayas, he told me.

Joginder sped along the toll road towards Agra. On either side of it, young eucalyptus trees, their branches entwined like a series of paper dolls, swayed together in the breeze. Their young leaves threshed it and made a moist, rustling sound. In the dividers in the middle, bougainvillea shrubs threw up blotches of colours: of pink and purple flowers. We passed towns haphazard and seamless, their faces slapped with nameboards.

'Could I have my notebook, please?' Dom said. 'And also a pen.' I took them out of our travel bag and gave them to him. He began to make notes, now and then studying what passed by outside his window. But for the trees, a few peasants ambling along the road and an old Muslim tomb painted a tentative yellow, there was nothing that was remarkable enough to remember.

'What are you writing?' I asked.

'All this.' He pointed to the window.

'There are only these eucalyptus trees. And those two skinny cows.'

'These trees don't belong here.'

'Obviously. They normally grow on the hills where it's cooler. These are newly planted.'

'In Coryate's time there must have been other kinds of trees. This entire area must have been a forest. I must find out what trees grew here.'

'Whatever for?'

He looked at me. 'We know that Coryate walked from Lahore to Agra. He called it the Long Walk. It was a straight road bordered by shady evergreen trees, and by villages and towns about every ten miles.' He turned to his notebook, muttered, 'This has changed.'

'What did you expect?'

He replied without looking up. 'Don't you see, Sarayu, we have only five letters that Coryate wrote from India. And some reminiscences by other people about him. Beyond this we have to reconstruct from available facts, reinvent his life all the time.'

'Reconstruct? Reinvent? How?'

He cast me a long troubled glance. He shook his head as though spinning the gloom and annoyance out of it. 'What the hell do you think we are going to be doing in Agra?'

'I haven't the faintest idea.' I laughed. His nostrils flared. Provoked, I teased, 'See the Taj Mahal? Buy *pethas*.'

'The Taj Mahal wasn't even built then. As for the pethas, I'm sure Coryate must have liked them as much as I do. Seriously, Sarayu, we are going to have to imagine a lot. Imagine Coryate is walking down a road in Agra. He wouldn't see a person for miles. Now imagine what we will see. Thousands of cars, millions of people, dirt everywhere.' Dom rolled down his window, lit a cigarette. A nerve twitched in his cheek. 'Sarayu, we must try to do Coryate some justice.'

In his eyes that looked into mine I detected a plea. 'We must look very carefully for the contrasts.'

'Contrasts?'

'Between modern and ancient India.'

I frowned. 'That's hardly difficult. It's all around us.'

'I'm not talking about that sort of a contrast, but one that shows similarities.' We passed a school with the board—Martin Luther High School. A few yards away from it was a shop called Cake Bank. Dom pointed to them, 'Look, this is not what Coryate saw. There are glaring contrasts between then and now. But there are tremendous similarities between the people.'

I found his explanation difficult to follow but I could see that it made some sort of vague sense. At this point I didn't know how or why it did. 'Similarities? I can't see any. How can you say people then and now haven't changed?'

'People in developed countries have changed because their countries have. India hasn't changed that much, so people haven't.' He thumped the seat with his hand. 'People here, Hindu or Muslim, are still religious and they believe what their ancestors did. People here were terrifyingly poor then and they still are. What's interesting is that their attitudes towards religion and poverty are slightly different now.'

Four wet heads of buffaloes thrust out of a pond in sequence; they ambled along the road whisking their tails above their rumps. A crow riding on the back of one of them, startled by a swished tail, flew away into the fields and perched on top of a dome of an old Muslim tomb. We had passed similar structures built of brick and stone.

Dom must have noticed them. 'Coryate must have seen similar tombs in his time. I want you to remember something. Coryate thought rather stupidly that Muslims ran this country. He believed, they had always been here. He must have been surprised to find that a lot of people were not Muslims. They were Hindus and the country belonged to them.'

Cigarette smoke shaped a veil around Dom's face. He said, 'Don't you see, Sarayu, although there is a contrast between Hindus and Muslims, there is also a similarity, in their attitudes towards one another. Only, now, the situation has reversed. The Moguls were conquerors then.' His eyes crinkled cynically. 'Now the Hindus dictate terms. As always, the two groups are suspicious of each other.'

A new thought took root in Dom's mind. He wrinkled his nose. He drummed his fingers in the air before he raised his hand to ruffle my hair in a patronizing way. 'I am not saying this to undermine the Hindus, or you, but this is a part of history. When the English came to India they could understand the Muslims better than they could Hindus. Because to them the Muslims were more civilized, they had some form of etiquette that the English understood, and a concept of equality. The Hindus were divided into castes, which the English could never begin to understand, nor could they understand their numerous gods, customs or their extended family connections and their loyalty to them.'

He took a close look at his index finger. He said smiling at it, 'The fact that Juzer is a Muslim is a good thing for you.'

'Did you say *good*?' Both my eyebrows grew tall.

'*Very* good. He'll draw your attention to the contrasts and the similarities through the way he relates to people, and the way they relate to him.' He patted my hand with the fidgety finger, 'And the way you relate to each other.'

~

We did not stop at Agra but drove on to Aligarh. The road paved with stone was rough. Not only were the stones of different sizes, but many of them were also broken or simply absent. In their place were craters the size of a truck's wheel. It had rained heavily the previous night; the roads were wheel-deep in water. Vehicles stood in a long queue. Wobbling like some ship caught in a seastorm, each vehicle waded through gloomy chocolate-coloured water. It continued to rain.

We reached Aligarh later than we expected. 'I am sure Juzer hasn't come in yet,' I remarked as we checked in at the hotel. It was as I opened the door to Dom's room that Juzer sauntered out of the adjoining one in the same white kurta and pyjama that clothed him with dignity.

'I told you, I'd be here before you,' he grinned, combing his beard with a finger. 'I've just finished offering my prayers.' His feet were clad in white bedroom slippers.

Dom waited for me to walk into the room, but Juzer was the first one in. 'I hope you had lunch,' I said following him, 'we were about to order sandwiches and coffee.'

Juzer stuck his tongue out, shook his head assertively. 'No-no-no! I am fasting.' He raised a finger in the air. 'No food. No water even. After sunrise and before sunset.'

'I hope this is only for today?' Dom looked apprehensive. 'Is it Ramzan already?'

'I am fasting for one whole month.' Juzer clucked with his tongue. 'This is not a compulsory fast like the one for Ramzan. I am keeping it of my own accord. It books my place in heaven.'

I stared dubiously at him. 'Heaven?' I laughed. 'How can you be so certain there is one?'

Juzer wore a tough look. 'Of course, of course, there is, there is. I know even what heaven is like,' he said wrapping his beard around a finger. 'I have the knowledge. I know exactly when Adam was born. I know when the Judgement Day will happen.'

'You do?' I said. 'When? Tell me.'

'I can't tell you. This knowledge comes automatically to those who are enlightened only. I know everything, but I can't tell anyone. But ...'

Dom, slightly alarmed, raised his hand as if to stop him, 'What have you been up to since you arrived?'

'I missed the bus.'

Dom looked startled. He laughed. 'Did you really?'

'So I came by train,' Juzer said. 'I left my luggage here and went to the internet cafe down the street.'

Dom studied him reflectively. 'Don't work so hard.'

'I wanted to check my mail. I have many e-mail girl friends.' He smiled. 'I met an English professor there. He had to fill up an application on the net for a job. He didn't know how to do it. I helped him.' Juzer's eyes sparkled. 'But sir, this professor had not even heard about Coryati.'

Dom was amused. 'You shouldn't expect everyone in this region to know of Coryate.'

I added with a grin, 'After all, he's not Jehangir.'

'But he knew about Mildenhall,' said Juzer extracting some invisible particle from his beard. 'He told me to look up his tomb in the Roman Catholic cemetery in Agra where many English people are buried. His tomb is the oldest English monument in India.'

I asked, 'Who was Mildenhall?'

Juzer adopted a knowing air. 'He was a buggering crook. He came to India with stolen goods in 1611. That bloody crook wanted to sell them in India. He fell sick in Ajmer and died. He was Catholic, so his body was taken to Agra.

He was buried in the Roman Catholic cemetery. He was the first Englishman ever to reach India over land. He was also perhaps the first Englishman to have married an Indian woman and have children by her.'

Juzer's eyes drooped. 'I thought Coryati was the first.' He raised his eyes to Dom. 'Sorry sir.'

'That's all right, Juzer,' Dom replied. 'But please remember that our man's name is Cor-Yet. Not Cor-Ya-Ti.'

~

The different departments of the Aligarh Muslim University were set in a huge campus more full of trees than students. It was the wrong season perhaps for the latter. A stray student pointed out the Department of History and Professor Irfan Habib's room to us. Juzer hurried ahead to its first floor, stood before the door looking puzzled. His head was capless; he rubbed it. He pointed to the bolted door as we reached his side. 'For nothing we came all this way,' he said.

We traced our way back down the corridor. I heard loud guffaws of laughter from a room we had passed. The door was partly open. I peeped in and saw the back of a woman; a middle-aged man sat in a chair against the wall mounted with a blackboard on which was scribbled two words: Demand and Supply. On a bench near the window was an elderly man with hair as white as fleece. Next to him, leaning against a steel almirah, was a foreigner straight out of a book on ancient adventurers. His leg was outstretched; it was clad in thick plaster. A wooden walking stick rested against it.

So engrossed was I in studying the contents of the room that I didn't notice the middle-aged man looking enquiringly at me. But no sooner had Dom's face appeared next to mine, he stood up. 'Please, please, come in, come in,' he said raising both his hands, then indicating the bench in front of the desk, 'I didn't realize it was already time. I am Irfan Habib.'

Dom waited for me to walk in first. I walked into a pile of books on the floor. Moving them aside I stepped into another. The bench was stacked with more books. 'Please find some place to sit,' the professor offered as the woman, dressed in a white salwar-kameez, pushed the books to one side. 'This is Professor Shireen Moosvi,' Habib pointed to her, 'this is her room. I thought this would be a better place for us to meet. It has more space for all of us to sit,' he laughed heartily, 'and,' he raised a finger as he sat down, 'she has the facilities to make us tea, and the gracious inclination to prepare it.' Turning to her, he said, 'Now that they are here, do you think we could have that promised tea?'

He introduced us to the other professor with silvery hair and a wide smile. 'And this,' he pointed to the man with the plastered foot, 'is our Simon Digby.' Digby was stout in a pleasant way and almost bald, and out of his chin, in a hesitant cascade, tumbled a white beard that ended in a point. He started to talk almost immediately to Dom even before he had sat down. His accent was that of an educated, itinerant Englishman. Dom paid rapt attention to what he was saying. It later occurred to me that he hadn't had much choice.

Professor Moosvi had retreated behind a door, which I presumed was the kitchenette; she returned with cups of tea. She held out one to me; I accepted eagerly. A hot cup of tea was exactly what I needed after the awful drive and Juzer's incessant chatter with Joginder. Half way through, Dom had fallen into undisturbed slumber emitting an unlimited ration of not-so-peaceful snores.

Taking the cup offered to him, Habib said to me, 'Have you ever seen a kitchen fitted in a toilet? This one is. Ingenious.

And out of it, we are able to get this wonderful tea.' He took a long sip. For some reason I was not as eager as I had been a minute ago. I looked into the cup; shreds of cream floated to the top. I drank it quickly. It was tepid.

Meanwhile, Digby had stopped talking. I think his foot hurt. Dom sipped his tea suspiciously, much as I did mine. Had it been wine, he surely would have gulped it down. Finding an attentive audience, he cleared his throat. 'I would have thought that the arrival of the Englishmen at Jehangir's court would have aroused some curiosity ...'

'That's the trouble,' Habib said, 'Jehangir never mentions Coryate in the *Jehangirnama*. The *Akbarnama* mentions a Portuguese couple—man and wife. Akbar tells them that monogamy was a very good thing for them. One god and one wife. Akbar added that he "preferred his three hundred wives to the Christian ideal of only having one."'

Habib laughed. 'The only reference to the English in the *Jehangirnama* is about a conflict between the Portuguese and English in Surat. *Rangrez,* they called the English that.'

Digby interrupted, '*Angreja* is a Portuguese word. *Angrej* is derived from it. It is curious that in the very same period a man called Usman from Gazipur writes about the "ships of angreja". Usman lived far away from Surat, but it is possible that he could have travelled down the Ganges into Surat and heard that word . . .'

'The English don't seem to have been very popular then,' Habib added. 'The Dutch were more important.'

'Coryate had a meeting with Jehangir,' Dom said. 'What and who would he have seen in Jehangir's court?'

'I don't think that Coryate would have met Jehangir at all,' Habib was quick to add. 'It was not easy to meet the Emperor. Jehangir gave an audience from his *jharoka*—

the upper window of his court. People gathered below the window, made petitions to him. I think Coryate must have done that. There is an account of how he submitted a petition to Jehangir; he asked for money. Sir Thomas Roe scolded him. "Beggar," he said, "filthy fellow." But Coryate writes, "I answered the ambassador stoutly." He must have been terribly hurt by Roe. My sympathies are entirely with him.

'If you want to know about Mogul society, Pelsaert's book—*Jehangir's India*—gives a vivid description of it in Agra. It has been reprinted many times. Pirated editions are also available. Simon himself is a pirate.' He pointed a finger at Digby. 'He lives in the Channel Islands. In a magical house he inherited from his aunt. But it has no furniture, only books all over the floor and wooden crates and cardboard boxes with more books. They are his furniture.'

Dom asked, 'Is it possible that Coryate came by ship from Delhi to Agra?'

'It is possible,' Simon said.

'But unless Coryate has written this, you can't assume it.' Habib added. 'I can see why you are asking this question. Very often, in the absence of details, we are compelled to assume certain things. But only if we are absolutely sure. At that time, they normally travelled by road to Patna and then by boat to Calcutta. Shah Jehan went by boat to Agra, yes.'

Dom said, 'A pity, because it would have been interesting if he had travelled by river. There's another bit that puzzles us. Where did Coryate go when he left Roe in Ajmer? It is mysterious; he disappeared for a year.'

Juzer, who had been sitting quietly until now, his pen poised over his notepad, suddenly put up a hand, as we did at school. 'Sir, according to Coryate's last letter, he leaves Ajmer on September 1616 and reappears in Mandu in September

1617. Do you think he would have encountered the plague during this year? We know that Jehangir went to Ahmedabad to escape the plague and returned, as per the Gregorian calendar, in 1618.'

Habib clicked his tongue. 'Jehangir used to go to Kashmir via Lahore every year. The plague started in Punjab in 1616 and slowly spread into Agra and even perhaps Delhi. After 1616, Jehangir never went south. And even if you consider the Gregorian calendar, the difference is only eight to ten days.'

Juzer persisted. 'According to Roe, in September-October of 1616, he was in Ajmer. It is possible that Jehangir went to Ahmedabad. Roe went with him, and then they went to Ajmer and later to Agra.'

'Don't forget, at that time, the Christian year began in April. Not January. That is how we got our financial year end as March,' Habib said.

Juzer continued, 'Also, Coryate is said to have gone to Haridwar, Rishikesh and Jwalamukhi. We don't know whether he got there. If he did, how?'

'He must have gone by the same route as Akbar who went to Jwalamukhi from Haridwar. Jehangir also went to Haridwar. He distributed money there,' Habib said.

'There is a possibility that Coryate saw the Kumbh Mela. The question is, did he see it in Haridwar or Allahabad?' Juzer added, 'The last Kumbh Mela happened in 2001.'

Professor Habib waved a hand at him. 'Forget that. Kumbh Mela was not important in those days. There were so many fairs then and the Kumbh was just another one.'

'But sir, Huien Tsang has recorded the Kumbh Mela in his account. He went to it with King Harshavardhan and there were 500,000 people, he wrote.'

'I don't think you should take any historian's account or their numbers seriously. How do we know how many were there? It is merely a notion. You must try and understand the psychology of the travellers and their accounts. Today 500,000 people are many. At that time even a hundred would have been many. People didn't rush to the Kumbh Mela from all over the country or world then as they did recently. They did not have any great fervour as they have today.'

'Sir, what I was trying to ask you is, if the Kumbh Mela happened in 2001, then we can calculate backwards to determine if Coryate could have seen it. But there is a slight problem. The Kumbh Mela didn't happen exactly every twelve solar years. For example it should have happened in 1954, but it did in 1953. So ...'

'As I said, forget it.'

Digby was giving Dom accounts from various academic papers that he had written. Habib laughed. 'You should publish all your papers in a book, Simon. Call it *Inconsequential Curiosities*.' Turning to Dom he said, 'Can you come back about three? I will show you some panels. We prepared them for an exhibition of miniatures from Akbar and Jehangir's time. They might help you.'

Juzer left us to our own resources for lunch. 'I am going to the mosque,' he said waving to us, 'it is time for my afternoon prayers. I will be here at three.' Joginder knew no restaurants in the city. 'First time,' he explained, then stopped a young man on the road and asked him for a hotel. Following his instructions, we drove to Natraj Hotal at the end of the road. The man behind the counter said, 'Only sleeping here, no eating. Go to Novelty Cinema.'

'But we don't want to see a film,' I said, 'food, food, we want *khana*.' I put my hand to my mouth several times.

'Go to Novelty Cinema. India Hotal there.'

We drove back the way we had come. It was close to two. Dom spotted an advertisement of India Hotel fixed to a lamppost. Half an hour later, following a series of lampposts, we arrived opposite Novelty Cinema. It was showing a B-grade film and exhibited a poster of a half naked woman on its facade. The road was full of slush that smelled of piss.

We opened the door to the restaurant; the front room was flooded. A waiter put three plastic Pepsi crates upside down on the floor and indicated we use them as steps to the inner room. It was pitch dark in keeping with the seventies' style. I could make out two men in the corner, drinking.

Dom ordered a drink. I felt like one but declined Dom's offer. The waiter held out the menu and a candle. I ordered dal and nan. It was the safest food in such a place. I could see rats darting about. To my astonishment, Dom ordered kadai mutton. I begged him to reconsider, but he laughed. 'Don't worry. I doubt if it's rat. It may be goat, of course.'

In the light of the candle the mutton was nearly black. Dom finished most of it. 'See, it wasn't bad,' he remarked thirty minutes later as we drove back to the university. We left for Agra the next day.

~

At breakfast, Dom was white as a sheet. He stared fixedly at his order of fried eggs; the twin yolks matched the colour of his eyes. He clutched his stomach, groaned with pain. I was tempted to say, 'I warned you,' but I let it pass. I gave him some tablets to ease the ache. He returned to bed.

Juzer and I went in search of bookshops. We found an old one stacked with dust-ridden books. The owner, an old Sikh, tall though frail, welcomed us, eyes warm behind thick glasses. We enquired about books on Jehangir. We showed him the list Irfan Habib had given us. He couldn't find the books we wanted but showed us others. Some minutes later he called for tea and settled down, prepared for conversation.

'My Sikh people are democratic. They have no castes. You Muslims,' he said looking pointedly at Juzer, 'say you have no caste system like the Hindus, and yet you do. You have your own divisions within yourselves.' He blew on his glass of tea and then drank some. 'Maybe that is why both you people and the Hindus have both persecuted us. You are interested in Jehangir and you say he was a good king. But Jehangir was an utter villain. He liked to watch men and animals fight. He liked it when animals tore up men. He liked it very much when a lion slowly ate up a man. He was very violent. As you should know, he ate pork in public and refused to fast during the month of Ramadan even.

'Many years ago, the Muslims under Jehangir started to persecute the Sikhs. Under Aurangzeb, it became worse. Even our gurus were killed. This has become a tradition in India. When the Muslims are not following it, the Hindus do. Look at 1984 and everything that happened after that year. Look at how we fought the Hindus as we fought the Muslims under Jehangir.' He fixed us with the eye of a turbaned Ancient Mariner.

As we left sometime later, Juzer took a slip of paper from his pocket. Noted on it was the address of an old singer. Juzer insisted that we pay him a visit. I declined to do so. 'But you asked me to find someone to tell us about the Mogul harem, eunuchs, prostitutes. You wanted to know what Coryate could have seen. Besides his good voice, this bugger is a learned bugger.'

We walked a long way through narrow alleys paved with

brick. Old houses squatted along either sides, falling apart like well-used teeth. And like them, they smelled foul. We stood before a blue coloured door. It was open. Beyond it was an open court paved with stone. In the veranda abutting it, covered by timber rafters and tiles, was an old bald man. He stumbled up and down with the help of a walker. He was dressed in a frayed vest and a white dhoti.

He welcomed Juzer with unusual delight. His hands shook; his eyes tried to focus, the folds of skin around them crinkled like tissue. He led us to a table at the end of the veranda. No sooner had we sat down, a woman, her head covered with the end of her saree, placed before him a plate of rotis, dal and vegetables. 'I am sorry,' Sharmaji said, 'I have to eat. I have to take injection. Diabetes, you know.'

After he had finished his meal, and after one of his sons had given him the shot in his thigh, he started to talk about the old *gharanas* of Hindustani classical music. He rounded his mouth over each word as though his lips were halves of a musical instrument. Now and then he broke into a song. Undoubtedly, he possessed a good singing voice but I wasn't keen on songs. Moreover, I was anxious about Dom. I tried to catch Juzer's eye but he had them shut and his head bobbed to the song; his cap followed suit. Sharmaji finished a verse, and before he could start another, I asked him about Jehangir's harem. His mouth paused for moments in an 'O'.

He answered with a question. 'Do you know why the Moguls had harems? So that they were not tempted by any single woman's charms and they could have sex on demand. And what a huge and splendid place the harem was. *Subhan allah. Subhan allah.* It was like an amusement park, a fairyland, a place of high security and stringent rules of discipline. Every lady of the harem had her own splendid apartment with ponds and running fountains, streams, gardens, shady retreats and underground structures. An average Muslim harem in India accommodated 2000 women, some of them of different nationalities. The women provided the men with fun and dance, equally the men tried every trick to amuse and arouse them. The upkeep of the harem cost the kings a tremendous amount of money. Akbar had 5000 women in his harem, and Jehingir, his son, had 6000. *Kya baat thi. Wah-wah.* Imagine even King Solomon's harem had only 1000 women.

'These women were kept closely guarded and secluded. Naturally, because the king couldn't satisfy all of them, women could start loving women. Such activity was not allowed. *Chi-chi-chi.* So they were locked into the harem and had to observe purdah even there. Any wrong thing done, woman to woman, then straight execution. It was like that.

'The Moguls kept eunuchs as guards. It was a custom followed in Persia. They castrated hundreds of young men to make them eunuchs. *Bechare.* Some times they were even given as dowry when a girl was married. These eunuchs were harmless; they didn't need sex. But they knew all the art of being erotic, and taught the harem ladies many, many things. The chief eunuch selected the woman for the night for the king and he dressed her up himself. Rose water, sandalwood, scented oils, flowers, henna, kajal, this and that.

'Also the best jewellery. Big, big diamonds, rubies and shining gold. The eunuchs also knew about aphrodisiacs, drugs like opium, and wine. They were excellent cooks even. *Subhan allah*! Young pigeons, chickens, sparrows, this, that. Very delicious. And what clothes the women of the harem wore, *wah-wah*, pure muslin from Bengal, so fine, so transparent that even when clothed they seemed naked.

'What wine! What music! Flowing, flowing through the night. And dancing girls also. Absolute professionals called *kanchanis*. These kanchanis were essentially cultivated prostitutes, who could sing and dance. And the king and his women showered trays of gold and silver coins on them.

'It was absolutely paradise. You see, the real Paradise, the Muslims believe, is a place of polygamy. So men could indulge in a lot of sex and women were obliged to please them. So making earth just like paradise was to them being faithful to their religion. Yes, Muslims are very fond of beautiful women, wine and sex.' He licked his lips.

I asked him if we could arrange for us to meet some hijras and prostitutes. He shook his head ferociously. 'No, no, no, but I will tell you about them,' he said. 'Prostitution has been a centuries-old tradition among the Bedias, who live in Agra ...' An hour later, we extricated ourselves.

In the hotel, Dom seemed better, or worse, depending on how you looked at it. The condition of his stomach had improved, but he had acquired a bottle of whisky, and his spirit level was high. 'It's wonderful,' he kept saying.

Already exhausted by Sharmaji, I was understandably irritable. 'What's so wonderful?' I demanded, and he replied with an angelic smile, which annoyed me further, 'Why, that professors in India, including an Englishman, are curious about where Coryate went and what he did, four centuries after he died. It's a triumph for Thomas, don't you see?'

9

A Demon and Two Priests

Agra was a crowded city sprawled out on either bank of the Jamuna river. A great fortress in red sandstone stood on a rise above it and dominated everything else. 'That,' said Mustapha, 'is the Red Fort of Akbar who, by the grace of god, was our emperor. He was Jehangir's father, a wise ruler, though he favoured the kafirs, the Hindu infidels, may they be cursed by Allah.' He spat in the roadside dust. 'Akbar had a prime minister, Birbal, who was very wise, though he often behaved like a clown. I will tell you some tales of Akbar and Birbal. He did so, laughing very loudly at the climax of each. Coryate, as courtesy demanded, also laughed, on a less raucous note. Also out of courtesy, he curbed the long stride that always surprised people in a man so short. This enabled his loquacious companion to keep up with him.

The caravan had shed many of its members on the road to Agra, for here its trip, which Coryate had thought endless, ended, and he no longer had a home. No goodbyes were said, but he was sorry to part with these rough and seasoned men whose faces had become familiar to him over the months, though he had only spoken to a few of them and had known the names of even fewer. They had understood what hardships the world created for travellers upon its surface, and accepted him because they knew he also knew.

Mustapha led him to a sarai where they could live cheaply. The weather was now warm and Coryate had no need of blankets, nor of any pillow beyond the small bundle that contained his few clothes and his many papers: most already covered with his sprawling childlike scrawl.

They explored the town, and Mustapha showed him the river. Coryate was amazed. He had never seen such a waterway in Europe. The Jamuna was full of vessels of varying sizes, barges carrying trade goods of all kinds, but mainly cloth, and passenger boats under brightly coloured sails. 'They say,' Mustapha told him, 'that once people could cross the river by stepping from the deck of one ship to the next. Now because of pirates, most people travel by caravan. But see, see, Koryati, how much wealth there is in this land!'

It had not percolated down to Mustapha, an unsuccessful trader who lived in a village north of Agra. He was a poor man, but seemed to have widespread contacts, perhaps because, as he explained, he came of a well-known family. He took Coryate to teashops where they were fed simply but amply without being required to pay. Agra was famous for petha, a crisply textured and expensive delicacy made of sugared pumpkin. Mustapha knew a sweetmeat seller who gave them a small quantity.

The two friends walked by the ship-filled river and shared the petha and Coryate, who had always wanted affection and not acquired much so far, felt warmth well up in him for the emaciated, bearded Indian who had befriended and helped him for no reason but human kindness.

'Did I not tell you of the whores of Agra, Koryati?'

Mustapha said. 'Eating this sweetmeat of pumpkins reminds me of the taste of their breasts. But their favours come expensive. I have little money these days, and you none. Still, we can enjoy their bodies with our eyes. A friend of mine owns a *kotah* where beautiful whores dance and he will allow us to come there as his guests.' He led Coryate through a tangle of alleys to a shabby house and knocked on the door. A gawky person dressed and made up as a woman, but with stubble on her face, opened it. She seemed to expect them.

Coryate stared at her, fascinated. 'She is a eunuch,' muttered Mustapha in his ear. 'They are not uncommon here.' A whine of music and the dolorous wail of voices raised in what Coryate supposed to be song drifted down from the floor above. The eunuch led them upstairs.

There a large room was filled with smoke from braziers and the smell of incense. In one corner, seated on what appeared to be a dirty tablecloth, Coryate saw a group of white-clad musicians. The instruments they played did not resemble any that he had seen in Europe. The rest of the room was filled with men more affluently clad.

Their attention was concentrated upon a fat woman, wreathed in scarves and veils over a long tunic and skirt. She writhed her hips and heaved her large, though copiously covered, breasts as she danced. Now and then her enraptured audience shouted '*Wah! Wah!*' and threw canvas pouches of coins at her. They were snatched up from the floor and carried off by a small girl. She smiled triumphantly, old beyond her years, as she scurried away with her booty.

As one dancer succeeded another, each a clone of her predecessor, the same procedure was followed. 'The child will count all the money given to each dancer,' Mustapha whispered. 'The purses the men throw are marked with their names. He who has given the most to each dancer will spend the night in her bed.'

Coryate was not really listening; nor was he watching the dancers, whose obesity disgusted him. He was trying to sit comfortably on the floor, cross-legged, like the other men, a posture to which he was wholly unaccustomed. Soon he began to feel considerable physical discomfort. Time passed; he shifted from haunch to haunch, and from side to side, but his efforts to ease his hardships didn't work. After two hours in the hot and smoke-filled room, his nose and eyes were running, and his joints hurt. When the performance ended, Mustapha had to help him, groaning, to his feet.

They went back to their sarai. Mustapha rhapsodized about the dancing they had seen and in particular about the dancers. 'What women, Koryati!' he exclaimed. The one in blue, did you see her breasts? I would pay thousands, if I had them, for a single night with her, and then die happy!'

Coryate decided not to reply.

~

Next day, after they had breakfast of unleavened bread and a soup of lambs' trotters, Mustapha said awkwardly, 'Koryati, the time has come for me to leave you. Today I must return to my village, where my business lies untended. I would ask you to live in my house as my brother. But I know the desire that burns in you to reach Ajmer and have speech with the Emperor. There is one last thing I can do for you, my friend, and I will do it today.'

Once more they walked through the cobweb of streets, but this time into a part of town that Coryate had never seen before. They reached a field with a small stone house beside it. He saw a cross atop the house and tombstones and more crosses in the field, all in the red sandstone of the area. The crosses were Armenian, but it was clear that this was a Christian church, with a Christian cemetery beside it.

'I was told of this place last year,' Mustapha said expansively. 'I did not know of it till then. Here there are some Nazrani priests, Koryati, though they are not angrez like you. But they worship, I think, the same gods. They pray to Isa, who is one of our prophets. In this graveyard an angrez is buried, your countryman, Koryati. It is good in a strange country to find people of your own faith. Therefore, I brought you here, so that you should not feel lonely when I depart. This is the last act of friendship I can offer you. I go to my village this afternoon. I must leave you now to make my arrangements for travel.'

Mustapha touched his brow and his heart, and then hugged Coryate in bear-like arms. 'Farewell, my friend,' he said, and turned away. 'I will find someone to guide you.' At the entrance of the cemetery he spoke to a scruffy young man who loitered there, gave him some coins, and pointed at Coryate. Then he walked resolutely on towards the town. Coryate stared after his receding back, and felt wholly forsaken. The scruffy young man came towards him, smiling with black and broken teeth. 'I am Abdul,' he said. 'I am a Christian like you. Your friend gave me money to take you to the padres. But it was very little. You will give me more?'

The padres were presumably in the church, which was perhaps a hundred yards away. 'No,' said Coryate. 'I will give you nothing, because I have nothing to give.' He was a resilient man. Mustapha had left him, but he had fended for himself all his life and he was accustomed to loneliness.

But Coryate was also incorrigibly inquisitive and he asked a question that he later regretted. 'How come you, fellow,' he inquired, 'with a name like yours, claim to be a Christian?' Abdul again bared his tarnished teeth, which now seemed unusually long, like a wolf's. Great and quintessential evil transformed his face like a mask. A feral smell filled the air around them. 'I am whatever I choose to be,' he whispered, and suddenly Coryate was terrified.

'You will not give me money, eh?' Abdul hissed. 'Then I will tell you what will become of you. You will yearn for your home, but you will never return there. You will suffer more pain than you ever thought was possible, and then you will die far from your friends and kin, and once you are dead and food for vermin, no man will ever know where your corpse lies under earth.'

Then, with an abrupt swivel of his thin body, he scampered away from Coryate, whose eyes, bulbous, blue, and somehow always innocent, followed his uncomely shape as it hopped like a toad between the tombstones, then disappeared into the distance. Coryate sank down on a rock and sat there for a long time. He was trembling all over, in spite of the heat. When he looked skyward, even the sun seemed sullenly darkened. 'Who was that?' he asked aloud. 'Mother of God, Master Jonson, Master Donne, what was that?'

~

Two Jesuit priests ministered to the Catholic church by the cemetery, both Portuguese. Coryate ardently hated Papists; it had been part of what he had learnt at the vicarage in Odcombe, now distant and perhaps unreachable forever, then at Oxford and the court. But now he needed some human company and did not berate them as he might easily have done otherwise. They all sat in a long bare room as darkness dropped over the world outside, and its realities vanished, to be explored by their voices under the cloak of the dark.

The Portuguese were old, but not very, yet were already worn out and frail after a few years in this place. The conversation between them and Coryate was not as difficult as it might have turned out to be. Since none of them knew each other's language properly, they had to speak in Hindustani—a mixture of Hindi (versions of which were spoken all over northern India) and Urdu, a dialect created in the military camps of the Moguls. There were a number of halts and stutters in their talk. Sometimes Coryate saw the dark eyes of the priests flicker over his face. He realized that they hated Protestants as much as he hated Papists. The only reason they could talk together was because they had all come here from the same continent; because all their skins were white.

This was not exactly true, he reflected. They had all been white when they first came to India. Now Coryate was as red as a boiled lobster, his skin mutilated by the sun and rain under which he had walked endlessly for months. The naturally sallow, brindled skins of the Portuguese had turned to a dark yellowish colour, like ancient parchments he had seen in the older abbeys of Somerset. He listened carefully to the two priests. 'There are devils abroad in this land,' said the elder, Father Mateus. 'The people are terrified of ghosts and evil spirits, and I doubt not but in this place they exist.

'For there is an endless mixture here of malign forces. Know you not, Senor Tomas, that for thousands of years this land was the land of the Hindus? They worshipped apes, elephants, rats and snakes and they had laws that kept many people at the status of animals. No man not Hindu can pretend to understand the intricacies of philosophy in which they believed. Because of their divisions, they collapsed when the Muslims came. The Muslims believed all men were equal. They were barbarians, from countries that had no cultures. But the Muslims were fighters, and the Hindus, because they were divided into what they call varnas, were soft.'

Coryate looked through the windows and saw only darkness. The smells that came out of this darkness were of exotic flowers, cows, unwashed human and animal bodies and their excrement. 'There is a belief here,' said the other priest, Brother Mario, 'because the Moguls are now rulers, and the Hindus subservient, this state of affairs will go on forever. But the Hindus greatly outnumber the Muslims, and if they can unite they may be moved to rebellion. Then there will be killing and bloodshed not to be imagined. Senor, even now they hate each other. But both say they do not, because of expediency.'

Father Mateus rubbed his bald pate, which already shone like a boiled egg. 'What has complicated it further is that after all these years the Muslims have become Indian. Many of them now are converts from Hinduism. The Indians, whether Hindu or Muslim, will do anything that will serve their own interests. It is of no use to us to make converts. No Indian believes in anything that does not help him or his relatives personally. Here we Christian priests are altogether useless.' Then he looked at Coryate's tired face and said, 'It is far from the city, and darkness has fallen. Why do you not sleep here tonight? It will save you a long walk.' He obviously did not know his guest's habits.

Coryate needed to shake off the accumulated depressions and fears that the day had brought him. It was very dark outside, and tonight he feared darkness. He accepted. Father Mateus showed him to a bleak and doorless room. The only furniture was a native *charpai*. Coryate did not doubt that the Papist priests had similar accommodation. Mateus gave him a candle.

'An hour before dawn we take our morning meal,' he said. 'All we eat is Indian bread with a little milk. Do you Protestants have food requirements that we of the true faith do not know about?' Coryate shook his head.

'Very well, then,' said Mateus. 'We shall speak further tomorrow.'

~

It was still dark when Coryate awoke next day, and he had forgotten where he was. This was a commonplace of his existence, and didn't alarm him. He allowed himself to wake completely, and then remembered. He also remembered the face of the creature that called itself Abdul and what it had said. He shuddered, rose, washed from the bowl of water the priests had provided and joined them outside to eat. He liked them though they were Papists; he even said Grace to please them before he took his first mouthful.

He asked, 'Yesterday my friend told me that an Englishman lay buried in your cemetery. Mayhap he died after you had come here. Could you tell me his name, or aught else about him? For he was my countryman.'

'Yes,' Mateus said, 'He did not die in this place, but in some village not far off of fever and the flux. The villagers brought the body here. So we prayed over it and buried it. Later some English came and put a stone on the grave. I cannot well pronounce his name, it's difficult, but we can show you the place, if you so desire. Since then I have seen some other English in the town. I think many more will come here for trade, and so many more will die here.'

Coryate once more remembered Abdul. He flinched a little, then composed himself and said, 'I would much like to see where he lies. Doubtless his name will be on the tombstone?' The priests nodded. 'It will soon be day,' Mario said. 'When it is full light, we can take you to the grave.' A little later, though the light was still dim, the priests rose and said to Coryate, 'Come.'

Outside, aviaries of birds shrieked and shrilled, and the sound of wingbeats filled the still air. Dusky clouds cluttered the sky overhead. 'Soon the rains will come,' said Mateus. 'There will be much water and the villages will be flooded. Everything in this land of devils comes in excess; if it rains, there are floods; if it does not rain, there is drought. I am sorry for the people, for though they are heathens, some have good hearts and souls worth the saving.'

'There are many good people in this place,' Coryate agreed. 'I met many as I walked. When I was hungry, they fed me. When I was naked, they clothed me. I do not think this is a land of devils, good Father.' Then he thought of Abdul, and added, 'But truly, often I cannot tell.'

They stumbled over tussocks and stones as they crossed the cemetery field. Near a decayed edifice, obviously old, Mario stopped and pointed to a tombstone. 'This is where your countryman lies.' Coryate stared at it and saw the name on it: John Mildenhall. He remembered Steele in the hills, who had spoken as though the man now underneath the tombstone was still alive.

Mildenhall had been a rogue and a thief, but for some reason Coryate felt grief for him. He had come very far from England and had presumably hoped to return to it. It seemed a sorry end to a life that, however ignoble, had been full of aspirations: to lie unknown and unmourned under a cheap tombstone in a field full of rocks and turds, thousands of miles from home.

'You seem much moved. You knew this man?' asked Mario sympathetically, but Coryate shook his head. 'It is only that he was my countryman,' he said. On the way back to the church they passed the spot where he had met Abdul. Coryate inquired if the priests knew him. Both made the sign of the cross. 'No,' said Mateus. 'God be thanked. But the natives speak of him. They say he is often seen in the cemetery. He comes and goes. They speak of him with great dread. They say he is *shaitan,* the devil himself.'

They walked on in silence.

~

The two Jesuits invited Coryate to stay with them. He was glad of the invitation, which eased his pinched purse. Mateus and Mario were Papists, and Portuguese to boot, categories of the human race that he had been brought up to dislike and distrust. But since those early Odcombe days, travel had made him forget such matters, and Mateus and Mario became his friends. He used to shop in the town markets with them for the simple provisions they needed. Though in features and complexion they might have passed for Indian, their black cassocks made them conspicuous. Coryate was surprised at the respect that the people, Hindus and Muslims equally, showed the Christian priests.

Coryate dressed in Indian clothes, seldom very clean, but his blonde hair and beard marked him as a foreigner. Though the natives were friendly towards him, and often helpful, he received no respect from them. Indeed, in the teeming city, very few people did, unless they were obviously rich. But even in the most crowded thoroughfares, people made way for the priests and saluted them courteously. He was puzzled about this, and asked Mateus.

'Ah!' said the old priest. 'The Indians have usually respected us. There have been no martyrdoms in India since the Brahmins killed St Thomas in Madras, more than a thousand years ago. The last Mogul, Akbar, invited the Jesuits to his court, and they debated religion there with the Mohammedan prelates. The ambition of the good fathers was to convert Akbar himself, but in this they failed. When he saw what they wanted, he became a little cold towards them. But our cassocks have been seen in Agra for many years.'

'You said, before, that Christian priests were useless here.'

'Tomas, know that I am a Jesuit. I speak on many levels.' His bald head shone with sweat. The wrinkles and furrows in his round face showed not only his years, but that he had had to endure much as they passed, under many desolate suns. 'Because of Akbar's patronage, and Jehangir's, we are physically accepted and respected. But our religion is not. What our Hindu converts represent is not our triumph but the failure of the caste system. Only those of low caste, who are treated as less than human, like beasts, decide to become Christian, so that they can rise in status and be treated as men. Muslims are proud people and will not convert. We need to convert powerful, wealthy people. *They* will not convert. That is why we are useless here.'

They were walking through the rough, rocky field under which the bones of Mildenhall and a handful of unknown Armenians lay. A few crosses reared up from the earth, as though the field had become a pirates' map for hidden treasures scattered widely: 'X marks the spot'. Mario had been silent as they walked, out of respect for his senior. But he now addressed Mateus. 'Good father, you regret that our converts are of low caste: But the first converts Peter made in Rome, were they not slaves? Only later were powerful and wealthy Romans converted. And all Italy now belongs to the true faith.'

'You are younger than I, and not so tired,' Mateus sighed, 'but this whole land is full of heathen religions. Tomas, there are the fire worshippers, the Zoroastrians who came from Persia. There are innumerable Hindu sects. The Muslims are divided into two groups, the Shias and the Sunnis. I admit, so are we Christians. But in India the religions are as many as wasps on a wall in a Lisbon summer. There are also Buddhists, Jains, and the tribe of Sikhs.'

'Sikhs?' Coryate asked. 'I have heard of the others, and mayhap I have met some too, but of them I have not heard. Are there any in Agra?'

'Their country is north, in the Land of the Five Rivers,' Mateus said. 'But a few live in Agra, and I can call one or two, Tomas, if you wish to write about them in your book.' They had entered the cool shadows of the church, and Mateus sat down on a chair, wiping his brow on the sleeve of his cassock, apparently oblivious to the others. 'I have only been here seven years,' he said to the sluggish air that cloaked them, 'and I am already so tired. Oh Jesus, my Lord, my Saviour, help me. I am so tired.' The air smelt of his tiredness.

~

Next day a man of strange appearance called at the church. He was tall and gaunt, clad like most Indians in loose white clothes, but he also flaunted a blue turban and a long, wild, beard. A scabbard belted to his waist contained nearly a yard of assiduously honed and sharpened metal, and he wore an iron bangle round his wrist. His eyes were large, bloodshot and wild and, for a man his size, he had a curiously high, womanish voice. 'He is Jagjit Singh, Tomas,' Father Mateus said. 'He is one of the Sikhs we talked of. He is a carpenter who works for us now and then. Brother Mario speaks his dialect somewhat.'

Mario said, 'Only enough for us to understand each other. I will tell him that you are interested in his religion.' Coryate surveyed the Sikh with interest. He had seen a few other such turbaned and bearded men in the towns through which he had passed, but had never known they had a religion of their own; nor had he met one before. Mario and the Sikh conversed at some length.

Finally the priest turned to Coryate and said, 'The home of his people is in Punjab, north of this place. The land is very fertile, and enriched by five rivers. The Sikhs, he says, are all farmers. Some time ago they broke away from Hinduism, mainly because the caste system disgusted them. They formed a religion that is more like a brotherhood.' They spoke in Hindustani, and the Sikh understood what they said and showed it with nods of his turbaned head.

'You will be interested to hear him, Tomas. So far all you have seen of these lands has been peaceful, and the people have seemed to you well settled in life. It is not so with these Sikhs. They call their religious leader the guru, and each guru is to them, if it be not blasphemy to say so, what our Pope is to us. Recently one such guru, Arjun, from the village of Gobindwal on the banks of a river called Beas, was taken and imprisoned by order of the Emperor, and most cruelly tortured before he was killed.

'I know not exactly what Jagjit means, but he says that a book this Arjun wrote so enraged Jehangir that he wreaked vengeance upon the holy man. So now the whole Sikh nation is in an uproar, for Arjun was considered a great leader of his people. We had not heard of this incident before, but we have always heard that the Sikhs were troublesome to the Emperor, and he dislikes them. So you see, Tomas, these lands are not as peaceful as they seem.'

Coryate asked a few more questions about Punjab and the Sikhs, and the answers so fascinated him that, as he told Mario, he had resolved to walk north once he had met Jehangir. Jagjit had been watching him closely, a slight smile on his bearded lips. When Mario told him this, Jagjit pointed a finger at Coryate and burst into bellows of laughter. Mario translated what he said.

'He says he likes you. But you are underfed, like a calf that has lost its dam. He wants to take you to his mother's house in Punjab. She will feed you corn bread and spinach, which seems a favoured dish there, and you will soon turn into a bull. He says you should tell him when you go to Punjab. He will guide you, for he must also go there soon when the time comes to fight in a war upon the Mogul.'

~

From Agra, Coryate made side trips to places which strangers told him would interest him. He knew that they did not properly know what might interest him, but often followed their advice. His methods of travel had always been chancy, his destinations usually dependent on wayside talk.

Now he walked alone, as he had done when he started on the trip, though these were Mogul highways. There were other men on the road as well as a variety of beasts—camels and elephants, trained bears and monkeys—and their keepers. The men came from different professions: carpenters and blacksmiths were common, as they walked from village to village, plying their trade. Here and there groups of uniformed Mogul soldiers rode high on their horses. Smells of human and animal excrement and flowering wayside plants filled the air. Drums and cymbals were constantly beaten, flutes played.

He also observed people who puzzled him. They wore white muslin masks that covered their noses and mouths. 'They are Jains,' he was told when he asked the keeper of a wayside stall. The man was surprised that he did not know. 'They do not want to take life in any form,' he explained, 'not even the lives of insects. Therefore, they wear a finely woven cloth upon their faces, so that they do not inhale even the smallest insects, and unknowingly cause them to die.'

Coryate observed the stallkeeper's surprise at his question. He had thought the Englishman an Indian like himself; and certes, Coryate reasoned, with so many people of different sorts abroad upon the road, nearly all of them natives of the country, why should he think otherwise? They differed in complexion and features; even in the languages they spoke. He was dimly aware by now that India did not have one language, but many, and that not all the people could understand each other, truly like the tower of Babel.

He watched others on the road who whipped themselves or were whipped by others as they walked. They were Muslims, he was told, but how was this any proof that they were barbarous? Christians in Europe flagellated themselves in penance for their sins. The eyes of these Muslim flagellants were glazed and swollen, as though the sting of the lash caused them not pain but an almost pleasurable stupour. Maybe the eyes of Christians looked like this when they whipped themselves or had others whip them.

He made these side trips because he had heard many stories of the Hindu god, Krishna. Krishna had been born a cowherd and, as a very small boy, had liked to sport with the pretty milkmaids of his village, Vrindavan. He watched them bathe in the river and then stole their clothes. The stories he was told about Krishna fascinated Coryate. To him, the Hindu god seemed as unashamed in his amorous adventures as some of the Greek deities. Temples had been raised in his honour at Vrindavan and Mathura, and Coryate decided to visit them, even though they were out of his way.

He was sorely disappointed. The Krishna stories he had heard had been pastoral myths. The blue-skinned boy had played his flute by clear waters rinsed by the whiteness of the milkmaids' flesh. Amidst green fields and flowering trees, magnificent cattle had pastured. But the cows in Vrindavan and Mathura were flea-bitten, sad cadavers, fit only for the butcher's hatchet, and the towns were crowded with pilgrims and priests. As for the great temples, Indian architecture had never appealed to Coryate, apart from the pillar in Delhi.

He came to the temple towns down stony, dusty roads. The countryside around had forgotten Krishna, and had become a barren wilderness of thorn and rock. The temples themselves smelt of dead flowers, incense, bodies. Many withered rose-petals and dry marigolds were scattered around. The priests had the faces of minor but dangerous predators, made more frightening by the caste marks daubed on their faces.

~

Coryate always thought best on the road. The customs and habits of people had always intrigued him, and in the temple towns he had perceived what seemed to him an enigma. As he came back by tortuous ways towards the highway that led to Ajmer, his mind followed paths equally tortuous. He had questions to ask, but nobody to answer them. London, when he first came there from Odcombe, had seemed to him a filthy town. The people were not scrupulous about bathing or wearing fresh clothes, and the great city reflected their habits. Country people were cleaner.

Yet, whether in town or country, they kept their places of worship scrubbed and swept. The Indians were a cleanly race, but their temples and mosques, and most public areas, were filthy beyond belief. It occurred to him that this might be because, except when it came to religion, most Indians he had met had been concerned with themselves as individuals, and not moved by any idea of collective responsibility. And why should they be so moved? he inquired of himself. From all he had found, Indians were unlike others in that they did not feel they had a country, as people in Europe did.

The Indians belonged to religions; to villages or towns, or to small provinces. The Hindus within the area ruled by the Moguls would never acknowledge loyalty to the Emperor, but had no language to link them with other Hindus beyond the borders. The Muslims could hardly be expected to protect Hindu interests that conflicted with their own, and had their own divisive sects, as the Hindus had castes.

The empire, moreover, did not prevail all over the country; outside its borders many independent kings—Hindu and Muslim—ran their own states. The Indians did not believe that they belonged to a country, because they had never had one. This was the source of all their sorrows, Coryate concluded. As he strode along, cursing the thorns and nettles that pestered his legs, he became proud of his theory.

Finally on the road to Ajmer, he forgot all about it.

10

Diary Five

September 2002

Agra–Mathura–Vrindavan

We reached Agra late in the night. It was still dark when, several hours later, I was aroused in my hotel room by the unmistakable sound of Juzer's voice outside. I glanced at my watch. It was half past four in the morning. I opened the door to find a waiter with a tray. Juzer was screaming at him. Dressed in a crisp kurta-pyjama, cap perched on his head, his arms flailed about. He grabbed the tray from the waiter, then slammed the door in his face. The man remained fixed to the spot, still hoping for a tip. I returned to bed.

We had decided to get an early start. But both Dom and I woke up late. We had no time for breakfast, so after coffee, we waited for Juzer in the hotel lobby. Dom lit a cigarette. 'For a person who doesn't eat breakfast, let alone lunch or dinner, Juzer certainly takes his time,' he observed.

Soon, Juzer panted up to us in through the front door. 'I went to the mosque to offer morning prayers. I also found out the way to the cemetery where Mildenhall is buried.'

When we reached the cemetery we found out it was the wrong one. We turned back and drove in the opposite direction. We came to a Bhagwan Talkies and stopped to ask for directions. Juzer asked an old man selling peanuts on the pavement. He had cataracts in both eyes. But even through opaque eyeballs, his confusion was clearly visible. He shook his head, 'No-no. You don't mean cemetery.' He pointed to Juzer's cap. 'You mean *dargah*. It is down the other way, son. You will make it just in time for namaz.'

The old cemetery was at the end of a narrow lane. A rusted square board of the Archaeological Survey, tilted towards the closed wooden gates. Juzer knocked on the small door that was fixed into the gate. A young boy opened the door. He was short and wiry with sad indolent eyes from which sleep had been recently rubbed. They lit up at once as they focused on Juzer's face.

'Come in. My name Shankar. I am speaking Hindi and English. I am Mohammedan and Christian. I am taking you to big tomb and temple now.'

It had rained and the path was covered with a greenish slime. Snails wormed their way across tombstones, leaving gleaming white trails behind; and pink fleshy earthworms slimed out of holes in the ground and across the path. Juzer asked Shankar, 'Do you know John Mildenhall's tomb?' 'Come in,' replied Shankar, 'I show you big tomb and temple. This is all right?'

'No, no,' Juzer yelled at him. 'Show me Mildenhall's tomb. Do you know where it is?'

I pointed to a large tomb building in red sandstone built in typical Mogul style. Shankar led us up some steps to it. It was the tomb of one Colonel John William Hessing who had died in 1803. He served in the army of Mahadji Sindhia and fought in many battles, and ultimately retired to Agra as the commander of the fort.

Shankar said, 'This very bestest tomb. This is all right?' He scurried down the steps. 'Now I take you see temple.' We walked past rows of tombstones, most of them broken.

'This is an Armenian temple,' Juzer studied the names of priests on the inside wall; they were buried there. The Armenians were the first merchants to carry back from India spices, muslin and precious stones to Europe and the Middle East. Akbar invited them to settle in Agra.' He added, 'Mirza, who set up a college in Agra, was the most distinguished Armenian in India. He was a strict Christian all his life.' Juzer laughed heartily, 'Jehangir tried to convince Mirza and his brother Iskanderus to become Muslims. But they didn't, so Jehangir had them forcibly circumcized.

'But Akbar was tolerant,' Juzer offered hastily. 'He even married an Armenian, Mariam Zamani Begum. In Fatehpur Sikri, there is a four-room building known as Mariam's House. Akbar built it for her. Akbar also built her a church. It is called Akbari Church. But I don't know yet where it is.'

Shankar said to him, 'This is all right?'

'This is not all right!' snarled Dom, who was standing entrenched in a puddle of water, his shoes coated with mud. 'Do you know where Mildenhall's tomb is or don't you?'

Shankar smiled. 'I know everythin. Yes-yes. Welcum. I show more more tombs. Very good.'

'Sir, you wait here,' Juzer said.

'Here!' Dom looked down at his feet.

'I'll look for Mildenhall's tomb.' Juzer jumped over a bush and ran towards the other end of the cemetery. It took him all of half an hour to locate it. It was a small marble slab set on a grey mortar base broken all along the edges. A red sandstone tablet marked the spot. Carved on it was a cross that was faintly visible since it had eroded. Weeds grew around it. From a clump of wild grass I plucked a purple flower and gave it to Dom.

We walked back to the gate. Shankar was nowhere around. 'One would have thought that idiot would pester us for money,' Dom chuckled.

Just as we reached the gate, we saw Shankar charging towards us. He shouted, 'Welcum sir, thank you, come in next time. I show very old tomb. Milt-ta-alls. I know where it is. I know everythin.'

Swaying like a pendulum, his hands behind his back, he stood looking up at Dom. He held out a hand, and in it were a bunch of purple flowers. He thrust them into Dom's hand. 'That's all,' he smiled, 'sir, welcum, thank you.' Dom warmed to him. 'Thank *you,* Shankar, for these.' He held the flowers to his chest, patted them with the other hand. '*Thank* you *very* much.'

Shankar put out a hand, 'Mention no! Only fifty rupees. It's all right?'

~

Juzer had arranged for us to meet Dr Ram Nath, a local historian and an author of many books about Mogul architecture. He was a small man with long grey hair and a thin pointed moustache. Clumps of hair spurted out of his ears; surprisingly they were black. We sat in his living room enclosed by walls painted a greenish blue. The room had a few chairs, a bed against one wall and a steel almirah.

'Yes, sir,' Ram Nath stretched out his legs in front of him, 'your researcher told me you are here to find out about Thomas Coryate. What do you want to know from me?' His wife bought us tea and snacks.

Dom leaned forward and said, 'I'm curious. Where do you think Coryate would have stayed in Agra?'

'Eh? Oh! Well ...' Ram Nath pulled back his legs. 'I don't know.' He appeared confused. 'Very, very good question. I'm very sorry but ...'

'It's all right. Can you tell me what Agra was like in Coryate's time?'

'Oh yes! That I'll tell you. Some travellers compared Agra to London and Paris. Everywhere gardens-gardens. Babur built Char Baug—the pleasure garden. Everywhere big mansions and little streets. There were many mosques. There is the mosque of Mokhannisan, which is a special one for eunuchs. There were huge mausoleums, tombs. Also orchards, *hamams* or public baths, and sarais. The Fort had large open grounds where elephants were made to fight. There were bazaars, chowks, and many-many shops. You see, all along the streets rich traders built their houses with their shops facing the front. Then there was *nakhas*—a market where horses, camels, oxen, tents, cotton goods were sold.'

'Because it was so hot,' Ram Nath said, 'the elites built their mansions along the banks of the Jamuna. The ceilings of these mansions were beautifully painted and were made of a special plaster of lime, milk, gum and raw sugar. The plaster was smooth as a woman's cheek and it was polished so much that it shone like her eyes. The rooms were fitted with *khas-khas* curtains and *pankhas* that servants sitting outside the room would operate by pulling on a rope with their toes. The lords had three-four wives, and each wife had separate apartments for herself and her slaves, sometimes ten, sometimes twenty or even hundred. Many of these mansions were occupied only occasionally and they were often rented out to travellers and visitors. Often the factors of European companies stayed in them.' He nodded his head, 'I am thinking now, maybe Coryate stayed like that?'

Dom shook his head. His reply was curt. 'He had no money.'

Ram Nath scratched his head. 'Yes, he could have stayed in the old mohallas. You see, the trading community of Agra was wealthy. They were both Hindus and Muslims and they were called *sarrafs* or *shroffs*. They acted as bankers and moneylenders. Some of them lived with other rich Hindus in large houses along the narrow and crooked streets paved with brick. These houses did not have windows facing the street. But within the front wall there were courtyards with ornamental gardens, tanks, fountains and fish ponds lined with different coloured tiles. The bazaars were located within the narrow streets so people didn't have to go far to shop for daily necessities. These narrow streets, of course, puzzled the European travellers. But they were needed because of the seclusion of women and to foster a stronger sense of community feeling. It enabled people from the same professions and castes to live together. This was very good. But how was the western traveller to appreciate all this?'

'So you think Coryate would have stayed in these mohallas?' Dom asked.

Ram Nath rubbed a finger on the ridge of his nose, repeating, 'Where, where, where.' He seemed to remember something. 'You see, at that time there were many Jesuit fathers and other Catholic peoples who were involved with missionary work. They were given special sites to build their residences. They made a residential complex called the *padri tola*. They even constructed a college and a church there. Foreigners could have stayed there. Coryate could also have stayed there.'

His eyes wandered around the floor and rested pensively on the tile lines, moving up and down along them. He said without looking up, 'Actually there should have been no problem of staying. You see, in Agra at that time, there were too many sarais. Jehangir ordered the rich people to build sarais, dig wells and build mosques all along the roads. Akbar built many sarais in which food and lodging was free for the poorer people. It is possible Coryate stayed in one of these free places.'

He clicked a finger in the air. 'Oh yes! Nur Jehan built many sarais. The Nur Mahal ki Sarai was only two miles from Agra and Peter Mundy stayed in it in 1632. Coryate may have stayed in it.' He smiled at Dom and added as if to reassure him, 'It was built of solid stone and could accommodate 3000 people and five hundred horses.' He hesitated, 'But who knows if Coryate would have liked it. You see, in all sarais one had to use one's own bedding and eat one's own food. These sarais were meant for Indian communal way of life. They didn't suit European peoples. They want too much privacy and independence. Some of them even described the sarais as barns where people had to sleep together with animals. But I think the main objection of the Europeans was that they were untidy and there was too much noise.'

Dom grunted. 'This hasn't changed much, has it?'

Ram Nath slapped his thigh several times, laughing, 'Good joke.' His eyes lit up like bulbs, he said, 'One more thing of interest I want to tell you. Sarais created a new class of caretakers. They were called Bhatiyaras.'

'Who? What?'

'The Bhatiyaras were mainly Muslims. It seems that after the Sur dynasty was finished, its household servants had to leave royal service. So they began to take care of travellers. Caste laws and so many taboos made it difficult for Hindu families to prepare food for everyone. Sarai life was very interesting but I think the best part was that it provided nice gossip about everyone who had stayed there.' He laughed, slapping his thigh again. 'I am thinking, that if Coryate had stayed there, there must be stories about him.' He sunk his head into his chin. 'Where, where? But there was not just road travel in those days, you see,' he added, shaking his head. 'A large volume of trade was carried on by river between Agra and the eastern provinces. It was cheaper to send things by river than land. Such large boats sailed on the Jamuna river. They saved time by half. And on both sides of the river there were big landing ghats. Entire armies could land there, even elephants.'

Dom asked, 'Do you think Coryate came by river?'

'Why not? Why not?'

'That still doesn't tell us where he could have stayed,' Dom said.

'Please take,' Ram Nath said pointing to the samosas. 'It must have become cold.'

Dom shook his head. 'I wonder what Coryate would have eaten. And where? He did not have much money.'

'No problem,' Ram Nath clicked his fingers. 'There were many *langarkhanas* in the city. They were free kitchens meant for the poor. In Akbar's time there were three. One for Hindus, one for Muslims, and a third for Jogis.' He clasped his fingers, glanced out of the window. It was dark. The streetlights had come on. A haze of insects swarmed around the light outside the gate.

Ram Nath scratched his head. An expression of helplessness spread over his face. 'I am sorry I couldn't tell you about Coryate. He went to meet Jehangir at the court, this much I know.' Ram Nath covered his mouth with a hand and giggled. He sounded like a squeaky door hinge. 'There were lots of amusements in the Mogul court. One, *gap-bazi*.' He giggled. 'Jehangir indulged in this a lot. He had hired a professional storyteller, Mulla Asad, who entertained the king with his gossip. Once the king was so pleased with his story that he awarded him rupees equal to his weight—almost four thousand four hundred rupees. I think Coryate was also a court jester. Asad was not like an English clown or court jester, but a personal friend who amused the king.'

'Could I have some salt?' Juzer said. 'I need some salt to break my fast. Also a glass of water.' When they were offered to him, he put a pinch of salt on his tongue and washed it down with water.

'Take,' Ram Nath held out the plate of samosas. 'You must be so hungry.' He called out to his wife. 'I'll ask her to make some hot ones.'

'If you don't mind, sir,' Juzer said, pushing the plate away, 'they are too much oily. I will eat what I have brought with me. The hotel packed it specially for me.'

Ram Nath chuckled, covering his mouth with his hand. 'You are talking like upper caste Hindu. They never touch anything in a stranger's house.'

I cannot clearly explain this, but I helped myself to a cold samosa. It was perhaps because I didn't want to hurt Ram Nath's feelings. Oil soaked my fingers. Following my example, Dom picked up a samosa and bit into it. 'Very good,' he muttered, 'Please thank your wife for us.'

Juzer took out an aluminium foil parcel from his bag. He shifted his chair so he didn't face us. He pulled the small side table towards him. He opened the foil, then spread it on the table. He laid out four sets of sandwiches packed in paper that was completely drenched in grease.

A dog started to bark. A car honked. A gate whined open. A child cried. The thin, nasal call of the muezzin floated through the air.

Juzer eagerly began to devour his cold and oleaginous repast.

~

The plan for the next day was to look at old localities from Coryate's time. Ram Nath had given us a list of some of them. But once more, Juzer was missing. We waited for him in the hotel lobby. He rushed in half an hour later with his pair of binoculars suspended around his neck. 'I went to the internet shop,' he said smiling happily, 'I got so many mails from my electronic girlfriends. I also went to St Peter's Cathedral. Akbar's church is in there. An old man in a green shirt who was standing near the gate told me about it. I was so lucky to find this bugger. He knows a lot about old localities. I told him I would return at once.' He consulted his watch. 'Come, come, let's go quickly,' he said decisively, 'We don't want to lose him.'

Outside St Peter's Cathedral, Juzer asked a cycle rickshaw driver parked near the gate if he had seen the old man in a green shirt. 'That madman,' he laughed. 'He often stands here in the morning looking up at the cathedral and shouting.'

Juzer groped for words, he shook his head vigorously instead. The rickshaw driver laughed again, 'Sahib, every other person in Agra pretends to be a guide. A man has to earn a living and look after his family, no? So he will tell you a lot of stories. So you pay for the entertainment. I can show you many places and I can tell you whatever you want to know about them.' He fastened pleading eyes on Juzer. 'I have four children and an old mother to feed. Also, of course, my wife. She is sickly.'

'Such sadly unsuccessful cheats,' said Dom walking through the gates. Akbar's Church was a bluish white and yellow building with a large dome. Surprisingly, it was similar to the churches in Goa and not crammed with Mogul features, as I had expected. The window and door details in red sandstone, however, were typically Mogul in style. As we waited for Juzer to fetch someone to open the church, an old woman appeared. She knelt on the ground in front of the closed door. She appeared to be praying to a column in front of her.

An incredibly old man took us into the church. His skin had crinkled with age and resembled crushed brown paper. Inside, the floor displayed the tombstones of a number of European priests who had died a long time ago. Apart from these, it was covered with a red carpet. 'Akbar built this church for his wife Mariam,' the old man said as he leaned against the altar. He had a beet red mole positioned delicately at the tip of his nose. I shot a photograph of him, and in my mind I impulsively captioned it: *Beetmole Man.*

He walked us to the back of the altar, to a sealed door. 'Mariam came from the Fort through a tunnel to this door. She prayed in this church. Now this tunnel has been closed for seventeen years. Animals and children got trapped inside. It was very dark. There were too many bats. So the church sealed it.'

His back was bent as though under some unbearable burden as he led us to the small graveyard at the back of the church. Many of the graves were of women and small children. There were several tombs of an entire family of Lyons. One of them in black granite was that of Stephen Anthony Lyons.

This tombstone particularly distressed me. The person underneath had died at the age of one year, eight months and fourteen days. Dom was equally but impassively upset. 'It's sad what some English women had to go through in this country for the sake of trade,' he said. 'For various reasons their children could not survive the weather, the food or the way they had to live here. So many died young.'

We walked away hurriedly as if we wanted to get away from the tomb. 'The English women not only had a tough time here,' Dom sighed, 'they also gave their men a difficult time.' He stumbled over a broken edge of a tomb of a five-month baby; he quickly steadied himself. 'When the British first came,' he said, 'they had relations with Indian women. Many wanted to legitimize their relationship but they couldn't since no priest from any religion would marry them. So when the Englishmen brought their women with them, there was immediate conflict. Bloody women,' he added, with one of his more annoying smiles, 'they seldom cause anything but trouble.'

We were still stumbling about amidst tombstones and mud, and the smell of the mud was like the smell of the pitiful corpses it contained. One of Dom's more horrible habits is that he thinks and talks to himself under any circumstances one is in. He continued to lecture me on race relations in Victorian India as we walked between the tombs.

'European men may have thought that Africans looked different from them, but they didn't think Indians were all that different; their features were more or less alike; only the Indians had got a bit tanned, no wonder with all that sun. It was the Englishwomen who forced their men to feel the difference between the natives and themselves. They started colour prejudice.' Dom sighed.

'If you think of white as a colour, it's OK for houses and maybe Utrillo, but not all that hot as a colour for people. Many Indians had skins much closer to white than any European. Forster called the European skin pinko-grey. But I don't think anyone would have thought of it when Coryate was here.'

'Are there services in this church now?' I asked the beetmole man.

'Yes. Every day. No fail.'

'We saw an old woman praying outside the door. Do you pray here?'

'No.' He looked puzzled. 'I too am a convert. I am Hindu first. Now I am Mohammedan. My wife Christian. She used to work here. Now dead. Gone to her heaven.'

~

Juzer walked with the beetmole man to the small office next to the cathedral. 'I was right, madam,' he said when he returned. His nostrils flared righteously. 'I asked the bishop's secretary about the man in the green shirt. Yes, he used to be a guide. She also told me about another guide who can take us to areas that Coryate may have seen. He is a Muslim bugger. His name is Iqbal. We have to pick him up from the Fort.'

'I thought I made myself clear, Juzer, we don't want any guides,' Dom retorted, then added gently, 'in the absence of much material about Coryate, what I want, Juzer, is to be in the same place as Coryate may have been. I want to feel him with me. I want to shut my eyes and imagine Coryate there. I don't want some idiot guide faking history for a few rupees.'

Juzer was adamant. 'He's good, sir. Let's try.'

No sooner had we stopped opposite the Fort than half a dozen guides beat at the doors of the car. Dom glowered at them in an attempt to shoo them away. Vendors held up mini Taj Mahals made of soft stone, key chains and other brass artefacts. Dom picked up the book he had got with him and pretended to read it. Juzer rolled down his glass and asked each one of the men about Iqbal the guide, but none of them seemed to have heard of him. 'Even if they do, they would hardly tell us,' I said, as the men got rowdy.

'There is an office inside the Fort,' Juzer got out of the car, 'I'll go ask there.' Juzer pushed through the people who pressed against him. A bus shrieked to a halt; a large crowd tumbled out of its door. Four donkeys ambled past, one behind the other, carrying sacks of bricks. A car braked as a young boy dashed across. Someone screamed. A crowd gathered out of nowhere. The dirt crust broke under their feet and every moving thing lifted the dust. The sharp sun illuminated it, before it turned into a cloud. The dust clouds pushed towards the Fort paled by the fierce sun. The wind grew strong and hard and worked at the dust, lashing it up like grey plumes of smoke. I could feel the grit between my teeth.

Dom coughed; he screwed his eyes. 'It can't have changed in four centuries, all this fucking chaos. And those poor donkeys hauling bricks. And the dust.'

The sun was red as new blood. Juzer walked towards the Fort. Some of the guides followed him. One of them grabbed his sleeve. Another tapped his shoulder. Suddenly, Juzer turned. Even from where I sat I could see his eyes full of wrath. He struck a man with his arm, then pushed him aside with a loud yell.

The dust rose higher; the wind whisked it about leaving craters through which I could see the bronzed walls of the Fort. Dom said, tormented by the sun and noise, 'Where the hell has Juzer gone in this fucking place?'

Juzer darted across the road waving a piece of paper above his cap. 'I've got Iqbal guide's address,' he said.

Joginder started the car. 'Where?' He looked at Juzer. 'Vazirpura.'

'Vazirpura?' He switched the engine off. 'It's a terrible place, sir. The lanes there are narrow and filthy. I can't take the car through them, meddem.' He turned to look at me.

'Can't or won't?' Juzer asked and burst into a shrill laugh, which Joginder did not seem to enjoy as we drove on. He slapped his forehead in despair several times as he drove through lanes full of people, bicycles, cars, carts, cows and pigs setting forth in every direction. His hand was fixed to the horn. He muttered constantly; now and then he rolled down his window to yell at whatever or whoever blocked his way. Juzer started to tell me a long story about Akbar's eight wives.

Joginder switched off the engine. 'Meddem, I'm not going any further.' He said to Dom, 'Please you walk, sir. If anything happens to the vehicle I will have to answer my boss. This is my daily living.'

We turned into a narrow alley paved with bricks. Garbage rotted in the gutters along either side of the lane; doughballs of shit dotted the pathway. Even as we walked on, children squatted on the lane, in twos and threes, talking, singing, *itna itna pani, gol gol rani,* and defecating. Pigs snorted past, dipping their noses into the gutters overflowing with green slush.

Unperturbed by all this, Juzer continued to tell me about Sheikh Salim Chishti, the Sufi who was Akbar's adviser. 'Despite the eight wives, Akbar went to him because he could not produce a male heir,' Juzer said. 'According to William Finch, Akbar, like our own Coryate, made a foot pilgrimage all the way to Ajmer. He had pillars built along the route, called *kos-minar,* at each *kos,* and a mahal to accommodate sixteen beautiful women at every eight kos.' He stressed the alphabets. 'It seems after Akbar returned from his foot pilgrimage, he got three sons.'

Juzer was surprised when Dom, unamused by his tale, asked, 'How much is a kos?'

'About two miles.'

'And Akbar walked all the way to Ajmer?'

An entire family of pigs obstructed our way, their snouts covered with black mud. Juzer made a strange snarling noise at them. He laughed as they moved away to one side. 'Even pigs are scared of me!' The youngest one fell into the gutter.

Dom scowled. 'Have there always been so many pigs in Agra?'

Juzer said, 'You see, Akbar was a vegetarian and ...'

'I was not asking about Akbar,' Dom retorted. 'I was asking about these pigs!'

At the corner where the lane turned, inside a small shop, mutton shanks hung from hooks. Flies covered their flesh as though they were original skin. In a quadrangle, biryani cooked in large vessels. Loudspeakers tied to trees spewed loud film music into the air. Young girls and boys wriggled their hips to the scratchy tune: *ye kali kali aankhen, ye gore gore gaal.* Some men were putting up a bamboo fence and a brightly coloured awning.

'There's going to be a wedding tonight,' Juzer said as he checked the number on a door, then knocked on it. A hefty man appeared dressed in a brown and green striped shirt and a checked lungi; his hair was smeared with a paste of henna.

'Yes, I am Iqbal Sheik,' he said when Juzer asked for him. Behind him, in the inner courtyard, two young girls washed utensils. A goat tied to the leg of a coir bed pulled at the rope, tossing its head about and frightened the parrot in a cage. As Dom walked past the cage he muttered something privately to the parrot. Although it shook its head several times, the parrot didn't seem to understand what he said.

Iqbal led us into a room that was like an excellent art film set. It depicted the possessions, contentment and resignation of a poor middle class man. A high bed with tall drawers occupied most of the room. A steel cupboard was pushed into the wall. Next to it was an old Singer sewing machine similar to one my grandmother had. Facing the bed were two chairs and a small fridge. A television set was perched on top of the fridge. A green frosted glass lemonade set and some cups and saucers with pink roses on them were neatly arranged in a shelf on the wall. And Iqbal, the family man, sat with pride and diffidence on his bed. A blob of henna dropped on his shoulder.

'For how long have you been in this line?' Juzer asked him.

'I am in this service for fourteen years. Employed by the Archaeological Survey. My father was also in same service. And my elder brother also. It is family tradition.'

'Ask him how old this area is?' Dom said to Juzer.

Iqbal replied, 'Vazirpura is almost four hundred years old. During Jehangir's time *vazirs* used to stay here in large havelis. They were the king's ministers.'

'It's like this,' Juzer tried to explain, 'my boss wants to see something that is very very old. Can you show us an old haveli?'

'All the havelis have been divided into small quarters. Many have been broken down and new buildings have come up. This one used to be a part of a haveli. Look at it now. In shambles.' He patted his hair, then wiped his fingers on his lungi. He said seriously, 'If you want to see something old then why don't you see the Taj Mahal?'

Juzer slapped his thigh, 'That's a good joke. Ha-ha-ha, but it wasn't there four hundred years ago! It's like this, chacha. An Englishman, walked to Agra to meet king Jehangir four hundred years ago. Now we want to know where he would have stayed in Agra. We have a list of old localities here. He could have stayed in one of them.'

'From England you say he was. Then a Christian he must be.' Iqbal began to shuffle his feet and shake his head in rhythm. 'Oh! Why didn't you come a month ago? Then you could have met Sylvador. Best guide he was. He has his house in padri tola. Christians lived there from long time ago. He could tell you everything. Maybe your Englishman stayed in padri tola. Sylvador must have surely known about him. Sylvador wrote detailed notes of everything.' He scratched his thigh. 'If you had only come a month ago, you could have talked to him.'

'Where has he gone?' I asked.

'Gone up there.' He pointed to the ceiling. 'But his daughter is here. She may have the notes. Ask her. She teaches in a local school.' He scratched the other thigh. His skin seemed to be sensitive, and concentration appeared to bring on a prickly itch. 'You should go to the old villages behind the Taj Mahal. They existed even before the Taj Mahal was built. Go to village Katchpura. Humayun's Mosque is there. And in the next village you can see Babri Masjid. This is older than the Babri Masjid in Ayodhya.' He scratched his chin, 'I can't tell you more than this.'

'Chacha, we were told that you knew a lot about the old areas,' Juzer said accusingly.

Iqbal laughed, 'Who told you that? I am sorry your visit

here has been a waste of time. But tell me who sent you to me?' He scratched his head. His fingers were covered with henna.

'The bishop's secretary,' Juzer said, 'she told me you were the best guide in Agra.'

Iqbal looked puzzled. 'Guide? I am not a guide, sahib. I am only a watchman at the Fort. Like my father and my brother. It is family tradition.'

11

Waiting for Sir Thomas

His encounter with the Sikh, and the conversation about other parts of this enormous land, eventually made Coryate move on towards Ajmer. He was very comfortable as he was, and the priests liked him; he was in danger of stasis. When he told them that he must leave, they seemed sad. But this only hardened his resolve that while he walked, he should drop no roots. Where and when they threatened to develop, he must toughen himself and pull them up.

A visitor from Portugal had brought the priests some *bacalhao,* salt cod, which they had hoarded with miserly possessiveness for the past two years. But on Coryate's last night at the church they ate it all, and next day stood at the door and waved till his figure had become dim in the distance.

On the road to Ajmer, he met two Englishmen. They were charred and welted by the sun and their hair was long and dirty, but Coryate recognized them as countrymen even before he heard them speak. He was not surprised to find them slouching down a dusty Indian road; he could not now be surprised by anything in this country. Their names were Young and Whitington, and Coryate, studying Whitington's long, skewed face and small gleaming eyes, felt he would come to no good end. But the three Englishmen slept that night in the same sarai. It was hot and airless; mosquitoes troubled them. Whitington drank a lot of some local liquor.

They seemed, like other Englishmen in India, to be remotely related to the Company, but also engaged in some mysterious and secret form of private enterprise. Coryate asked them what places they had seen in India, but they were not clear about this. 'I have seen Venice,' Coryate told them, eager to start an intellectual discussion, 'but in India the only fair architecture I have come on is a pillar in Delhi, that I believe to have been set in place there by Alexander the Macedonian.' They seemed not to have heard of Alexander and not to want to hear of him. The conversation faltered and failed and at last died into the nasal tympanics of insects and the snores of sleepers.

Coryate, encompassed by the colossal darkness of the country, wondered what made him different from all others he came across, English or Indian. Master John Donne had written that no man was an island, but he, Tom Coryate, seemed to be one, set afloat by God's hand in an ocean created for him to float in alone, with no single other living thing nearby that was recognizably related to him. He lay in the dark and thought, 'I am Tom Coryate, but what is Tom Coryate, that I should live in him and not know who he is?'

~

Coryate followed the road for more than a week, till it slewed and started to climb a rugged mountainside. At the top were fortress walls of cyclopean dimensions and sentry towers, each with its garrison of guards. Inside Taragarh fort, a city teemed and pullulated, but seemed quiet after the road. In a ragged collection of tents near the Emperor's palace, Coryate saw white faces and men in English breeches and coats. Though he was dishevelled, dirty and in native dress, they perceived him to be English and he was led to a man whose clothes hung loosely on him but whose complexion was apoplectic. 'I am William Edwards,' said the man. 'I am the factor here. Whatever you have come here to do, you are a countryman, so we will lodge you and feed you, till our leader Sir Thomas Roe comes to take command of us.'

There were a dozen of them, pleased to see another Englishman, though they could not help taking note of his vagrant state and treated him with amused curiosity. But they found Coryate a corner in one of the tents and offered him food. It was the first time in months that he had eaten roast fowl and vegetables cooked in the English fashion. He was grateful, and explained that he had come to write a book. They could not understand this, but were kind to him.

These servants of the Company were nearly all vulgar fellows, he felt. They were uneducated, without any thoughts except how best they could keep their bodily wants satisfied for the present, and how, at last and with luck, they might make their fortunes in India. They had very little to do except await Roe's arrival, and were always idle and bored.

Before the rains, the weather was stiflingly hot, but they dressed, under orders, in woollen English clothes. As a result, they suffered, sweated and most developed skin diseases. They had one means of relief. Most of them had learnt broken Hindustani, enough to carouse with the whores of the town, and by nightfall each day they were nearly all drunk. Several men also picked up the pox.

Coryate's only friend in the camp was the chaplain, Peter Rogers, a small, rotund man in a constant and understandable state of agitation. 'As Englishmen,' he complained to Coryate, 'we should be examples to the heathens around us, but they hold us in contempt and derision. I pray daily that Sir Thomas will come and set these matters in order, but weeks pass and he does not come. And, alas, I have some small skills as an apothecary, so I am called to treat the disgusting disorders of the men.'

Skin diseases, stomach ailments and venereal infections were not all that Rogers had to deal with. The Englishmen were often embroiled in disputes with one another, mostly over small wagers lost and won. One day a man of Essex, Thomas Mitford, stabbed Edwards in the arm. The camp was in uproar. Edwards ordered Mitford's arrest but nobody would obey his orders. 'More bloodshed will surely follow,' said a woebegone Rogers to Coryate, 'if Sir Thomas come not in haste.'

~

Every day Coryate contemplated the ramparts of Jehangir's palace. The Emperor and he were physically close, they even breathed the same air, but those ramparts were an irrevocable barrier between them. Sometimes Jehangir came out into the city, perched on an elephant and heavily guarded. Coryate could not form any idea of what the monarch looked like; distance reduced him to the size of a gilded doll. Coryate wanted to speak to him about many matters; he wanted Jehangir to help him walk on to China.

'Be sure he will refuse you audience,' Rogers warned. 'Why, he will not speak to any man of the Company of lesser stature than Roe, and you are not even of the Company. When Sir Thomas comes, perhaps he will help you get audience with the Emperor; but until then, friend, you can only have patience. All of us need it in this place.'

But as yet there was no definite time known for Roe's arrival. Instead of staying in the camp, Coryate started to tramp around the city. He especially liked to frequent the bazaar, though its narrow lanes were crowded and filthy. It provided him with a sense of Indian life that he had not had before. The different kinds of shops were crammed into an individual area, the shops that sold meat set a little apart from the rest. Coryate had been told that the Hindus were vegetarians. But he saw as many Hindus in the bazaar as he did Muslims; possibly more. He had learnt to tell them apart.

The Muslims were taller, with paler skins and sharper features. Their clothes were different; their language also. The Hindus talked more, and louder. Coryate had realized by now that his original concept of the country had been completely false. The Hindus, with their gods, had been here for thousands of years. It was the Muslims who were the newcomers, interlopers and invaders. They had conquered the Hindus and now ruled them, though much outnumbered.

He was surprised that in this situation the two peoples appeared to be on equal terms. The Muslims did not visibly dominate the Hindus. The Hindus did not treat them as overlords. He learnt more about the country every day, for he could now speak Hindustani better than before, and he found almost everyone willing to talk to him, though they could not place him. Most people in Ajmer had seen the English, with their red faces and cumbersome clothes, but Coryate was clad like a poor Hindu and behaved like one. He became known in the bazaar as the white fakir, and was often offered small gifts of cooked food and sweetmeats.

He also visited the enormous dargah, the main place of worship for the Muslims. Here, in a high courtyard, two great brass utensils simmered, full of food for the poor. Coryate scrambled for his bowls of curry and rice pudding with the rest, even though he observed that some of them were lepers. It was good food, and also free. So was the food at the camp, but he had developed a slight aversion to dining with his compatriots, and stayed away from them except when he needed to sleep. Some of the priests and worshippers at the dargah came to know his face well. They greeted him in the elaborate Muslim manner.

One day, an old white-bearded moulvi came up to him in the courtyard. 'I have watched you day after day, feringhee,' he said. 'I have wondered why you visit this place so often, and it has come to my mind that perhaps you desire to be instructed in Islam, the true faith, and become one of us. My name is Ashraf. Come with me to my house so that we may talk. If you become a Muslim, it will be to you like sweet water to one lost in the desert. Come with me now.'

Coryate was astonished. He had always hated those who followed Islam. His outburst at Multan had not been entirely due to humiliation and rage; part of it had been heartfelt. He had certainly never contemplated conversion to Islam. But in the last few days he had brushed shoulders with many Indians—some of them Muslims—and his hatred had subsided. Ashraf also had a distinguished air about him and a kind face. Coryate badly needed to talk to an intelligent Muslim. Ashraf had come to him by accident, but it seemed a benevolent accident, and he followed the old priest home up a rough, stony hillside beyond the bazaar.

The white-washed brick house where Ashraf lived had only one floor, but seemed to contain several rooms. A veiled woman in a black burqa served them tea and sticky sweetmeats. She was one of Ashraf's three wives but it was impossible to see how old she was through all her clothes.

Ashraf was solicitous; he insisted that his guest ate and drank before they started to talk. Coryate was surprised to find the old Muslim priest very curious about English life.

He attempted to explain it, but the priest did not understand, or had no desire to. 'So your people are all idolators and unbelievers,' Ashraf said finally. He clicked his tongue in disapprobation. 'They are not unlike the Hindus here.' Coryate felt compelled to defend his nation. 'There is no comparison, sahib,' he protested. 'My people do not worship animals, but the Lord Issa, who is one of the prophets in Islam.' Ashraf only smiled and shook his head.

'For thousands of years,' he said in the manner of a lecturer, 'the Hindus ruled their own land. But they were divided as a people. Under Islam all men are as brothers. The Hindus have their varnas, their castes, under which some men are lower than beasts. Have you not seen in the bazaar how some men ring bells and cry out aloud as they walk? They are warning other Hindus that they are untouchable. Anyone who touches them will be defiled.

'The Hindus are divided. Even the rulers of different kingdoms would not aid each other when we, the Muslims, came. And now they outnumber us fifty to one, yet are still too divided to drive us out. Many of their lower castes have converted, but still they outnumber us. And still they cannot drive us out, because we shall not go from this place, and we are united under Allah.'

Then he began to discuss Coryate's imminent conversion. Coryate tried at first to be polite in his refusals, but when told he would have to be circumcized to be accepted into Islam, became vehement in his assertions that he wanted to remain Christian. If Ashraf was irritated by this waste of his time, he was too courteous to show it. But he inquired, 'Tell me, angrez, why have so many of your people started to come to this place? You say you have come to write a book, and I believe you. The reason I thought you wished to convert was that I perceive you to be honest. But the others are not. They say they have come for trade. But I think they have come to try and take this country from us.'

As Coryate trudged back toward the English camp, he laughed inwardly at the absurdity of Ashraf's notion.

The rains were late that year, everyone said. Though low, sullen clouds obscured the colour of the sky, the heat swelled in the blood of the Englishmen till it was difficult for them to move freely by day or sleep at night. Then one day, the clouds burst and a rage of rain burst over the city. Coryate had never seen or imagined such rain. Every so often the sky whitened with explosions of electricity, and thunderclaps like cannon fire made the air vibrate. Dense slanted masses of water slashed down in such quantities that within an hour the earth underfoot had become slush.

After that first storm, though the clouds stayed perpetually overhead, only a few showers fell, comparatively mild. But a miasmic heat enfolded the city, and a plague of geckoes and mosquitoes descended upon the English tents. Glutinous mud surrounded them and through it scuttered black rats of unbelievable size. Coryate's companions swore, drank and quarrelled, except for Peter Rogers who prayed. Sometimes after too much native liquor had been swilled, the knives came out, but nobody was much damaged. 'Oh, Thomas,' the round priest wailed, 'why hath God brought Englishmen here, to suffer such privations in such a place?' Coryate had already started to ask himself this question.

Around the encampment was a convolution of hamlets where poor people lived. Normally a great deal of noise came from them and continued deep into the dark: the thuds and squeals of musical instruments whose names were unknown to men from the English shires, accompanied by shrill, dirge-like ululations, which Coryate had been told were expressive of happiness. Since the rains had come, the whole city had been silent, except for the wet sounds of the weather, the insistent chorus of insects, the rats' squeals.

Once at midnight Coryate lay awake as usual. He scratched his louse-ridden scalp and his now gaunt body, where the mosquitoes had fed on him. His belly was a knot of pain, for over the last weeks he had developed a bloody flux. Suddenly he heard loud screams in Hindustani, drums began to beat, and above all this came a squalling like that of an angry cat, except that this sound was harsher than that of a normal cat, more like iron under a saw. The night around had come alive with many flames. He lurched from his tent to find Rogers outside. In the adjoining hamlet he saw villagers who shouted loudly, beat drums, flourished burning brands.

'Oh God, spare us all!' Rogers cried. 'Thomas, Thomas, are the heathen coming to kill us? I knew one day they would.' The others had come out of their tents, half-naked, bewildered by the commotion. Some carried their cutlasses. A turbaned man ran towards them from the village, his face contorted, crying out plaintively as he came.

Edwards' bull-bellow rose above the din. 'Hew the black arsewipe down, before they are all at our throats!' And the hairy dwarf Coryate, who lived on the charity of the Company, guts in knots, flesh aflame from the depredations of innumerable insects, raised his arms and cried, 'No!' He did not know why, but he felt noble. 'He asks for our aid! A leopard or tiger, I know not which, is abroad in the village.'

The Englishmen, carrying their cutlasses, ran down to the torch-lit hamlet. The leopard had been driven, through fear of the flames, into a tiny granary, shaped like a beehive. It was a small animal, not fully grown, and now covered in its own blood. It was too weakened to roar, but still hissed and spat at the enemies who pelted it with stones. They screamed in triumph, because it carried too many wounds to fight any more. Its green eyes gleamed from the granary, and Coryate thought them beautiful.

He said in Hindustani to the villager beside him, 'Why do you not spare the beast? It has done no harm. Let it go.'

The man grinned at him as though he were mad, then threw another stone. The leopard fell over on its side. It was no longer making any sound. But the villagers waited for some time. At length, the braver ones entered the granary with clubs and, though they showed circumspection, beat it till they were certain it was dead. Some of them went for skinning knives. Others beat drums, and the singing started.

The Englishmen were offered liquor and food, accepted by all except Coryate. The leopard's flayed corpse had been dragged out of the granary and lay in the mud outside. It was unrecognizable as a thing that had until recently been alive. Coryate could not bear to look at it. Out of the corner of his eye he saw several large rats, very cautiously, come out of the shadows. He stood under a sky that showed no stars, and cursed them, the villagers and the world he breathed.

~

By September the rains had dwindled to fitful spatters, but the heat, which had never left, intensified, and so did the number of insects. The Englishmen scratched and fretted but a message came from the western coast to raise their spirits. Roe had landed in Surat at last and was coming with an entourage to Ajmer. Edwards was simultaneously greatly relieved and further burdened, for he would now have to give his master some account of his stewardship. Since the leopard episode, the men had often complained of having to live in unprotected tents. Edwards had not listened then, but he now set them to building small huts with locally made bricks, helped by the villagers. When Roe arrived he would find the English lodged in the semblance of a settlement.

Coryate assisted the others, but his mind was not on manual labour. He was filled with inward excitement. He had awaited Roe's arrival more eagerly than anyone else. Through Roe, he would meet Jehangir, and he hoped for much advancement from the Emperor. It was, therefore, vital to Coryate that he should impress Roe, who had already probably heard of him, through Ned Phelips and perhaps through perusal of *Crudities,* for people equal in eminence to Roe, like the Shirleys, had read his books. The journey from Surat would take many days and Coryate spent much time in the composition of an oration with which he would welcome the new leader of the Company to Ajmer.

Messages came from Roe every few days to indicate his progress. The weather was now benevolent, crisp and dry and cool after twilight; greenery surrounded the camp. One day, immediately after Coryate had written out a fair copy of his oration, another messenger arrived. He brought news that Roe lay within two days march of Ajmer and would come there after that time. Frenzied efforts were made to tidy up the camp. But the huts and storehouses were not yet quite finished, and the ground was strewn with debris. Edwards ordered every man to help scrub and sweep, and sent out scouts to report Roe's approach. Word came from the palace to say that certain Mogul noblemen would visit the camp to welcome the English envoy once he had come.

Three days after the last message, the scouts came back to report that Roe would enter Ajmer the next morning. The men dressed in their least shabby clothes and gathered at the city gates. Coryate stood with them, his scrolled ovation clutched to his breast. Edwards had said he could read it aloud when Roe came; he had no better way to show his master respect—no guard of honour, no musicians. The oration was all he had, and it would have to do.

As the morning sun acquired power, the watchers at the gates saw a cloud of dust on the Agra road. As it approached the foot of Taragarh, it became a group of men: Mogul footsoldiers and a couple of mounted officers, also a few Englishmen—in coats and breeches—on horseback. The faces of the Englishmen were red and shone with sweat, though their features could not be deciphered. Edwards led his followers down to the plain to offer them welcome.

When the cavalcade reached the fortress gates, where the small party of Englishmen waited, the leader pulled up his horse. There was no doubt that this was Roe; he had the mien of a master. He towered above them on horseback, but Coryate reckoned him to be of no more than medium stature. He had thinning brown hair and a brindled beard. His features were not unhandsome, but hard, and his pale blue eyes surveyed the poorly clad welcoming committee with what appeared to be disdain. Edwards stepped forward, hat in hand, and bowed deeply as he introduced himself, and then Coryate.

Coryate had no hat, but he also bowed. 'Master Coryate has prepared a fair ovation with which to welcome you, your lordship,' Edwards said, 'and he desires to recite it aloud to you.' Coryate, miserably aware of Roe's gelid eyes upon him, started to recite his oration from memory, as he had learned at Henry's court. It was, he thought, one of his best efforts: the style was his most orotund and flamboyant, and peppered with quotations from Greek and Latin writers. The Englishmen with Roe sniggered among themselves; their leader remained impassive upon his horse.

Crowds had emerged from the town and watched the scene. Coryate suddenly realized how absurd a spectacle this must present. Carrion hawks and crows flew above the heads of the Englishmen. They were gathered under a hill, at the gates of a great fortress, the tainted Indian plain spread out below them, under the cyclopean eye of the sun. His must be the most absurd figure of all, a dwarf in native dress, shouting unintelligibly up at a man on horseback who wore finery that came from another country.

He had recited his speech for perhaps a quarter hour when Roe suddenly held up his hand. 'Enough,' he said curtly. 'It is foolery to sit here in the sun and listen to all this spate of words. Let us go forward to the camp.' Coryate felt not only ridiculous but also ashamed. But before Roe urged his horse onward through the gateway, he looked down once more at Coryate with a not unfriendly eye. 'Master ... Coryate, Thomas Coryate, is it?' he said. 'If I mistake not, I have heard you spoken of in England. We shall have speech later, Master Coryate. Do not take it amiss if I say this is neither the place nor time for your orations.'

~

Coryate had never served as a soldier, nor was he familiar with any form of military activity. But as he observed Roe over the next few days, he became convinced that this was a man born to command troops. The more ignorant and brutal the troops were, the better. The men in the camp were of this kind, and Roe terrified them without effort. He usually spoke in a low, muted voice, with an educated accent. But when he was angry, he rasped his words in the ill-bred accents of the rabble he commanded. He showed his contempt for the men by a descent to their level.

In the first few days, he was often angry, mainly with Edwards, because of the unkempt and disorderly state into which he had allowed the camp and the men to fall. On the evening of his arrival, some of the Emperor's courtiers came to welcome him; they talked for hours, and the next day a force of local labourers and masons arrived. Edwards' half-built huts were destroyed and new, more solid houses were built. This was achieved quickly and with minimal fuss. Within a few days, Roe had had audience of Jehangir and it seemed that they established a rapport almost at once.

In the camp itself, he went through Edwards' account books with savage thoroughness. After this, it was rumoured in the camp that Edwards would soon be sent back to England, the worst fate that could befall a man who desired to make a speedy fortune. Certainly, Roe treated him like a pariah and scarcely spoke to him. He hardly spoke to Coryate either, but Coryate could see why. Roe was, for the moment, obsessed by his work. His new responsibilities had put him under intense pressure. But Joseph Salbank, one of Roe's entourage, assured Coryate that his time would come.

Salbank was a man to be trusted. He was less uncouth than the others who had come with Roe, and knowledgeable. He had been a London tradesman, but had thrown up his trade to venture all in India. They enjoyed the conversations they had daily, and these were different from any other conversations Coryate had had in the two years since he had left England. Moreover, Salbank developed the kind of affection for Coryate that he might have had for an eccentric brother. They were of the same age, nearly forty.

Coryate told his new friend of his long walk to India and also of his ambition to continue it into Tartary and China. Salbank, a religious man, not only worried about what might happen to Coryate in his farings, but also prayed for him.

~

The Ajmer masons, working at inconceivable speed, did well by Roe. Only a few days after they started work, a neat English settlement had appeared where there had been ragged tents and partially completed hovels. Coryate had discovered that dust and mould, in their separate seasons, quickly infiltrated every dwelling place in India, and if left to accumulate, would do so with malign permanence. His opinion of Roe increased when he ordered daily cleaning details in the camp, with untouchables to do the tasks others declined, like the collection and disposal of night soil.

Coryate observed these men and women with interest. They kept their eyes averted from their employers, in subservience or even perhaps shame. They were not ill favoured. Though they dressed more shabbily then other Hindus, some had delicate features and intelligent eyes, and a few younger women were beautiful by any standards. They had full breasts, clearly revealed because they wore no blouses. Many Hindus wanted and used their bodies.

What the priest Ashraf had told him was true. The higher caste Hindus saw the untouchables as lower than slaves. Outside the camp, when they walked abroad in the city, they rang small bells to warn those of higher caste of their arrival.

In any case, they emanated the noxious stench of their trade; they had been forced into it by their birth.

He pitied them in an abstract way, but they puzzled him. Other Hindus despised them, treated them less kindly than animals; how had they come to be in this situation? Were they Hindus at all, or the remnant of another race the Hindus had once enslaved and degraded? Indian history seemed more complicated and mysterious than any European could imagine, and Coryate could find no answers because no caste Hindu was anxious to provide them.

Now that the houses were built, he had a more private and convenient lodging than before and shared it with his friend, Salbank. Salbank was shrewd and slow, the kind of man Roe instinctively trusted, and he was often with his employer. That left Coryate with plenty of time to himself, and he was glad of it, since he could collate his voluminous notes and add to them. One afternoon, he was thinking that he must question one of the untouchables to find the answers he needed, when a young sweeper woman passed the house. Coryate called her in.

She came with a look of terror in her large eyes: a fine looking wench, no more than twenty years old at most. Coryate tried to reassure her with a smile, and then asked her what she knew of the traditions of her people. From where did they come? Were they in fact Hindus? It transpired, to his annoyance, that she spoke some kind of dialect, so neither of them could understand what the other said. But the girl with a sudden movement unwreathed the tattered saree, her only garment, from her body, and stood before him naked. What she expected him to do to her was clear, and for one moment Coryate was sorely tempted.

For she had golden, taut skin, a delicate beauty of feature, and the voluptuous fullness of breast and hip that he had seen in Hindu temple statues. Between her thighs was a plump mound thatched with thick silky black hair. She attempted to cover it with her hands. The gesture aroused Coryate. But, for all her beauty, she stank like a sewer and trembled like a dove in a trap. Besides, he had resolved on a monastic life till he should once more see Anne Harcourt.

He gestured that she should dress once more and leave, but she did not at first understand what he meant. When at last she did, she smiled, and wrapped her saree round her body. Then she came towards Coryate, bowed low, and touched his feet before she glided out of the room.

It was the gesture that the Indians made to another person as a token of deep respect and to show gratitude.

~

Coryate had become increasingly fretful. Weeks had passed, and though Roe, when they passed in the compound, always nodded and sometimes smiled, the audience he had been promised had not materialized. 'Honest Tom, it will most certainly come about,' Salbank said. 'I remind him every day. But he has many grave matters on his mind. He came here to arrange matters of trade between the Company and the Indies, but now he is involved in matters of state. Jehangir, or Salim, as he is privately called, desires the aid of our ships against the Portuguese in Goa. Sir Thomas has sent word on this matter to His Majesty in London. Meanwhile, Salim and he have become very close.'

The news delighted Coryate. The closer Roe and Salim became, the more likely the Great Mogul was to grant favours to another eminent Englishman: himself. He had maps, of Tartary and China, and often busied himself looking up the routes he would take, once he had Salim's help. But

Salbank said, 'It is no joy to be close to Salim. The longer I see this place, Tom, the more convinced I am of the hypocritish disposition of these Indians and their Emperor. Salim is a Mussulman who has forsworn the use of liquor. But thrice a week when he calls Sir Thomas to council, in his private quarters, he offers him wine and fiery spirits.'

Salbank had a broad simple face, and the quality of dismay in it was almost laughable. 'The other day,' he said, 'we were near to a scandal; for Salim, by night and privily, sent Sir Thomas a courtesan, for his enjoyment of her flesh. That night we lodged her and her attendants secretly in a house apart and treated her like an English lady; my master never went near her, and at dawn, before anyone saw, sent her back untouched to the palace. Courtly behaviour, Tom, was it not, and Christian too? And yet this heathen Salim took offence.'

Coryate listened attentively to these tales. Clearly, Roe had many troubles and his audience would have to wait. He was delighted and amazed when one night Salbank, returning from his work, announced that Roe would see him next day.

~

In this season, the nights had chilled; for the first time since Coryate had entered the Mogul's lands, the sun once risen became a comforter rather than a tormentor. He dressed in his cleanest clothes and walked over to Roe's house, the largest in the compound, the only one that looked substantial. But it was sparsely furnished and Coryate felt bleakness in the air when he entered it, which, perhaps, reflected the character of its inhabitant. Salbank led him directly to the room where Roe sat, writing at a desk. A smaller desk had been provided for Salbank in a smaller and darker comer of the room, fit only for an industrious mouse.

Salbank said, 'Sir Thomas, I bring Master Thomas Coryate, as you commanded.' Roe glanced up, nodded Coryate to a stool placed in front of his desk, and then continued to write. At last, he looked up and smiled with his teeth. Seen close his face was harder and more wrinkled than Coryate had thought it was. 'Joseph says that you have had to wait to speak to me, Master Coryate,' he said. 'But you understand that some of us have more responsibilities to fulfil and less time to waste on talk than others.'

Coryate felt a chilly shock. Then Roe smiled in a quite human fashion. 'But I have heard of you. Ned Phelips told me of you and your books. I have not seen them, but I know you to be a learned man. Also it does you much credit that you have walked to the Indies without money, as Joseph tells me. You may be of great help to me in this place. I shall consult with you about the country as you have seen it, for you have seen it more closely than any other Englishman alive. At the end, I shall send you safe home to—Somerset, is it not?—a fine county, though I have no palate for cider.'

'Sir Thomas,' Coryate said, wishing that he had spared the time to compose another oration before this encounter, 'after this trip, it is to Tartary and Cathay that I would go, on foot as I came here. This is why, of your kindness I need to have audience of the Emperor Jehangir, or Salim, as you call him. But while I am here, Sir Thomas, I will help you as well as I can, and stand like Salbank at your right hand.'

Roe pinched his underlip between finger and thumb. He said, 'You misunderstand me. You will talk to me, but you will not speak to Salim. Master Coryate, I wish the Indians to respect us. I wish them to see us dignified, clean and clad as Englishmen should be. And you are not any of those. If Salim should see a ragged fellow like you, and this fellow proclaims himself an Englishman, he would lose all respect for us. I will arrange for you to witness the wonders within the court. But if you try and see Salim, I will throw you out on the Indian roads. Meanwhile help me, and I shall see to your necessities. Is that plainly understood? I trust it is.' He rose and left.

Salbank's newly cut quill, scratching mouse-like in its corner, stopped. He rose from his stool and came to put his hand on Coryate's shoulder, for his friend was weeping.

12

Diary Six

September 2002

Agra–Pushkar–Ajmer

The streets in padri tola were clean and empty. We stopped to ask an old man where Sylvador's house was. His eyes turned into large rounds; he slapped his mouth with his hand. 'Oh no! You mean, you didn't know. Sylvador died, just few weeks ago. Was he your friend?'

A stout lady joined us. She plucked some tissues from under the neckline of her dress. She dabbed her nose with them and then her eyes. 'He was a good man. God bless him.' She pointed out Sylvador's house to us.

A woman dressed in a cotton nightgown with lace around the neck opened the door. When we were seated in the tidy, uncluttered living room she took an album from a shelf and showed us photographs of her father. 'He was a good man,' she said, 'he would have been so happy to help you.' She spoke in faultless Hindi laced with Urdu words.

'That part of the house is old,' she pointed to the bedroom, 'more than four hundred years.'

The plaster on the walls had peeled; I could see the slim bricks used during the Mogul times. I asked to see Sylvador's notebook. She seemed confused.

'You are his daughter?' I asked, 'You are a school teacher?'

'No.' She smiled. 'That's my younger sister. She has moved to Delhi. She has taken all her things with her.'

Juzer said as we walked back to the car, 'She speaks such good Hindi. Almost as good as me. She's Christian.'

'Her family was either Muslim or Hindu before it was converted,' Dom said. 'Hindi must have been their language. Long ago when the missionaries came to India, they were made to learn the local language. They were told that it was required to convert people and talk to the newly converted ones and the faithful. They would tell them stories, fairy tales about God in the local language. But when the British came, they began to educate the local people. So the fathers, who were either Italians or Spanish, began to speak to people in broken English.'

Dom lit a cigarette. He blew smoke into the air. 'I don't believe in a religion but I think it's very important to keep languages alive even if it is through religion.'

~

Humayun's Mosque was on a small hill at one end of Katchpura village. The five-arched brick mosque was built in AD 1530 under Humayun's order for the religious needs of the Moguls who had set up their residences along the banks of the River Jamuna. The cupola on the southern side was entirely broken revealing the brickwork and variegated veins of mudmortar. It was held up by a number of wooden pillars.

In the central nave, four men knelt on the floor offering prayers. One man, who was seemingly the priest, knelt in the front and the other three in a row behind him. The garden in front of the mosque was full of fruit trees—pomegranate, date and guava. The parijat or harsingar tree, with delicately scented white flowers and flame orange stems, was in full bloom. 'I am sure Coryate must have come here,' Dom said. He put his feet together and looked up at the mosque.

When they had finished their prayers, the priest stepped out, clutched Juzer's hand in both his and exchanged holy greetings. The other men did what he did. Then the priest clutched my hand in both his. 'Assalam alaekeum,' he said to me. The other men did the same, saying, 'Assalam alaekeum, assalam alaekeum.' Then they moved on to Dom.

Juzer asked the priest about the village. His straggly egg-white beard matched the white cap on his head. 'This village existed before the Taj Mahal,' he said dusting his white kurta. 'The houses were built with old Lahori bricks which were thinner than the bricks used now. But they have all broken down,' he said touching his forehead. 'Ah, but there is one house left next to the mosque. It belongs to the Patil. He owns most of the houses in this village.'

He took us through a small wicket gate to an open courtyard shared by three houses. A buffalo was tied to a post in one corner. Part of the wall in front of us was built of small Lahori bricks. Dom walked up to it and ran a hand over its surface.

Had Coryate touched this wall? I knew this was what he was thinking. As if to unravel a hidden code, Dom ran his fingertips over the mortar grooves. He looked at the particles of mud on his fingertips; each grain containing a speck of the past. I couldn't help thinking then how links in history accrue, how they seem more familiar and yet become more distanced. Dom smelled the mud on his fingers. He raised them to his ear; I thought he could hear the accumulations of dead voices.

From where I stood I could look into Patil's house. The walls inside were plastered and painted in two colours, green below and a violent blue above sill level. Two old women were fast asleep on a high cot. A young boy who sat between them watched a small black-and-white TV. A cricket match was on. Coryate wouldn't have seen that.

We drove to another village not far away. The Babri Masjid was a large mosque set in a compound with tall walls. It was built in red sandstone and brick that was plastered and painted a bright blue. The main doorway had been, not long ago, ornamented with pieces of coloured glazed tiles. We told a robust man in a white kurta and pyjama that we wished to see the maulana. He flung a green scarf over his shoulder. 'You want to know about this mosque, then ask me. Why ask the maulana? All he knows is to pray. He can't even protect this mosque. I have had to fight for it. I went to court for it. My name is Sultan Ahmed. I am the secretary of Babri Masjid. This mosque was built in Babur's time.'

He took us up a flight of steps to the terrace. Dom decided not to come. 'You see all this area,' Sultan Ahmed said. 'It belonged to the mosque. But since the BJP (Bharatiya Janata Party) came to power, their people have stolen all this land from us. Now they have built that factory on our land. I am going to fight this. Agra is a city created by the Moguls, and we Muslims are its caretakers. But we just stood by and let the city be ripped apart piece by piece. The old localities, the bazaars, the old havelis have all been destroyed. The history of Moguls in this city has been wiped out. Only Taj Mahal is left. Ah! But this is seen as a monument belonging to India. Not Muslims.

'Babur had built a large garden called Aram Baug. There was a board outside it with this name. The BJP changed the board and called it Ram Baug. I am going to fight about this too. It is Babur's garden. How can it become Ram's garden suddenly? Now they say this mosque is not even Babri Masjid. I am the caretaker of this mosque and I'm going to fight for it.'

'Do you live in this village?' I asked Sultan Ahmed.

'Yes, just this side of the Jamuna.'

'Was your father also a caretaker of this mosque?' I asked.

'I have no shame in telling you this. My father was a barber.'

'And you?' Juzer asked.

'I have no shame in telling you this either. I am also a barber. In fact I come from a family of barbers.'

Juzer stroked his beard as he looked at two old men who joined us. He said, 'Ah! Look at these two old Muslim men, Sultan sahib. They are loyal Muslims. They have kept their beards like I have. But you, the caretaker of this mosque, the one who is going to fight for it, you claim to be a devout Muslim, still you have shaved your beard?'

Sultan Ahmed nodded, stroked his clean chin, 'I may be a good Muslim and a caretaker,' he laughed, 'but you must remember, I am also a barber.'

~

We were back in the world of choices and decisions. Juzer chose to go to Mathura and Vrindavan. 'I am quite certain Coryate went there,' he said. 'I know that he would have been curious to see Krishna, because since the time he left Lahore, that would have been his first contact with a Hindu god. He may have met the widows in Vrindavan. But I am not sure of this. Because I think at that time they were following sati. The women would have jumped into their dead husbands' funeral pyres. Coryate was here to write a book on India and he would have been concerned about all this. And remember he had a lot of time in Agra.'

It had started to rain. Closer to Mathura, we passed a village where several huts along the road had advertisements of Rupa underwear and baniyan painted on their walls. Amidst them, keeping up with the native trend, on a wall of a temple, was a large red and white advertisement for Coca-Cola.

It was pouring by the time we reached Mathura. A landscape of filth and stench seemed to be rolling towards us like an uninterrupted ball. Religious towns, I had assumed, were meant to be humbler than assertive, and definitely not as revolting as this. Mud and water churned in deep puddles. The lane was strewn with layers of garbage and rotting flowers. Overhead wires crisscrossed. Little boys sold coconut slices. Cows, tractors and beggars ambled down the lane. STD booths and guides were all over the place, as also wayside vendors selling sugar balls and puffed rice. Guards with guns stood outside the Krishna Janmabhoomi area where Joginder stopped the car.

'I'm not stepping out in this filth and rain,' Dom grunted.

From where we had parked, I could see the temple and the green dome of the Masjid next to it. 'See. See how their walls touch,' Joginder exclaimed. 'That is why the Hindus are very angry with the Muslims. That's why all these guards have to be here.'

It rained harder. 'Let's go to Vrindavan,' I said. As we turned onto the road to Vrindavan, a swami on a motorbike zipped past us. The car was forced into a gutter. I caught sight of his face as he turned back and waved a hand. Joginder cursed, jumped out to inspect the damage. We got out and walked through the winding narrow street to the main temple. We left our shoes with two old women in white sarees at the temple. Their skins were shrivelled like salted prunes. They clutched our footwear to their breasts. The morning aarti was over; the temple floor was being washed with a hosepipe. Water gushed out of the temple into the street already full with rain.

I noticed two pujaris inside. The extremely well fed one was facing me. His paunch rose to his chin. His beard was scruffy and his moustache resembled that of a Hindi movie villain. The leaner one turned and I recognized him. He was the one on the motorbike who had caused the car to swerve into the gutter. Dom stood by the wall, plucked a cigarette from the box. I asked Juzer to stand by the door as I stepped inside to talk to the lean pujari. The pujari didn't recognize me. To my surprise, he beckoned Juzer to enter. Juzer cast a glance at me, then at the pujari and pointed to his cap and beard.

'King Akbar came to this temple,' the pujari said. 'If he can, so can you.' Juzer adapted a virtuous look.

The pujari said, 'Akbar even paid for the temple's upkeep. There was the great singer here, Swami Haridas. Lamps lit up when he sang. Clouds burst. And springs came alive. He was the guru of the great singer, Tansen. When Akbar heard of Tansen, he came to hear him. Akbar asked Tansen to serve in his court.'

The pujari talked about Krishna as though he knew him intimately. 'Krishna never spends the nights here,' he whispered this private information into Juzer's ears. 'He spends it with the gopis in Nathdwara. He returns early next morning.

But we know about this because there is mud on his chariot wheel. And when we bathe him in the morning, his body is so dusty. Also he is so completely exhausted. What must he have been doing, we tease him.' The pujari sang praises of Vrindavan. 'The water in Vrindavana is pure nectar. When it rains the sound is sweet. The lake of Vrindavan is surrounded by green grasses. Beautiful lotus flowers bloom in it. The air blowing in Vrindavan carries the aromatic scent of these flowers. Sandal-skinned deer are hopping. Birds are chirping. Peacocks are dancing. Bees are humming. The cuckoos sing nicely in five kinds of tunes. Vrindavan is a natural forest of desire trees. In Vrindavan there are cows that fulfil all desire. They graze from forest to forest giving purest milk.'

Coryate sang praises of his Odcombe. The pujari sounded like him.

Dom was in serious conversation with a young man with a carefree expression. 'Must be a reporter, he has that kind of air,' Juzer screwed his eyes. 'Must be from a local paper only.'

'This is Gopal,' Dom introduced him. 'He has lived here since his birth. He speaks very good English, but I am, amazed how well he can speak French.' Dom hesitated. 'He was telling me about the widows of Vrindavan.'

'Which paper?' Juzer asked.

Dom said, 'He is a guide.'

'Ah!' Juzer stuttered. 'I hear there are as many as 5000. Yes?'

'Guides?' Dom's spectacles slid down his nose.

'Oh-no. I mean widows.'

'Two thousand, maybe more,' Gopal said. 'They are thrown out by their families, so they come here. The widows believe that they can break the cycle of birth and rebirth by dying in Vrindavan.'

'Someone looks after them here?' Dom enquired.

'There are free chowltries. Some widows stay in them.'

'What do they do?' Dom asked.

'They wear white sarees, always cover their heads.'

'But what do they do?'

'Nothing. They sit around the idol of Krishna and pray from morning till night. Each widow is given two rupees every evening and a cupful of uncooked rice and lentils, enough for one meal. Before they begin their prayers, many women clean temples and they are paid a monthly salary. Not much. Half of this goes to rent one room that is shared by two-three widows. Some are too ill to work. They are very weak. They're not allowed to eat non-vegetarian food because eating meat arouses sexual desire. One widow here, she is very old, above seventy. She was married off when she was five years old. Her husband, whom she never saw, was thirteen and he died one month after the wedding. So she came here when she was a girl. She is sick; she will die soon. She has prayed for so many years, she will surely not be reborn.'

Juzer put an arm around Gopal's shoulder, 'Gopal, brother, tell me one thing, I read in a magazine that the younger widows in the chowltry are forced to do bad-bad things. Is this true?' Juzer held his shoulder tight. 'I also read that they are now selling the rice and lentils they get so they can leave the chowltry, rent a safe place to stay. It seems they are saying that they would prefer to starve then lose their honour. It seems they live like slum people beneath stairwells, on verandas or in makeshift shelters, using old jute matting or bed covers. Also that slum landlords harass them and try to evict them to make housing for the thousands of young westerners who come as Krishna devotees. Is this all not true, my brother?' Juzer's hand tightened around Gopal's arm.

Gopal gave him a solemn look, 'My brother,' he hesitated, then said in a tough voice, 'I don't know.'

~

We set out early next morning for Ajmer. Juzer had worked out a route that went through a number of villages. It was the old route and one that Coryate would have taken. 'We go up to Fatehpur Sikri on the highway then take the old road,' Juzer announced. Joginder did not conceal his displeasure. Dom was silent. He clutched his stomach, shut his eyes.

We were out of Agra. 'Look, look,' Juzer called out, positioning his binoculars. I turned to look but couldn't see anything but two women in kitschy clothes sitting on a culvert. 'Bedia women. Prostitutes,' Juzer said.

'How can you tell?' I asked.

'They were making signals at me.'

Half an hour later, I was engrossed in a book, when, 'Look, look,' Juzer shouted, his binoculars stuck to his eyes; I clearly saw a huge black bear standing upright in the middle of the road. As the car came closer, a young man appeared from behind the bear, waving out to us to stop. Joginder swerved the car, sped. 'They are scoundrels,' Joginder cursed. 'They stop tourists, foreigners, they show them bear tricks and when they take photographs of them, they force them to pay five, six hundred rupees. Cheats!'

'It might be interesting to talk to one of them,' Dom, who had woken up, said. We passed another dozen bears on the road. As we drove past Gorai village, we saw an old man squatting under a tree with his bear. Dom said, 'That old man seems harmless. So does the bear. Let's talk to him.'

I got out of the car, sat beside the old man. His bear sniffed at my toe. Then making up its mind about something or the other, it moved away to sniff at the bark of a young tree. I talked to the old man. He was dressed in a white kurta and pyjama; his head was shaved and his white beard was trimmed. His name was Umar Mohammed. He was sixty years old, he told me. Bear-keeping was a traditional job and his father, grandfather, even his great-grandfather had kept bears. Most of the families of the village kept bears.

As a boy he had been told that, a long time ago, one of the villagers had brought a male bear when he returned from the forest. Another brought back a female bear. Since then these bears had been responsible for the great bear family.

He called out to the bear, hit the ground with his stick; the large animal bowed to me, then turned around a number of times. 'You can take photo,' the old man said to me. 'Many people want to photograph the bears. We make money like this. It is our livelihood. There's nothing else we can do. But recently some journalists came and reported about us. So the animal organizations came with police to take away our bears. We pleaded with them, so they left us alone. These bears are all we have. When we get our daughters married we give away a bear as dowry. Our fathers used to go to villages and towns with their bears and make them perform. Now we are invited to five star hotels. Our bears even dance to disco music for the foreigners. They like that very much. We are paid over five thousand rupees.'

As we talked, a large crowd had gathered around our car. There were at least ten bears amongst them, docile and uninterested in the conversation. Some of the men looked ferocious. They held wooden sticks in their hands which they thumped, as though in a rite, now and then, on the ground. Joginder started the car. 'Get in, meddem. Shut your door,' he said. I climbed in, asking Joginder how much to pay the old man. 'Two hundred, enough,' he said waving out to the three men positioned in front of the car to move.

They moved closer holding up their sticks. One of the young men with a daunting moustache said to me, 'We want five thousand rupees. You took video-audio.' Another man began to thump the car with his stick. I tried to explain that I did not have a video camera. 'Four thousand, then,' the man demanded.

Juzer started to talk to him. I took the cassette from the recorder and gave it to the moustached man with a five hundred rupee note, and as I tried to pull up the window he put out a hand to stop me.

Joginder called one of them to his window and said something. Suddenly, the men moved away. Joginder sped down the road.

'What did you tell him?' I asked.

'That sir is American journalist,' he said. He pointed to Juzer, 'He is TV reporter, and you, meddem, are related to a minister. I told them you would come back with the police and take away all the bears, and have the men put behind bars.' Joginder laughed.

'I better make some notes. What did the old man say the bear's name was?' I asked Juzer.

'Raju.'

'But he is a Muslim. Wouldn't he have given the bear a Muslim name?'

Juzer laughed. 'Not necessary. I may be wrong, but you see, biologically speaking, the bear falls in the pig family. According to the Koran, the pig is a bad animal. It is haram. If that old man had known this, he wouldn't have kept bears in the first place. Look, look,' he turned around, his binoculars on his nose. He pointed to a tall brick minar. It was one of the road markings that Akbar had built at every kos, he said.

We stopped at Kiraoli village. Juzer told us that it was the first post for travellers a long time ago. He asked a young woman on the road if there were any old buildings in the village. She looked at him, giggled and covered her face with her saree. Juzer asked an old man with a haggard goat. He pointed to a mud track. There was a very old masjid at the end of it, he told us. We walked to it. In the front room, there was a tomb painted green and covered with a cloth with pink and purple stripes. It was the grave of Feroz Shah Chisti Rehmatullah, a young man in a white kurta and pyjama, a cap on his head, told us.

He was Mohammad Altaf, the school teacher. He had come from Bhagalpur in Bihar to his uncle's home in Agra. He wanted to see the Taj Mahal. He came to this village to teach children for a month and earn some money and had stayed on for five years. The children were taught Hindi and English besides the Koran. Juzer asked the teacher, not too discreetly, how much he was paid. Two thousand rupees, he said.

He took us out to the masjid's courtyard where around fifty children were seated in two lines. They were from many villages. They lived at the masjid and were provided with food and clothes. As we left, Juzer asked the teacher what he intended to do in the future.

'Follow Allah's path,' he replied.

Juzer laughed. 'So did Osama bin Laden.'

We drove past more minars, more villages; row upon row of distinctive ugliness, all of which, struck by the eventuality of destruction and renovation, were an endless graveyard of building materials—sandstone, cement, marble, dust. Strewn here and there amidst them, like vouchers from the past, were eroded monuments and tombs.

In Sikandra, through Juzer's binoculars, we spied a fortress built by Jehangir atop a hill. I watched the glare fade. I saw silhouettes of hills and trees, gauze-like and forgettable. Dom began to feel terribly sick. I gave him some tablets and soon he was fast asleep. Juzer's head rolled and he too fell into a deep slumber. Now and then, as his head fell heavily to one side, he would abruptly awake as though to new life and begin to recite his prayers, then fall asleep once more.

It was late; the dimness all around had an immense power of emptiness. We were miles away from Ajmer. Joginder remarked, as he tried to navigate through sodden masses of loam and stone that overtaxed his nerves, 'We are not even halfway. What is the use of driving through this hell, if these two are asleep?'

He was wringing his hands over the steering wheel. His voice was beseeching as he turned back to look at me. 'From the next village, there is a link road to the highway …'

'Take it,' I said.

~

Stealthy as thieves, we drove through the dark. Shadows were rising from its depths. It was five minutes past midnight when we reached Ajmer. Dom and Juzer were fast asleep. Joginder cast a glance at them, remarked with a snort, 'What meddem, now that they have sold all their horses, are they snoring?'

Out of the window, I saw a hundred buses parked in an open area. Thousands of people slept out in the open, and above them, watching with flinty eyes, were half a million stars tacked to a violet chiffon sky.

Joginder made a noise through his nose that sounded like a horse's sneeze. 'What a time to come to Ajmer, meddem,' he said pointing to the people. 'So many come here now because of Urs.'

Juzer, when he was last awake, had talked about it. He had peered into his notes, said excitedly, 'So good that we are in Ajmer at this time. Coryate must have seen the Urs at both places, at the Dargah Sharif as well as at the Taragarh Mosque. Now we can see it too.'

Urs meant death anniversary, he told me. Over five lakh devotees came from all over the country to seek blessings at the Dargah Sharif, he said, where the Sufi saint Khwaja Moin-ud-din Chishti was buried.

Joginder drove on to Pushkar. He looked tired. In the darkness, the arms of hills wrapped around us. The wind seemed to entwine itself around these stone arms, in and out. For some inexplicable reason I remembered a girlhood song: *in and out the sparkling bluebells, I am your leader, tapitapitapitapi on your shoulder, I am your leader …*

Looking over Joginder's shoulder, I saw a line of lights like sparkling bluebells that climbed all the way to the top of a hill. I could make out the silhouette of a temple.

Next morning at the hotel, Dom braved an attempt at breakfast. His face was pale; his body burned with fever. We were seated in the opulent dining hall, just the two of us. Thirty-odd tables were draped in white linen, white napkins poised, and around them chairs decked in floral velvet. The ceiling above was busily painted, as also the walls around us, and hung with brass shields and swords. At the far end, the buffet had been laid out: a row of at least ten silver lidded vessels perched over stands. Over a hundred plates were stacked at one end of the table and an equal number of bowls and cups. The whole atmosphere was that of a pantomime, soundless, frozen, as though entrenched in the sense of absence was a perceived presence. And we were an essential part of it.

I walked to the buffet, lifted the lids one by one. They were empty. A bearer in a farcical imitation of Rajasthani costume was beside me, waving a menu card in my face. 'Only Hala Karti,' he said, 'bouffey not there.'

I asked him why not. His eyes narrowed. He put on a sad face. He seemed adept at it. 'No guests, meddem, after 9/11, all foreigners are scared to come. And now, with the threat of India-Pakistan war, no Indians come even. So only tables, only chairs, only two bearers, and sir and meddem. No booffey. No tips even.'

He asked cheerfully, 'What will have for break-faast? Aumlet, eggs-fry or Rajasthani puri-bhaji, very good, meddem, try.' We settled for cornflakes, toast and coffee. He was not pleased. He pestered us to reconsider. 'Eat more, then give more tip, no?' His sad look reappeared.

He brought us coffee with the same face. When I asked him about the temple on the hill, he brightened. 'That is goddess Saraswati temple. Long ago Brahma, god of creation, was flying on his swan scattering lotus petals on earth. One of the petals fell at Pushkar and became a lake. It was the perfect spot to start the world. Priests lit sacrificial fire, and they were ready to perform the ritual, but Brahma's wife Saraswati was not there. What to do? Auspicious hour was over, almost. The priests got hold of a young milkmaid, Gayatri, to take her place and performed the rites. When Saraswati returned, she became very angry. She cursed that Pushkar would be the only place where Brahma would be worshiped and that too, only four days every year. Then she went to that hill. She's there only in a temple. Very angry still.'

~

Soon we descended the hills towards Ajmer which, until 1192, was ruled by the great Raja Prithviraj Chauhan, the last Hindu king of Delhi. After having changed hands several times, Ajmer finally came under the Mogul emperor, Akbar, in 1556, who used it as the headquarters for his vitally important operations in Rajasthan. It was here, a generation later, that the first British Ambassador, Sir Thomas Roe, had an historic meeting with Emperor Jehangir in 1615. In the nineteenth century, Ajmer became a little British enclave, from where the British Chief Commissioner for Rajputana kept an eagle eye on all the Rajput kingdoms.

Dom was keen to go to Taragarh Fort built by the Chauhan dynasty of Rajputs in the seventh century. On the hill, was also the shrine of Miran Sayyed Hussain, the first Muslim governor of the hill fort. A line of buses snaked their way up ahead of us, cars honked behind us, and people walked alongside. Some of the passengers from the bus in the front got off and started walking; the village men in bright red turbans and their women in bright skirts carrying cloth bundles on their heads. Dom pointed out a woman amidst them in a bright yellow skirt, a red blouse, swaying her hips to the wind. Balanced on her head was a single ripe tomato.

The road ended in a large open ground full of vehicles. Joginder drove into a narrow lane ahead. We passed a blue door with the sign:

OH! MY DEAR. PARKING HERE.

We parked.

'Would you like to go inside,' the old man behind us asked.

'I am Sayid, the caretaker.' He was dressed in a white kurta-pyjama, a short black coat, and on his head was perched a khaki cap. 'I can tell you the history of Taragarh.'

Dom put up a hand as he started to speak. 'Juzer, I want you to ask him,' he said pointing to the crowd around, 'I'm surprised because many of these people appear to me to be Hindus. Do many Hindus come here? Was there any problem during the communal riots?'

Sayid replied when Juzer asked him, 'All this Hindu-Muslim fight is recent only. They used to live peacefully together. But they must understand,' he ran a hand over his face, 'how can the Hindus forget the years of Muslim supremacy just like that? And the Muslims in India, they cannot ignore the feelings of the Hindus just like that. It's simple, we were the rulers and they are the majority.'

He shook his head, 'What to do, such different religions we have, sometimes we don't know what to believe even. We have the same sky, same moon, sun and stars, then how can our gods be different? See, Islam says that Allah is the only God. It says believers of all other religions are infidels. But these Hindus, they pray to some million gods and goddesses. They say we Muslims are unclean and unholy. If we turn to the west to pray, they face east. We write from right to left, they write from left to right. They love the saffron colour, we like green. The Koran condemns idol worship. It says to the faithful to kill infidels. And these Hindus, they are sitting and sitting and waiting and waiting for the Kalki avatar so it can redeem the world of the unholy. They mean us Muslims,' he thrashed his chest. 'So Hindus, Muslims, they fight like cats and dogs. It is natural, no?' He took off his cap, scratched his head.

He turned to Juzer. 'But what is so unnatural, my fellow mate, is that we Muslim-Muslim fight. You, I presume, are a Shia, I am also,' he slapped his chest again, wobbled his head, left to right. Look at the Shias and Sunnis, they are also fighting like animals, like cats and dogs only. When we Shias observe *maatam*, beat our chests, these Sunnis say it is wrong. What is wrong? When you are distressed, you show it by hitting your chest, no? It's natural. You do this when you are happy also. People who go to watch cricket, or go to conference, meeting, party, weddings, tell me, they clap their hands so hard no, so that their hands become red? But these Sunnis don't say anything to them. But they will argue with us, that self-flagellation is haram because it causes pain to the body. But don't people hit their foreheads when they hear sad news?'

Juzer nodded, pinching his chin thoughtfully. Dom said with a sardonic smile, 'I may be wrong, but I read an account of some Muslim pulling out all his teeth when he heard that two teeth of the prophet were broken in some battle. That must have been terribly painful. This is more extreme than beating oneself with knives and chains I think,' he said, his hand pressed to his jaw. 'I had my molar removed a month ago. It was awful.'

Sayid said something to Juzer. Juzer nodded. 'The Taragarh Mosque is maintained by Shias. They prepare kheer in the large deg and distribute to the devotees. But the Sunnis allege that the Shias spit into the food so that everyone who eats it automatically is converted to a Shia. This is how, they accuse, we are trying to increase the Shia population. But these Sunni buggers happily queue up for this khefer, and eat for free. Then why complain!'

Sayid laughed loud. There were very few teeth in his mouth. One front tooth was long, capped with gold. 'If there was a sense of brotherhood, then this nation would be okay.

But now people don't have food to eat but they want things, more and more things. If people had more knowledge and more faith it would be okay. But people want more from God even. Everyone wants to fulfill his or her wishes and their demands at holy places rise.' He pointed to the crowd, 'That is why they are all here, Hindus, Muslims, Christians, they go to all the gods, Ram, Allah, Jesus, to get all their wants.'

A deep breath, and then he said, 'You must go also inside. Pay respects to the tomb of the saint. All your desires will be fulfilled.' He put out a hand as if to bless us, then raised a finger, 'Don't forget to see the unusual tomb that faces the Kibla. Come, let me take you. You can donate whatever you want for the upkeep of the shrine.'

I pressed some notes into his palm. 'May Allah bless your soul. This is for the mosque,' he said putting the notes into his pocket. He extended his palm towards me. I put some more notes into it. He touched the money to his chest, stuffed it into his shirt pocket.

We walked to the back of the shrine where the hill rose then flattened. The wind wailed in our ears, made our eyes water and tore at our shirts. 'What is Kibla?' I asked Juzer.

'Oh! Have you not seen my Kibla-finder? It's a silvery compass that I use when I pray. Kibla is the direction towards the Kabba in Mecca. All graves should be perpendicular to this direction.' He hesitated, laughed, 'Not only graves, ma'am. When we answer nature's call, we cannot face in the Kibla direction. When having sex even, we can't lie down in that direction. But the grave in this shrine faces the Kabba. This is never so.'

Juzer's face grew energetic. He said to Dom, 'Imagine, sir, Coryate walked through Middle East, Allepo, Syria, Turkey, Persia, Afghanisthan, Sind, Punjab, nowhere would have seen a grave facing the Kabba. But here he would have. Imagine how surprised he would have been. Don't you want to see it?'

Dom declined. Juzer looked away. 'Look, look, there,' he pointed out to a sheet of white, far away. 'Those are the sand dunes.'

Dom looked at the stretch of white sands undulating like a chain of endless camel humps. He sighed. 'I'm not sure he would have seen this grave of yours, but Coryate could have stood here. He would have seen the sand dunes from here.'

Dom bent down, picked up some mud, crumbled it in his hand. A pair of ants moved away from the mud in his palm and progressed up his wrist. Dom watched them. Gently he blew the ants away.

13

Exile

Coryate had no idea what had happened to the papers he had asked various people to convey to England. He was not fool enough to expect that he would receive acknowledgments, but the absence of any nagged at him continually. He had images in his mind of Jonson poring over his work in the Mermaid, holding the papers in one hairy hand while the fingers of the other explored the body of some pretty, buxom barmaid. Sometimes the poet might stop his reading, though not the other activity, to quote aloud to the members of the Mermaid Club from a page of the manuscript, saying, perhaps, 'Is this passage not one of great splendour?' His audience, awestruck, would nod, and concur.

But then the nightmare thought would come: what if his papers had never reached England? What if they had been lost in some mishap? What if (but he made efforts to put this fear away, for it was too much to bear) they had never been sent at all? Perhaps he had been a fool to entrust a manuscript to a man like Steele. It was during one of his cogitations over the fate of his papers, that he realized that his mother would have had no news of him for three years now.

Guilt filled him immediately. He went to Roe and said that he needed to send word to Somerset. Roe advised him to entrust his letters to the reliable Peter Rogers, who was to go home soon on an East Indiaman from Surat. Rogers assured his friend that he would see the letters reached Gertrude safely. 'But make haste, good Tom, and compose them,' he adjured. 'I leave for Surat at the end of this very month.'

The camp, even under Roe's strict discipline, was a noisy and troublesome place. Coryate sought a haven where he would have peace of mind to write to his mother in suitably impressive style. A shopkeeper in the bazaar told him of a town called Pushkar, two days walk from Ajmer. 'It is a holy place, full of temples,' said the man. 'It is peaceful, though at this time of year they sell camels there.' Coryate started out for Pushkar next day, eager to write once more.

He found, when he reached it, that one side of the town faced a desert. Lion-coloured sand covered it and stretched away to the horizon. There, the local people told him, lay the country of the Rajputs, who were famous as warriors and saints. In the desert outside the town, Coryate saw hundreds of hobbled camels, grumbling to themselves. Sometimes one would raise its saurian head and emit loud snorts and then a deafening roar of complaint. The owners had put up an encampment of tents nearby. These men had bronzed, leathery skins, and looked more like Arabs than Indians.

Throughout the day, dealers from Pushkar and the towns around it, even from Ajmer, would haggle with the camel owners over the prices of the beasts. Towards evening, the owners would race the camels over a track demarcated by flags. Large numbers of local people collected to watch.

The spectacle of camels running, as though on stilts, the huge humps on their backs bouncing like women's breasts, was comic even to Coryate, whose sense of humour was limited. But the onlookers, many of whom had money on one or the other of the animals, took it very seriously. They roared wildly as the camels ran; afterwards they got drunk on the local liquor and fought with knives. This liquor was yellow and potent, and sometimes tasted of saffron or roses.

~

Pushkar was surprisingly large in area, but otherwise little different from other such provincial towns that Coryate had passed through on his peregrinations around north India. The difference was that in the middle of the town was a lake. Its shores bore an enormous weight of stone, fretted and carved into temples. As happened in most Indian places of worship, their courtyards were crowded with mendicants, many of them cripples or lepers, holy men, pilgrims, food vendors and priests. By day, the courtyards filled with a susurration of sounds; but not after nightfall, except when the wind moved the lake water and lapped and slapped gently at its shores. Coryate slept by day in one of the sarais nearby.

At dusk he emerged and sat down by the lake. He had a bowl of oil by him, in which a kindled wick floated. By this faint, uncertain light, he wrote to his mother; he was not sure that she would ever read his words. After true darkness had set in, wild creatures came to the water to drink. Coryate would watch the delicate deer, the boar and the birds, and then go back to his work.

~

In Ajmer, Roe sat in his new-made house, the darkness in his mind as impenetrable as the night outside. He was up very late as usual, for he laboured long days. Jehangir was one of the most difficult men he had ever met, and since the Emperor made all the important decisions in the empire, Roe had to meet him incessantly. Jehangir liked to hunt, and often sent the envoy presents for his table, principally wild boar, for the Emperor himself, as a Muslim, could not eat it. He also invited Roe to drink with him after darkness concealed his bibulations, for, as a Muslim, alcohol was prohibited to him.

Roe supposed that they were friends, but he had not thought a friend would be so evasive. Jehangir wanted military help against the Portuguese, and Roe could not agree to it without some word from King James. But until it came, the Emperor would not set seal upon an agreement with the Company. Roe's principal task was to obtain this. But Jehangir made many excuses, mostly that he was too busy.

This, actually, was credible. Jehangir had to work very hard to be an emperor. He had to show himself to the people four times a day, once from each point of the compass. He had to hear their complaints and settle disputed issues. He had paperwork and rebels on his hands. Roe thought he was a good ruler, but in a style that would be deemed barbaric in England. He had heard of the tortures the Emperor had had inflicted upon those he considered disloyal. Certes, Roe thought, some of our own monarchs have done the same, but Jehangir's ancestors were brutish Mongol warlords, capable of any bestiality, and sometimes this showed in him.

Roe had another problem on his hands: Thomas Coryate. Coryate's conversation sometimes entertained him, though he could become repetitive, and when they met he beset Roe with pleas for an interview with Jehangir. The English envoy felt he must prevent this. Coryate was unpredictable; were he to be put into contact with Jehangir, an embarrassing situation might be created. Roe had asked Coryate to stay in his house after he returned from wherever he had gone. He had done this so that he could keep an eye on Coryate; but he was unsure that this had been a good idea, for Coryate could now make his demands daily, face to face.

Enfiladed by the Indian darkness, with its sounds of insects and unfamiliar nightbirds, indelibly strange odours brought to his nostrils by every shift of wind, Roe composed a letter to Lord Pembroke in London. Pembroke could never imagine what this country, its people, its emperor, or Thomas Coryate were like, nor any of the difficulties Roe had.

He wrote of Coryate, whose plans changed every day: 'He is now for Samarcand in Tartarya to kiss Tamberlans Tombe, from thence to Susa, and to Prester Jhon in Ethiopia, where he will see the Hill Amara, all afoote, and so foote it to Odcombe. His notes are already so great for Portage, some left at Aleppo, some at Hispan—enough to make any stationer an alderman that shall but serve the Printer with Paper. And his exercise here or recreation is making or repeating orations. Principally of my lady Harcourt.'

However, Roe wondered, as he put down his pen, had Anne Harcourt, one of the greatest beauties in England, come to know Coryate? It was as though a swan had befriended a Somerset crow. But it was no suitable hour to answer riddles. He yawned hugely, and went lonely to his hard bed.

~

Roe, as an English gentleman, kept most of his promises. He got Coryate admission into the palace so that he could see Jehangir from afar, if not actually have audience with him. Coryate invited Ashraf to accompany him. It turned out that Ashraf disapproved deeply of the ways in which Jehangir amused himself. At the great daily event to which the public was admitted—a fight between elephants—he told Coryate, 'This is no more than a farce.'

The battle of elephants took place in an arena within the palace area. Jehangir attended it daily, as part of his routine, but also for his own entertainment. But as Ashraf said, it was no more than a farce. The elephants were by nature peaceable beasts and would very seldom fight each other in the wild, except over females and territorial rights. 'In this,' Ashraf said, 'are they so unlike men?'

But these elephants were tame, and from Jehangir's stables. They were swathed in heavy brocaded padding to protect them from any harm from the tusks of an opponent. Their mahouts, perched on heavy saddles on their backs, tore their huge, delicate, leaflike ears with hooked rods to make them attack each other. But it was a desultory performance, and none of the beasts was ever seriously hurt or killed. They collided violently, then separated; that was all. Meanwhile, drums beat and cymbals clashed. 'A farce,' Ashraf repeated, mumbling the words into his beard.

'What is it that you would have wanted to happen?' Coryate asked. Ashraf shook his head. 'I would not have wanted anything to happen,' he said. 'These beasts would not fight unless they were forced to. But Jehangir would have liked to see blood. He is descended from Babur, who came from the high steppes in a northern country, brought up on the smell of blood and dying men.'

After the performance was over and they were seated in a teashop, Ashraf said mournfully 'Some say Islam is for warriors, but I do not think so. Our Prophet preached the equality of all men. He did not recommend enmity between them. But from what I hear, Jehangir likes to see brutality. I have been told he took great pleasure in the spectacle of a lion killing and eating a living man. Perhaps this is bred into the old blood from the steppes, but we should rid ourselves of it, Khoryath, for it is bad blood.'

Delicately he picked up a kebab made of calf brains and coriander from the dish on the table, and squelchily devoured it. 'Most of the trouble this country has, Khoryath, is that the seeds of violence are deeply embedded within it. We from the north, I regret to say, are a violent and bloodthirsty folk. Look what happened when Timur-i-Leng entered these lands; how many skulls were in the pyramid he raised outside the gates of Delhi?'

'He is famous enough in my country,' Coryate said. 'A man I knew, an angrez called Kit Marlowe, wrote a play about him. "Tamburlaine" it was called, and it was a true marvel.'

'This angrez,' Ashraf said bitterly, 'did he smell the blood and the shit men drop when they die by violence, or hear the widows and the children weep? Khoryath, our religion has been misread and we have become a race of soldiers and proselytizers. This is not what our Prophet meant, for he was gentle.'

Coryate cleared his throat in an English manner.

'Nay, if I become too impassioned, Khoryath, forgive me,' Ashraf said. 'It upsets me to think of these emperors. And this land holds much potential for violence. The Hindus and the rest seethe silently under our feet. We, the people of the book, tread on the crust of a volcano in these lands, and one day it will explode and all of us, we and the lesser races, will vanish in the lava and the ash.'

'It will explode because of cruelty,' he concluded. 'And there is cruelty, not in a race or religion, but in the minds of the men in this country, whether they are business people or circus actors or, for that matter, emperors.'

~

Roe was sitting at his desk one day, writing once more to Pembroke, when Salbank entered to say a messenger came from Jehangir. The messenger was a guards officer in a yellow uniform, a scimitar at his hip. An Armenian interpreter, who seemed frightened of Roe and shied back like a nervous horse whenever the Englishman spoke, accompanied him. Salbank said, 'Sir Thomas, it seems quite a serious matter. The Emperor wishes to bury a woman here, in our compound.'

'What woman?' asked Roe. 'Is she his relative? And why here, forsooth? Has he no other place in all his empire for the obsequies?' Salbank coughed politely behind his hand. 'Sir Thomas,' he said, 'it is not exactly as you might expect. He wishes to bury this woman while she still lives. Ah, it is intended as a kind of punishment.' Roe stared blankly at him.

While the guardsman waited for the foreigners' chatter to be over, the Armenian spoke. 'Sir Roe,' he said, 'this woman, Farida, has committed a grave offence. She is one of the court ladies, but she was involved with a eunuch. But she is the property of our lord Jehangir. When we questioned her under the lash and more delicate tortures, she said that she loved the eunuch, Usman. So we made her watch his death, long and terrible, and now she must also die. My master, the Padshah, Beloved of the World, wishes her to die amongst the English, so that the public does not hear her cries.'

Roe sat silent for a while, then slowly and reluctantly uttered the Hindustani word, '*Acchha*. Very well.'

Salbank stared at him in shock. When the visitors had left, he cried, 'Sir Thomas, this is monstrous! A woman to be killed in our compound! How can we abet a murder? How can you countenance this, sir? What will our own people think of this?'

'They will not know,' said Roe. 'Issue orders that the Mogul has some private work to do here and that no man should come out of his quarters for the rest of the day.'

'Sir?' said Salbank.

'What is it now?' asked Roe, who had become very pale.

'Sir, from all I am told by these men, if she is buried alive, her death may take much more than a day.'

'Go, man!' Roe shouted. 'Go, and issue my orders.'

~

The woman, Farida, was brought to the English in the late afternoon. The palace guards in their yellow uniforms, which reflected the colour of sunlight, brought her. She had been a very beautiful woman. Her long hair was dyed red with henna, her breasts were round and firm, and the rest of her body in proportion to them. Her skin was very white.

When she arrived, she was dishevelled, her clothes torn, and her face stained with tears of shock and shame. She had watched a person she loved tortured slowly by the professionals who served the Emperor, and then trampled to death by an elephant. Her joints hurt from the rack and her back bled from the whip. She had also had to submit to all the lustful whims of her guards, who were by no means as gentle in their ways as Usman.

In the meanwhile, a short distance from Roe's window, muscular workers had been employed digging a hole in the earth. It was about the size a small human body might occupy if it were standing up and was like a wound in the red soil.

When the guards brought Farida to her tomb, no

Englishman was visible. But Salbank had told Coryate what was to happen. Coryate did not feel bound by Roe's orders. He sat on the slope above the English settlement and watched as the guards pinched and fingered Farida's body one last time before they lowered her into the hole. Her arms and her head with its long red hair protruded from her newly dug grave and as the workmen spaded the earth in around her, she started to weep, also to scream in disbelief and terror.

Coryate stumbled downhill and entered Roe's house. The envoy was at his desk, trying to write, but his hands shook too much for him to do so and his face was ashen. So was Salbank's face, who sat opposite; for Farida's screams for succour echoed around the room, unanswered.

'Sir Thomas,' said Coryate. 'Know you not, hear you not, what occurs under your window? Will you not help this poor wretched woman? One word from you and she will be saved!'

Roe turned a pale, bleak face to him. 'Tom, I cannot. It is the Mogul's wish, and it is my duty to keep him in good humour with us, the English. Otherwise our trade with him will end and, God knows, we may suffer the same fate as the poor wretch outside. What am I to do, Tom? Salbank?'

'In all truth, I know not, Sir Thomas,' Salbank said. But in his sensible way, though he was an abstemious man, he went and fetched two bottles of Portugal brandy from the store Sir Thomas kept. The three men sat in the small, close room, sipping it and listening to the incoherent cries from outside. The sun fell, the moon rose. It became cold, and the screams died, to be replaced by hopeless sobs. The three men sat in place, like carved figurines. Only, now and then, their right hands rose and were lowered as they lifted and put down their pots. Towards dawn, the sounds from outside faded.

'Jesus be thanked,' Roe said. 'Her suffering is over.'

But as the room filled with light from a new sun, Farida started to cry out once more. Her voice no longer carried to them so clearly. *'Mera sirr,'* she cried, *'mera sir!* (My head! Oh, my head!)' and she called out a name. 'Usman!'

The sun climbed the sky and towards midday the cries ceased, and Coryate dared look out of the window for the first time in hours. Farida's head had fallen forward; her face was buried in the dirt. Vultures circled high above, scenting a feast to come, and the Emperor's guards, who had watched her death since it had started, came forward to see if she were truly dead. Once certain that she was, they called the labourers back to excavate her body, then lifted it from the earth, stained with soil, and carried it back to the palace.

'They will take their own time,' said Roe's jovial Muslim cook, who had brought food for his master. Roe had not eaten for several hours. Neither had the other men, but they were ignored. 'They may want to fuck her before they burn her. After all, she was from the Emperor's harem and, even dead, my masters, she'd be a fuck to remember.'

~

Coryate was by now assured that Roe would never countenance anything that might upset or offend Jehangir. He had, despite his occasionally erratic behaviour, a logical mind, and he drew a conclusion from this: Roe would never introduce him to the Emperor because Roe thought he might do both. If the meeting were to come about, Coryate would have to use his own initiative. Roe had ordered him not to try and meet Jehangir, but Coryate was not of the Company, and, therefore, not obliged to follow any edict issued by its envoy.

He made his plans carefully. In the mornings, Jehangir

appeared at his jharoka, a window overlooking the courtyard, and listened to the petitions of the people. The Emperor would then answer through one of his courtiers. He might also send a courtier down with a pouch of silver for the petitioner. Coryate strongly hoped this would happen to him.

He prepared a petition in ornate Urdu, a translation from his baroque English, and, one uncomfortably warm morning, stood in the crowd that filled the courtyard. It consisted mostly of good citizens, perfumed and robed, and Coryate was the worst dressed person there, though this was not unusual in any assembly. The crowd was respectfully silent until suddenly the air filled with the thunder of drums and the nasal whine of oriental oboes, and Jehangir appeared at his latticed window, looking down at his subjects.

He was a small man, dressed in brocade robes, with a round catlike face and a pale complexion. A great roar burst from the throats of the crowd. '*Padshah salamat*,' the people cried. 'Hail, Emperor!' Jehangir remained impassive. The music ceased; it was time for the petitions. The petitioners raised a forest of hands and a courtier chose the man who would speak and gestured that he should commence.

Perhaps because of Coryate's unusual appearance, he was almost immediately chosen. His petition was more of an oration; he lavished many flowery compliments upon the Emperor and introduced himself as a man who had come on foot, alone, penniless, friendless, all the way from England to look upon the face of Jehangir. He was composing a book on the country and wished to compose another on Cathay. Could the Emperor give him letters to the ruler of Cathay? And (Coryate's heart beat wildly) could the Emperor also provide him with money for his travels, since he had none?

A prolonged silence followed. Jehangir looked down

with some curiosity at the strange figure in the courtyard, and seemed to ponder. Then he murmured to a courtier. The courtier moved forward and proclaimed, 'We can give you no letters to the ruler of Cathay, who is not our friend. But we will give you the money that you ask.' A courtier came from the balcony with a purse and handed it to Coryate.

He knew that, within the hour, Roe would be told of what he had done and would consider it an outrage. Coryate would have to face his wrath and would almost certainly be ejected from the English camp. Now he did not care. He had got a little money and he could continue his travels in India. After he left the courtyard he counted what was in the purse.

Jehangir had given him a hundred rupees.

~

Though he was a lean man, Roe's face was almost apoplectic. It had turned purple under his tan. His whole body shook with fury as he stared across his desk at Coryate, who stood before him like a reprimanded schoolboy. 'Do you know what it is you have done, Coryate?' he demanded. 'In five minutes of foolishness, you have imperilled my entire mission, which is our King's work. I know not but that you have destroyed it utterly. Mayhap you have destroyed us all.

'Jehangir knows now that an Englishman may turn into a filthy fellow such as you are. That is bad enough, but it is worse still, that an Englishman should present himself to a foreign king in such a beggarly and poor fashion, and out of an insinuating humour crave money from him. What face have I left, now that he thinks our nation produces such creatures as you? I have laboured long months to win the favour of the Emperor, and you have undone all this today.'

Coryate's disappointment at the meagreness of Jehangir's

gift changed. It turned to a fury all his own, that suddenly boiled up in him, and he glared back at Roe. 'What are you but a Jew, who does all for money?' he said, forgetting that his anger was also connected with this commodity. Even in his rage, he used his oratorical powers. He did not shout; he spoke in a controlled voice that carried to several pairs of English ears avidly listening outside.

'What succour did you offer that wretched lady when she cried aloud in her agony under your very window? You said that you could not aid her because it would offend this tyrant, who tortures and murders all those who question him, whose raiment is stained with the blood of thousands he has made martyr. You are Sir Thomas Roe, and I am only Tom Coryate. But I ask you this. You do not wish to offend him because otherwise you could not trade. Is this the way of a Christian?' He paused for effect. 'Is this the way of a man?'

Coryate's fury had abated and he could now, standing a little way off from it, admire his own rhetoric. Cicero himself, he thought, could not have done better. The purple had drained from Roe's face and he looked not apoplectic but pale: as though he had received several successive shocks and needed to recover his balance on a violently spinning planet.

Coryate had compared him to a Jew, an unforgivable insult; but Roe, though a martinet, was a fair man. The anger had drained out of him as it had out of Coryate and, like Coryate, he began to move outside it and to see himself as a person once more, and Coryate also as a person, not a destructive creature the devil had sent to India to harass him.

A delicate knock rocked the already unsteady door. Salbank came in, gentle, dark, but with an English, not an Indian darkness, and his voice brought Roe and Coryate back to England, the shires and the trees and rivers in them, the little animals, night smells of herbs and weasels, and the birds flying, or, if they were swans, floating down the rippled rivers, their huge white wings folded quietly at their sides.

'Tom,' Salbank said, 'and Sir Thomas, we are all English here, amidst such a galaxy, as of stars, of people and things we do not know. Were it not better to be friends than opposed? For there are so few of us here, and of the others there are so many. Forgive Tom Coryate, and let us live together as happily as we can. Sir Thomas, will you not forgive him?'

'I am willing to part in peace,' Roe said. 'But part we must. I will not suffer this man in my camp for one more day. Go, Coryate, wander as you will, plague others, but by the sweet breath of Christ, no longer plague me. But if ever you fall in need, as well you may, come to me wherever I am, and I will look after you and see that you get safely home. As it is, the court moves next week to some other place, and I must oversee that my people and I will go with it, for I must stay with Jehangir till his seal is set upon the treaty for trade.'

~

Salbank took Coryate out into the small vegetable garden behind Roe's house. Coryate examined the little plots, defined by straw, with the interest of a countryman. He crumbled the earth in his hand, sniffed it, even savoured it slowly and carefully on his tongue, as though it were a fine wine. 'Why does Roe only plant English seed here?' he inquired of Salbank. 'This is very old soil, and overused, but it would answer better if he planted Indian vegetables. He does not know it.'

Salbank stared at his friend, crouched amidst Roe's tidy plants, with amazement. Coryate's features seemed to have defined themselves in the last few months: now they were more rugged and mature than when Salbank had first met him, and his yellow beard had become mostly white, though he was not yet forty. 'Perhaps,' Coryate said, 'there is much that he does not know. People do not live only for profit. But who am I to say so? Only Tom Coryate.'

'Where will you go now?' Salbank asked. 'This is so huge a land and so unknown to us. How will you go, and where?'

'I aim for the north,' said Coryate. 'I have heard of places where the Hindus pray in their millions, where there are holy men who live naked in mountain caves, places where gods walk who are made of ice and snow, others where fire leaps from the rocks. There is no end to the wonders of this land, and I need to see them, good Edward; I need to see them all. My heart will not rest until I have seen them all.'

Then he said, powdering the red earth between fingers that were surprisingly thin and delicate, 'As for how I will go, I will travel on my own two legs, as I always have. When I was a young man at Oxford, I called myself the Odcombensien Leg-Stretcher. It was my Latinate and youthful folly. The people of my village in Somerset called me Long Strider. I think that the better name.'

Around them, in the natural confusion and heat of the country, drums built up their beat, tambourines clashed, and harsh voices sang. Pariah dogs responded from Ajmer, jackals joined in from the forest beyond. Coryate's blue eyes were dark. 'Your long strides have taken you far,' said Salbank, who had always seen in his friend some quality that amused but beyond that, awed him. 'It *is* a better name.'

14

Diary Seven

September 2002

Ajmer–Pushkar

It was past nine in the morning. I went to look for Juzer. As I stood outside his room, I heard sounds from within that alternated between slaps and moans. Now and then I heard Juzer shouting aloud. Perplexed I walked back to the dining room and told Dom about the noises I had heard.

'Poor fellow,' Dom said, shaking his head.

'Whoever could it have been?'

'Surely a servant, being suitably punished.' Dom's face was inscrutable, though his lips twitched with laughter. 'He must have made a mistake with Juzer's sandwiches at dawn.'

A few minutes later, Juzer rushed into the room. Dom asked, 'Juzer, what was all that moaning from your room?'

Juzer blushed. 'Oh that! Sir, I was beating my chest.'

'Do you have a cold?'

Juzer laughed. 'No, no sir. I was doing maatam. It's like this, we Shias do maatam during Moharram. But I was doing it now because I am observing a fast. See,' he pulled his shirt open to reveal a reddened chest.

'Why?'

'To observe grief for Imam Hussain and the sacrifices of others.'

'Doesn't it hurt?' I asked.

'To feel pain is a sort of comfort.'

'Not if you ask me,' Dom said.

I said, 'But you were shouting …'

'I was reading aloud a prayer—*Saiyedas Shohadai*—as I beat my chest.' He smiled and added, 'When we go to the dargah now you may see others doing maatam.'

Joginder scowled when he was told to go to the dargah. He slapped his forehead several times as he drove. 'I am telling you,' he said, 'it is going to be so crowded.' He stopped the car at the start of the bazaar. He staunchly refused to go any further. Resolute, he got out of the car and began to inspect the tyres.

'How far?' Dom asked.

'Far,' Juzer replied as he led the way into the lane. We walked through the crowd that needed to be parted with our hands. People jostled one another, huddled together, like the cells of a living organism. The combined smell, emanating from the mass, of sour sweat, sweet attar and fervour, nauseated me. Rows of shops on either sides sold foodstuff that amplified the pervasive smell, felt not just through the nostrils but also through the eyes and ears. A cyclist with baskets of sweets hanging from every conceivable place of his vehicle manoeuvred through the crowd. He came straight at Dom, then unable to swerve, ran into him.

'Oh fuck!' Dom spurted out angrily. 'Shit. I'm not going

any further in this fucking place. Juzer please walk me back to the car. You wait here, Sarayu, Juzer will be back.'

I looked around at the people. Most of them were men with lewd stares. 'Why don't I walk back with you?' I asked.

'Don't be silly!' Dom replied, 'I thought you wanted to go to this mosque. Juzer will be back soon.' They walked away. I noticed a group of men watching me from the other side of the street. I turned, pretended to be busy; I picked a string of transparent heads, asked the old man what it was made of. I pointed to various strings, keeping aside those I wanted to buy. Juzer returned as the bead-seller held out my purchase. I opened my bag that contained all our travel funds.

Juzer swiftly zipped it up. 'Don't. Not here in the middle of the street. Here, let me pay.' I protested. Juzer smiled. He asked the shopkeeper the price and paid forty rupees. I was touched, and thanked him profusely.

Pilgrims carrying baskets of rose and jasmine flowers, sandalwood paste, perfumes and incense rushed past us. '*Nazrana*,' Juzer said, 'these will be offered at the tomb of the saint which has been washed with rose water, anointed with sandalwood paste and perfumes, then covered with an embroidered silk cloth.' A man walked past carrying on his head a large roll of pink satin with golden trimmings 'That is a *chadar,* also an offering. If we come back in the evening we will see the qawwals outside the dargah, singing in high-pitched voices. At night, *mehfils,* religious assemblies, will also be held in a large hall. After the mehfil there will be a mass prayer for eternal peace. Then *kheer,* cooked in two large cauldrons called *degs,* will be distributed to the devotees as sanctified food.'

Not far from us, people bathed in the middle of the road

with water from a large plastic tank. Further on young children shat, and next to them young men, sweat on their faces and hands, mixed masalas on chunks of mutton that turned dark purple as they impaled them with skewers. The same colour of the meat that Dom had eaten in India Hotel. A youth rushed past, wheeling a bicycle. Straddled over its carrier was a large ovine carcass. Blood dripped from it. A drop fell on my shoe. I stood still.

Closer to the dargah, beggars sat on the ground in a row as though in a game of musical chairs. They faced one way or the other, so no one would miss seeing them. Each one had a differing number of limbs: three, two, one-and-a-half, some with one eye, others with none. The film music that played was less blatant as the display of wretchedness around me.

Just as I wondered whether to go on, I saw a procession of men who were chanting. They held up a red chadar spread out like a canopy above their heads. The three men who led the group were bleeding profusely from their faces and necks.

Bringing up the rear was a fakir with a long beard as black as night. He wore a white kurta over a bright blue checked lungi. The white cap on his head rose tall, like a chef's. Numerous strings of red beads were thrown around his neck. Hung from his left shoulder was a blue bag: Singapore Airlines. He looked at us enquiringly, then stopped in front of us. He extended an open palm, then with the other raised above our heads, blessed us in Urdu. I asked Juzer to ask him about the bleeding men.

The fakir went into rhapsodies about Allah's faithful believers and their suffering in this world. 'These men have beaten their backs with whips and knives,' he said. 'Not because of Imam Hussain. No. They made a wish. Their wishes were not granted. So it is their way of showing their sorrow.' His hand remained outstretched. Juzer dropped a ten rupee note in it. His palm stayed open. Juzer pressed another note down. Not entirely satisfied, the fakir made his way behind the group. We walked behind him.

We followed the group into the dargah. We left our shoes at the door. 'Ma'am cover your head,' Juzer said, handing me a large handkerchief. I scrutinized it for its purity. Juzer pointed out the two cauldrons in the court. They were taller than me. 'This is for the blessed kheer,' Juzer said.

The group had stopped at the tomb. Loud chants filled the air. I heard screams. Juzer led me to one side so I could see the three men in the front. They slapped their chests furiously, moaning aloud. They continued to bleed. Then with a yell, the man in the middle jumped into the air, he fell on the ground, rolled and writhed, convulsed with electric energy. His body contorted and twitched, then it bent like a bow from the waist. His hands slapped the ground, his feet went awry; he foamed from the mouth.

'Look! He's possessed by the spirit,' Juzer exclaimed.

'I think he is having a fit,' I whispered. 'Why doesn't someone help him?'

'If anyone does he will become violent,' Juzer said. Presently, I watched three men carefully pinning his hands down. Two more held his feet, then together they lifted him up and put him down, his body bent over the tombstone, his head touching it.

'Let's go,' Juzer said urgently.

~

Dom had finished three-quarters of his detective story when we reached him. 'Just when I was about to find out who did it,' he said, putting his book away. 'Did you see anything interesting?'

'Not really,' I replied nonchalantly. 'A greedy fakir, a procession of bleeding men, one having a epileptic fit, plentiful shit around, bubbling milk pudding and a bloody piece of beef.' I felt extremely resentful when he replied, glancing at his book, 'What else did you expect to see?'

We drove to Daulat Khana, the residential palace of Akbar. It was now a museum housing Rajput and Mogul armoury, miniature paintings and sculptures. It was in the middle of the city, without fate or fact, choked by tousled lanes and dust: a travesty of historical anatomy. We drove into a narrow street. A family of pigs crossed it, once this way, then that way. They were covered with mud and looked like overgrown rats. Their cosy saunter made me laugh; I started humming: *three blind mice, see how they run …* A large garbage dump stood sentry to the palace. A tractor with a cart had been abandoned near it, half full of muck.

The ochre coloured board outside the palace read:

In this Fort, Sir Thomas Roe, the accredited ambassador of King James I of England, was given the first official audience by the Emperor Jehangir on January 10th 1616 AD.

Dom stood at a distance looking at it for a long time. His head was tilted to one side, sweat soaked his shirt, only because of the heat, but his face was devoid of emotion.

I moved away. I felt like an intruder in a time-endured relationship. But when I turned I noticed he was smiling at me. 'What is it?' I asked.

'Imagine Roe with Jehangir.' Dom laughed. 'Imagine them doing business together—a restrained Englishman and a demonstrative drunk king. Roe writes in his journal that as soon he had presented a case of European wine to Jehangir, business negotiations seemed to flow as smoothly as the wine. He's quite amusing about Jehangir's court. He says Jehangir was quite a nice fellow. One night, Jehangir urgently called Roe to his court for a drink. When he reached, the guests were all drunk. Jehangir himself was dead-drunk.' Dom glanced at Juzer to ensure he was not offended.

'Roe wrote also of how everyone was constantly eyeing his crates of baggage. Jehangir was known to have a hunger for gifts and European novelties and Roe grumbles about his having to part with his own personal possessions when he didn't have any more gifts to present.'

Juzer laughed, 'And, sir, that Jehangir even told Roe he wanted an horse. Pure English one.'

Dom laughed too. 'Jehangir liked European paintings and his artists made copies of them. When he arrived, Roe gave Jehangir an English painting. Jehangir was thrilled. He showed the painting to everyone. His artist told him that he could easily copy it. So Jehangir had a wager with Roe. On the appointed day, Jehangir called Roe to look at six paintings. He said five were copies. Roe couldn't identify the original.'

Juzer walked beyond the palace. He peeped into old and broken houses, one by one. 'I'm looking for Roe's residence,' he explained. 'He must have lived not far away from Jehangir. They were quite friendly. A number of English people would have lived around here. And sir,' he rushed towards Dom, 'somewhere here this Farida woman would have been buried alive. She was involved with a eunuch. Coryate must have seen her die. Or at least heard her screams.' Juzer's eyes were shining with the thrill of it all.

Dom asked quietly, 'Juzer, where's the jharoka? I'd like to see where Coryate may have made his plea to Jehangir.' We walked through large wooden gates painted red and held by iron clasps. On a concrete slab immediately behind them was an old board—Govt. of Rajasthan. NO PARKING.

Some feet from it, a watchman bundled in a reed chair snored sonorously. Juzer tapped his shoulder. He woke up with a start, shooing Juzer away with his hand as if he was a fly. 'Don't you see the museum is closed for lunch?'

~

Juzer wanted to go to Lake Foy Sagar. 'It is fully artificial,' he said. 'In the twelfth century, there was a very big famine and the lake was built by damming the river Luni. It was named after Foy, the British engineer who built it.'

A park with a series of marble pavilions overlooked the lake. Vendors with balloons, cigarettes, pan masalas, sweets and weighing machines strolled about. Young boys with a rag, brush and polish pestered men to get their boots polished. One of them came after me. I do not think I look like a man, but he eyed my leather shoes hopefully.

'What's your name?' I asked him as he tugged at my sleeve.

'Kadam. Didi, I'll polish your shoes for only two rupees.'

'But they are polished, baba.'

'But I will shine them like stars, didi. You will be able to see your face in them.'

'Okay,' I laughed and sat down on a parapet. I gave him my shoes. 'Do mine, then these men's. But make sure they can see their faces in their shoes. They'll be shocked.'

His eyes shone. He smiled as he got down to his job, 'Three pairs for only five rupees, didi. Special price for you only. I give one rupee discount.'

'Thanks,' I said as another boy picked up Dom's shoes, left by the wall. Kadam's eyes grew intense and like a chimpanzee he pounced on his competitor. '*Chal phut*, *ja- ja* (get lost, go, go),' he shouted as he shooed him away. The other boy squatted at a distance, watching in a wistful manner.

'These are my pairs, didi,' Kadam pulled all our shoes affectionately towards him, 'only I will do them. I have given you special price.'

'How much does he earn in a day?' Dom asked.

I asked him. 'Fifty or sixty rupees.' His father, he told me, was a cobbler. He had two sisters and a small brother. All three of them went to school. But he had quit midway. He didn't like to study and his mother hit him when he failed his exams. He had only been polishing shoes for five days.

'Do you know him?' Dom pointed to the boy sitting at a distance.

'He's my cousin.'

'Then why didn't you let him polish my shoes?'

'Why should I? He doesn't share his customers with me.' He frowned. 'He was going to school. Then his father saw me earn sixty rupees each day, so he sent him along with me. Now he's not going back to school.'

'When you are older what will you do?' Juzer asked.

'I will continue polishing.' He added defiantly, 'Why? Even big men polish shoes, no?'

'Of course,' Juzer smiled. 'Do you want something?'

'What?'

'Something that you want very much ...'

'Eh?'

'Say, like these binoculars. Shirt? Pant?'

'Yes. Ice cream.' We bought him some. The other boy watched enviously, and we bought him some too.

A man with a weighing machine came to me. 'Meddem, please weigh. Correct weight. Good weight. Weight please.'

I shook my head. He insisted, 'This shows exact weight, meddem. Less than all machines.'

Dom laughed. 'Good idea,' he said, 'then you can have a large dinner without fussing about your diet.' He asked Kadam, 'Do you know which country you live in?'

'I live here.'

'Which country?'

'Ajmer.'

Juzer persisted. 'Ajmer is your city. But which country?'

'This is my country.'

Juzer said, 'Have you heard of Bharat? Of Hindustan?'

Neither name seemed to register.

Dom asked, 'India?'

Kadam shook his head.

~

On the last day in Pushkar, Dom woke up sick. 'Why don't you go with Juzer to the temples? I think I'll sleep for a bit. But pick me up before you go to Jehangir's hunting lodge or residence or whatever. Coryate may have gone there.'

He touched my arm as I turned to go, 'Please be careful with Juzer,' he said. 'I'm nervous whenever you go with him to these very Hindu places. He has no control whatever over what he says, and I'm very afraid that he will come to harm.'

Joginder drove us to a street parallel to the temple lane. As soon as we got out of the car, a man dressed in a dhoti and a short black coat stopped me. 'I will take you to the Brahma temple ma'am,' he said. His English was remarkably good. I tried to walk away from him, but he followed me. 'I will tell you all about its history,' he pestered.

Juzer stepped between him and me. 'It's okay,' he put up

a hand. 'We know where the temple is, okay. And I know all about the temple. Okay.'

The man gave Juzer a cold stare. He walked to the other side, and all the way to the temple lane. It was lined with shops selling artefacts for rituals and prayer, apart from a lot else. Vendors called out to us; there were not many people on the street. Some of them called out in English. A young boy spoke French. The man beside me kept up his historical chatter, surprising me with a sentence in French.

'The Brahma temple is an important pilgrim centre for the Hindus,' he explained. 'Lord Brahma, together with all the gods and goddesses, performed a yagya here. A lotus fell from his hands and dropped into this valley. It became a lake. The Brahma temple is built with real marble and I will show you the silver turtle on the floor.'

At the entrance to the temple, I saw a swarm of pandits looking avariciously at us. 'Let's go,' I told Juzer, remembering Dom's warning. 'I think we don't have just company, we have a crowd waiting for us.' We turned around to return.

~

The sun had begun to blaze its way across the sky. Village women fluttered along the temple street like tropical birds. They wore peacock blue and parrot green veils and swirling skirts, their necks, arms and ears bedecked in silver jewellery. I dodged cows, their horns painted, hides daubed with colour. I paused at a sidewalk stall where I had tea and *bhajjias*.

Juzer had a long conversation with a shopkeeper who sold agate idols. Juzer told him boastfully of a business he had once had in agate lamps. To my surprise and slight annoyance he explained, 'But the man I was talking to in this five star hotel got fired and my lamp deal collapsed. Had my business gone well I would have been a rich man now. And then I wouldn't have been working on this book.'

Two hours later, on our way to Jehangir's residence, we picked up Dom. He seemed better. The complex was a number of pavilions set in a flattened valley peered over by eyebrows of hills. It was like being inside a giant navel. Some of the pavilions had come apart and their stones, like bones of a carcass, were lined up in rows according to size and shape. An acrid musty smell of dry shit pervaded the air. Dom strolled around the pavilion, touching walls and columns, apparently trying with his fingers to find traces of Coryate. 'Look, look,' Juzer cried out. He pointed to a banyan tree. Sitting under it was a yogi. The dogs around him barked.

'Will he talk to us?' I asked. 'He looks ferocious.'

'I'm more afraid of the dogs,' Juzer said as we walked towards him. The yogi was dressed in a white lungi; a white cloth was wrapped around his chest. His hair was long and matted. His legs locked into one another. His eyes were shut. Dom and I leant against the platform around the tree, a safe distance away. Juzer stood in front of him, petulantly tapping his shoe on the ground. He took off his cap, replaced it, and watched the yogi. The dogs had moved away, but continued to bark at Juzer from a distance. He tapped harder.

The yogi opened his eyes, then ignoring Juzer, he tried to light a match, then several others. All these attempts were unsuccessful. With his eighth matchstick, he lit a beedi. He sucked hard at it. His eyes were bulbous and bloodshot.

'Do you live here?' Juzer enquired.

'I come from Varanasi every year to Pushkar. This is an open ground. Good breeze. Quiet. I stay here.'

'But this is an old Muslim place?'

'So it is,' the yogi bobbed his head. 'At night I can hear the spirits screaming in pain. Muslim spirits, I'm sure.' He smiled. He raised his hands to the sky. 'But this air is not Muslim. Nor is it Hindu.' He slapped his thigh. 'Your problem is, son, like all others you think you have knowledge. People are all the time looking for differences in everything, in countries, in people, in religion, old and young. But why not look at similarities? This is what keeps us together.'

Dom didn't seem to be listening. What the yogi said was similar to what Dom had told me when we had started out on our journey. He had said, 'We must notice the differences between the places and people in Coryate's time and now, but what is more important is to look for the similarities.'

The yogi continued talking about similarities. 'Islam and Hinduism are not very different,' he said. 'All the thirty-three crore gods are nothing but the rays of one Paramatma. Islam believes in one God but he is addressed by ninety-nine other names.'

'But ...' Juzer said, and the yogi raised his hand.

'It is true that Islam abhors idol worship, and does not believe in form and symbol, and this is why the Moguls destroyed so many Hindu temples. But the Kaaba of Mecca is both a form and symbol.'

Juzer interrupted, 'But ...'

The yogi put up a hand, 'Muslims offer chadar at the dargah and the Hindus offer chunnis to the goddess Shakti. Did you know,' he looked at Juzer, 'namaaz comes, from two Sanskrit words: *nama* to worship and *yaja* to unite with God. And the name of the Islamic month of Ramadan comes from the Sanskrit word Rama-dhyan. Dhyan means to meditate and Ram in Sanskrit means the one who shines in the heart.'

'But Ramadan ...' Juzer said.

The yogi added, 'Your thirty days of prayer and fasting is

similar to our mandala puja. And think of this, Friday, the holiest day for Muslims, is also the holy day for Hindus to worship the goddess Shakti.

'Not just ...'

'In India, it was the saffron colour that stood out in the greenery of the Gangetic plains ...'

'But ...'

'Whereas the Arabs chose green, as it was seen from far in the deserts. Again, in the Hindu tradition the first born of God is Brahma and his wife is Saraswati; the first born of God in Islam, is known as Abraham, a-Brahma, and his wife is Sara.'

'I know this, but ...'

'Did you know that Mecca was also a holy place for Hindus?'

'Hindus?'

'The ancient Vedic scripture mentions that Lord Vishnu's footprints are consecrated at three holy sites, namely Gaya, Shukla and Mecca.'

Juzer started to speak, but the yogi raised an admonitory hand once more. 'Listen. The pedestal at the centre of the Kaaba is octagonal. The pedestal of Brahma, the creator, is octagonal. As in Hinduism, the custom of circumambulation of the shrine is practised at the Kaaba. Is that not so?'

He sucked at the beedi, then turning to look up at Juzer, he said, 'Does it matter that I live here near a Muslim monument. This air is not Muslim. Nor is it Hindu.'

~

We left the yogi with a packet of Dom's Benson and Hedges, a lighter and, much to Juzer's chagrin, a five hundred rupee note that he demanded. 'Fifty rupees was enough, ma'am,' Juzer complained. 'He's an absolute fraud.'

We headed straight for Pushkar Lake. All along its steps and under the trees were groups of foreigners. A young man with blue eyes and long matted hair leant against a tree close to us, played on a sitar accompanying an old villager who played on a folk string instrument. Dom sat back in his chair; the cool wind from the lake blew over us. I heard Dom, his eyes shut, humming softly to himself:

> '*O western wind, when wilt thou blow,*
> *Shaking the green leaf from the tree?*
> *O gentle death, when wilt thou come?*
> *For of this life I am weary …*'

I ordered tea. Juzer walked to the ghats. White women in wisps of clothing sat on the steps. Local women floated their offerings of marigold garlands on the lake's surface, then scooped the water into their hands. Sadhus with matted dreadlocks sat frozen on the banks. The sun was less fierce; a number of village women extravagant in mirrorwork skirts and men wearing enormous pink turbans had begun to dance to the rhythm of castanets and stringed instruments. Singers wailed out folk songs, mostly about unrequited love.

I saw a number of men around Juzer. He appeared to be giving them a lecture. I walked over to where they stood. As soon as the men saw me, they rushed towards me. They had kumkum marks on their forehead; they were pandas who performed rites on the ghats. Juzer, who had walked over, laughed. Pointing to them he said, 'They were telling me about the temples: this is the Brahma temple, this is this, this and this and so on. So I told them, "I know even better, I am a professional researcher. I will tell you," I said to them. "This is this, this is this …"'

One of the pandas pounced on Juzer. In a rage he said,

'What do you mean, this-this-this? Your mullahs near the mosques don't perform rites for money. Eh?'

Juzer, unfazed, smiled as the man held him by his sleeve. 'Of course, of course, they do. Where am I denying this?' He picked his cap off his head, pointed to it, 'But see, I am a Dawoodi Bohri Muslim. Not just any other Muslim.' Juzer plucked the panda's hands from his sleeve one by one. 'And we don't beg.'

15

The Roads of Torment

Salbank walked with Coryate as he left Ajmer. Coryate was in Indian clothes. He now had no other attire. His small bundle of possessions was strapped to his back. He looked so tired and bereft after his squabble with Sir Thomas and his expulsion from the English camp that Salbank's heart went out to him. Within the camp, Salbank felt safe; but to venture alone without adequate money into this huge, incomprehensible land seemed to him madness. He said so to Coryate, several times. 'I think Sir Thomas is already sorry for his words,' he pleaded. 'Make peace with him.' But Coryate shook his head and went on, trying his best to look proud and defiant.

At the gates, Salbank embraced him, and watched as he spoke in Hindustani to a group of travellers who waited to leave for Agra. Some of them were in oxcarts, some were on foot like Coryate; they had two armed horsemen with them to protect them, and they seemed willing enough to accept the feringhee into their company. Salbank walked away, thoughtful.

Several thousand miles away, Jonson sat at the Mermaid

with a pot of hot wine, properly sugared and spiced, in his hand. Opposite him sat the priest Peter Rogers, who differed from the other customers because his skin was reddened and browned by the sun of unfamiliar lands. He was drinking his fill of the Mermaid's finest Rhenish wine. Coryate had asked Jonson to serve it to him when his letters were delivered.

'Be assured that I will see this packet sent safely to his mother,' Jonson said. 'And my thanks, good sir, that you have delivered it to me, as Tom desired. From what I read he has had many travails, and little money, but is safe in body and soul. Tell me, Master Rogers, how was he in his mind, when you last had converse? The mind is a very delicate part of our good Tom's organism, as you may have found out.'

'He has seen a few terrible things,' Rogers ventured timidly. Jonson made him nervous, not only because of his fame, but tales he had heard in London of the poet's fierce humours. 'The Indies is a place where terrible things are common. But I think, Master Ben, that he is at peace in his mind, for as I told you he lies in comfort with the English in Asmere, and when I left it, Sir Thomas Roe was to take him into his household, where he will be safe, with no man to incommode him. But he was desirous also that news of this should go to Lady Harcourt, and I do not know any Lady Harcourt. Perchance you may have the news sent to her?'

Jonson shook his huge head. 'Not I,' he declared. 'I know her not at all, except by reputation, and from what I hear of her I do not wish to know her. Get the news to her by whatever means you will, but not by me. I am astonished that Tom Coryate ever came safe and hale to India, and pleased also, for he is a man of much worth. But I would not have him vex his heart with word of Lady Harcourt and her like. I will have these screeds copied before I send them to his mother and cause them to be printed. Many in this generation and in those yet to come will read them and so know Tom Coryate's name. But he himself will not. Let him be in the Indies while he may, for he will never return.'

'What!' cried the little priest in consternation. 'Master Jonson, if you wish him no ill, how say you so? He was in full health when I left him. Many have returned safely from the Indies, as I have done; there is no reason he should not.'

'He will not return,' said the poet. 'When last I set eyes upon him, in this very house, it was written in his face.'

~

Coryate's little group came safely into Agra, and at once he sought lodgings with the two Jesuits. They were glad to see him; he rested, but also, with native friends of the priests, he improved his Hindustani. The travel to come would tax him sorely, he realized, for whichever way he went, there were long walks ahead through unknown territory. It would be as well to better his knowledge of the language while he could.

When he told them about his experiences in Ajmer, the killing of the leopard, the living death of Farida, his speech to Jeharigir and the wrath of Roe, they shook their heads.

'All around you in this country, you see the teeming forms of life,' Mario said. 'There is a surfeit of them, so even if their religion tells them to, they have small respect for life. There are too many insects, too many plants and animals, too many people. The death of an animal or a person is scant cause for grief. Also, Tomas, women are hardly thought of as human. Burying a concubine alive, as a punishment for some treachery, may not be thought of as a monstrous action, but one justifiable and politic. The Hindus and Mussalmans alike have great respect for their mothers, but riot for any other women. The wives are treated as slaves during their lives, and only their children mourn them when they die.'

'In some cultures of northern Europe,' Mateo said in his learned manner, 'a dead man used to be buried or burnt with all his possessions around him. These sometimes included his wife. It is still so here. In some parts of this land, when a man dies, he is cremated with his wife. Even though she be still alive, she is compelled to mount the pyre with his corpse, whether she be willing or not. This act is called sati.'

The priests advised him about his destinations. 'If you wish to learn more about the Hindus,' Mateo said, 'there are famous shrines that you may reach afoot, not so very far from this place.' He asked a friend who had visited these places to draw Coryate a rough map of the route. The friend was a Hindu pandit, clad in a dhoti, his head shaved except for a topknot. His brow carried marks made in ash.

The pandit said, 'Haridwar is a great seat of learning. There are many holy men and temples, and our holy river Ganga flows through it. Hrishikesh is in the foothills. There also the Ganga flows, and there also you will find temples and holy men. Farther on, higher up, at Jwalamukhi, you will reach a temple where flames leap from the earth that are not kindled by any human hand. If you see all these wonders, and talk to the pandits, you will be enlightened in the spirit.'

'I have heard of these places,' said Coryate. 'My spirit is heavy within me, for my own people turn me away.' He added inquisitively, 'What are the marks upon your brow?'

'They tell my caste,' said the Brahmin, 'which is the most important part of any man. The brow is an important part of a man's body. Here, in men of holiness, the invisible third eye is seated. And here the future of a man is inscribed forever, from birth unto death, to those who can read.'

'Would it not be a long and complicated story,' Coryate asked sardonically, 'to be written in so small a space?'

The Brahmin smiled, but refused to say any more.

~

Coryate had to walk to Delhi to link up with the pilgrim road to Haridwar; but he did so in pleasant December weather, the air cool on his face, and the paved road underfoot smooth and without potholes. He recited Latin verse aloud as he went, oblivious to the startled faces of all those who passed him by. As he had first discovered in Somerset, now far, the roll of the hexameters helped his stride.

In the soil around Delhi he found—as he had found months earlier, when he approached it from the other direction—old, broken weapons in the dirt, and the bones of men killed on this plain before he had been born. He entered the city and found a sarai. Kashmiris, pale-skinned people from the north, ran it, and specialized in a herbal tea of which he drank several cupfuls over his kebabs and unleavened bread.

After this he felt in good spirits. It was late afternoon, and he asked one of the Kashmiris which way it was to Alexander's pillar. He had conceived a fondness for it. Nobody in the sarai had ever heard of it, nor to his dismay, of Alexander, though he repeated the Indian version of the name, Iskander, several times. 'He was the greatest man ever to visit your land,' Coryate said, 'though it was many years ago.'

The Kashmiris did not seem impressed. 'That may be,' said one. 'But if you want to see old places, feringhee, go to the tomb of the saint Nizamuddin Chisti. It is only a kos away, and it may be that the old men there will know of your Iskander.' Coryate walked to the tomb at twilight and found several white-clad men seated on stone parapets. They sat around a man-made tank of sweet water, which reflected hundreds of stars as they came out from under the early winter clouds. Coryate sat down among them, not unwelcome.

At first they continued to converse among themselves, but as Coryate had found was the Indian way, hearing that he could speak Hindustani in spite of his appearance, they included him in the talk. It was about the rising price of okra.

Coryate could not contribute much to this; but later one, who appeared to be a priest, asked if he were a Christian. He admitted to this fiercely, prepared to defend his faith, at least in dialogue. But the priest said, 'It is all one to us. We are Sufis from Persia, as was the saint who lies entombed here. We are Muslims, but not Muslims as they are in this country.'

'How are you different from them?' Coryate asked.

'The Muslims here remember the wars with the giaours when they rode to Palestine. They hate the Christians, and they look on the Hindus as barbaric, and try to convert them. We are not like that. Everyone is truly equal to us, which other Mussulmans do not believe in their hearts. We believe that Allah's breath is like sweet wine that all can drink. That is why we do not differentiate between believers and unbelievers, if they are good men, and that is why our poets call Allah an innkeeper, who serves heady liquors to all who come to his tavern.'

They murmured around him as the enormous night of India enclosed them all. Coryate listened for hours and felt at peace, as he looked into the dark sky, illuminated by the moon and the stars and the scattered powders left by falling stars.

~

The north Indian scenery was now familiar to Coryate and held no messages of importance. But as he walked towards the north from Delhi, on a route he had not taken before, it seemed to him that the nature of the people, rather than the landscape, changed. Their faces became harder and more cruel, and they appeared to be physically more bulky.

The nature of the vegetables in the village street markets also seemed to change. Huge phallic radishes of a dark red colour, swollen purple onions the size of a man's testicles, were displayed on sheets of cloth, with green peppers and other vegetables. These displays showed an eye for colour and arrangement. But the women who sold them were veiled and seemed more cowed than those he had observed farther south.

'Where you go is the Hindu heartland,' Mateo had told him in Delhi. 'There you will see the religion in the rituals and in the people. The people are violent folk, who solve many of their problems by murder. But the rituals can be beautiful to see.' Coryate had already seen some when he walked through Mathura and Vrindavan.

He soon realized that most of the others on the Haridwar road were pilgrims. They wore white, though that was not unusual in this country, and many carried parcels of food and drink. Some had beads around their necks, which they clicked rhythmically as they walked. Others rattled tambourines and clashed cymbals, and many chanted nasal and repetitive hymns in praise of one god or another, naming their qualities. They formed a kind of procession on the road, and the dust raised by their footsteps towered above them.

Coryate found this beautiful to see, though he was himself part of it and could not view it from outside. He also found it beautiful when groups of pilgrims separated from the main body and sat down by the wayside for refreshment. Many men and women who looked like peasants had brought no more with them than a single piece of unleavened bread, which they ate with an onion or a green chilli; they usually stopped at a well and drank the brackish water from it. He was himself very poor, but he felt humbled by their poverty.

So the pilgrims and Coryate came to Haridwar, a town of innumerable stone and plaster temples, most of them painted in lurid colours. Through this town ran the Ganges river, great and holy: stretches of ochre water and mudbanks. In front of most temples, ghats abutted on the water: stone platforms with steps that brought pilgrims down to the Ganges to bathe. Her holy waters would cleanse them of sin.

The men came down to the river in dhotis and loincloths, the women in white sarees. They immersed themselves in it; then rising to stand waist-deep in water, they prayed. As the brief Indian twilight darkened, small lamps were lit. They flickered on the ghats and in the river like fireflies, and a sound of singing came to Coryate where he watched all this from a hill on the far side of the river. Some people carried small earthen pots that they emptied into the water. Curious, he asked someone what these pots contained. 'The ashes of some relative,' the man said. 'Ashes, and a few bits of bone.'

Towards dawn, he was exhausted. His mother's blanket from Odcombe was in his bundle. He curled up in it, and slept, smelling his mother's body and his village, till day broke.

~

He came to Rishikesh up a forest path, on either side of which birds cried out as though in pain. Though he could not see them, he heard animals move amidst the trees: deer, most likely, some of them large. He had picked up a travelling companion in the woods, an enigmatic, etiolated man, Harish, who carried a thick staff. 'There are robbers in these woods,' Harish said. 'It is well to have a weapon.' But most of the time he said nothing, and his answer to Coryate's numerous questions was always, '*Ho sakta hai*,' which meant, 'It may be'.

At noon one day, they entered Rishikesh, another town full of temples, through which the Ganges flowed. It was in the foothills of the Himalayas and notably cooler than Haridwar. 'Are there good sarais here?' Coryate inquired. Harish had apparently been here before. But he only said 'Ho sakta.'

Temples did not much engage Coryate's attention. He had visited several by now, and sometimes the priests had allowed him entry. The interiors were invariably dark and oppressive, and seldom very clean. The courtyards outside were covered in trodden mud, whether or not it had rained, and flower petals. The outer walls of the temples were covered in friezes that to him were grotesque; though often there were sculptures of men with a noble appearance and beautiful, heavy-breasted women.

It struck him that the originals of these statues might belong to another, higher race, now defunct. He had met nobody on his travels that resembled the statues. But when he propounded this theory to Harish, the reply was, 'Ho sakta.' If Harish had any reservations about travelling with a feringhee who looked like a fakir, he did not reveal them. He accepted Coryate as he accepted everything else that happened to him.

There was one exception. When they reached the town, it was noon. Coryate was hungry, and though he had often been vegetarian in India, today his body craved for meat. After they had found a sarai where they would sleep, he asked Harish if he would like to eat. 'Ho sakta,' Harish replied. They went into the bazaar, where Coryate's nose led him to a Muslim food shop. Harish did not seem overjoyed, though Coryate knew he ate meat. '*Gandha jagah hain,*' he observed. 'It's a dirty place.'

This was immediately apparent, but Coryate had been to many worse. They entered a low shack, where cauldrons simmered on charcoal fires. Harish confined himself to daal and bread, but Coryate asked for mutton stew, and it was brought: lumps of tough meat in a black sauce. Harish, for the first time in their acquaintance, became agitated. 'No, no!' he advised Coryate. 'Don't eat that. It has a bad smell.'

Coryate had already become aware of this, but he had paid for the food. His inbred parsimony would not allow him to waste it, and moreover he was a stubborn man. He ate it all, with bread, though it had a peculiar texture and taste. Harish sat beside him, shaking his head in silent reproof.

Next day, Coryate awoke with a burning pain in his stomach, and in the privy discovered that his stool was discoloured with mucus and blood. He was not unduly alarmed. This country was such that illness came on one rapidly; he had already ridden out several fevers and fluxes and never had to take to bed. When the time came to leave for Jwalamukhi, he was ready, though much more silent than usual: a relief for Harish, who was not adept at conversation.

They walked up through wild, hilly country, where they saw many peacocks. Coryate's stomach hurt very much, and he frequently had to go into the forest to empty the blood and mucus from his bowels. Though Harish could not have failed to notice, he made no remark. Coryate was grateful.

At noon they went downhill to a village of slate-roofed houses with carved wooden walls. The village seemed empty, but on the far side of it the entire population had collected around a hut. The beat of drums and the clash of cymbals arose from the front of the crowd. 'Ahh!' said Harish. 'This is a sati. Do you not wish to watch it?' Coryate indicated assent. They joined the crowd around the hut, unquestioned.

People whispered information to Harish. He passed it on to his companion. 'The dead man has already been placed in this hut, on a charpai. Soon the wife will come. She is called Mala, they say.' Priests chanted, and now a group of white-clad men appeared; a buxom, pretty woman of about thirty was also with them. She wore a white saree and was laden with jewellery. But she had a vacant, sleepy look, as though she did not know what was happening. 'They may have given her opium to dull the pain of the fire,' said Harish, 'so that she does not resist and cause a scandal. Ho sakta.'

A group of men and women now gathered around Mala. She touched the feet of the men and embraced the women. 'Her relatives,' Harish explained. 'They are saying goodbye to her.' The white-clad men took her hands and led her towards the hut. It was made of wood and straw, and looked highly inflammable. Some trace of consciousness returned to Mala's face. Though she made no sound, she tried to pull away from the men holding her wrists, but feebly, as though she knew it was useless. Then she started to moan incoherent words and suddenly a river of tears ran down her cheeks.

With gold rings attached to her ears and nostrils, gold on her neck and arms and round her ankles, she looked like a gaudy doll. 'Her husband was a rich man, they say,' Harish murmured to Coryate. 'Ho sakta. Look at all that gold! It will melt in the fire, but its value will remain. Afterwards the priests will take it all, for that is their perquisite.'

Mala was forced into the hut. The white-clad men went with her. 'Now they will have to tie her to the bed with her husband.' She had started to scream like a child: loud, piercing shrieks, mingled with incoherent cries and sobs. The villagers whispered angrily together. 'They say that this is shameful behaviour. She has dishonoured her entire family.'

Flames leapt up inside the hut. At once the villagers uttered wails of grief, or wept noisily, and then the violent drumbeats and strident shrieks of flutes drowned out the shrieks of Mala from inside. It burned with loud crackling and popping sounds, as of fat in a hot pan, and above the stench of burning combustibles, a smell like roasted pork filled the air. 'She's dead by now,' said Harish comfortably.

The villagers were hospitable and invited them to a celebratory feast. Harish accepted, but Coryate refused. 'Perhaps we shall meet in Jwalamukhi,' he said to Harish.

'Ho sakta,' Harish replied, but without conviction.

~

Coryate went on into the hill country. In spite of the blue sky and the sunlight, it was quite cold. The architecture of the villages with their slate roofs and wooden walls and floors was completely different from that in the plains. The appearance of the people had changed also. The men wore caps, long woollen tunics and trousers, and the women similar tunics and long skirts. They were cheerful and friendly and greeted Coryate as they passed him on the road, either on foot or on muleback.

But they were also inquisitive and asked many questions, and Coryate felt that they had never seen a European before. With so many adventurers afoot in the plains, this surprised him. He was perhaps the first white man to have come into this country, and he felt privileged.

They were Hindus and spoke Hindustani, but had a

dialect of their own that he could not follow. They laughed more than the people of the plains and gladly directed him to Jwalamukhi, which they all knew and revered. One of them eventually led him there. The man, Hari, stopped in his village, and his wife fed Coryate unleavened bread and daal, and pickled porcupine. It was good but sat badly in his belly.

Over the meal, Hari said, 'Do you know how Jwalamukhi came to be? The goddess Parvati was once cut into pieces. Bits of her body fell all over these hills, but her tongue fell in Jwalamukhi, and fire leapt from the earth, many tongues of fire. So the king built a temple there, over where the fire leaps from the rock, and it will stand forever. We all go there to worship, and pilgrims too, from distant places. The Emperor Akbar came here once. He made a canal on the hill behind the temple, so that the water would quench the flames. But it did not. Then he gave a golden roof to the temple, but by Parvati's power it was turned into base metal.'

Coryate asked what became of the dissected goddess.

'She is a goddess, so none can kill her. She returned.'

~

Coryate lay in Hari's house that night. His host was a farmer, who cultivated wheat and barley in the fields beyond the village. He seemed comfortably off, and his wife, Priya, offered Coryate sweetened buttermilk for his breakfast. He had complained of his turbulent belly and she made him a herbal decoction, saying her mother had shown her how to make it.

'Women learn much from their mothers,' said Coryate, 'and so do men.' It was seldom in India that he could have speech with a woman, but these hill people seemed less hidebound by tradition than those who lived in the plains. He took the opportunity to talk of Gertrude, and Priya listened patiently and smiled, as he rambled on about her virtues.

When it was light, Hari took him to his field. On a slight elevation a mile or two away, he pointed out a white temple. 'Jwalamukhi,' he said. 'We shall go there presently, after I have attended to a few matters here.' About an hour later, they set out. It was not a long walk, and they arrived at the small village that had formed around the temple. Some of the temple attendants lived there, but it existed because of the pilgrim trade and most of the shops catered for them.

The temple itself was not large, austere in its construction, and from vents in the floor, odourless orange flames spurted out. Hari introduced him to an elderly priest. 'No man ever kindled these flames,' he said. 'These are sacred fires from Parvati. No man has ever fed them. They have fed themselves for centuries, and burn without cease.'

The priest's face was brown and wrinkled, his head shaved but for his Brahmin topknot. He wore a dhoti and a sacred thread, and was tall, a man of presence. He told Coryate that a record had been kept of all the visitors who had come here since the temple was built 'a thousand years ago.' As a favour, he brought out some ancient palm leaf scrolls covered with faded entries made in Sanskrit. Coryate could not read them, but he was impressed by their obvious antiquity.

'Many kings have come to worship here,' the priest said. 'For hundreds of years they have come here, from every part of Hindustan. Their names are all entered upon these scrolls.'

He seemed interested in Coryate, and asked him several questions about his religion and his country. 'You are the first white man I have ever set eyes on,' he declared. 'I desire more words with you.' Hari went back to his fields, but Coryate sat for most of the day with the priest, answered many questions about England and its customs, and asked some himself.

'If you like to visit our temples,' the old man said, 'you should go to Kashi, our most holy city, which some call Benaras. There are many temples there. Afterwards, travel to Allahabad, where in a little while there will be a great gathering of holy men and sadhus. That, you should see. If you travel in these lands, you will see much that will enlighten you.'

'You seem to me a good man,' said Coryate, whose stomach hurt more than ever, and he felt simultaneously an intense wish to relieve himself and an inability to do so. He wanted to go back to Hari's house and rest, but he felt that if he left, he might lose information that he badly wanted. 'Others of your faith whom I have met on my way seem to me good men. How then do you have these varnas, which elevate some people to a stature greater than kings and degrade others to less than the stature of animals?' The priest stared.

'Why do you ask me this? This is a very old country. The temples and towns, the villages, the rocks and the rivers, all are very old. When we say that some are superior men and some are lower than beasts, it is for a reason. It was decreed so by the creator Brahma, at the time when Time began.'

He raised a hand. 'I cannot tell you more. This is a very old country, and our laws were made at the time that it was very young. We cannot change them or question them. This is a very old country. So the faith we follow is also very old.'

~

Coryate trod the long road to Agra with a burning belly and a squirting sphincter. He did not try and find travelling companions, for he was ashamed to display his physical weakness before others. But he was still the Long Strider, and his feet took him onward, even while his belly betrayed him.

Even so, he walked more slowly than before and made more halts. He had also become reluctant to enter villages. One of the first he paused at on the road was a village he recollected. He had passed through it on his way to the hills. It lay amidst green fields by a river and had seemed prosperous. This time many of the inhabitants had red eyes and looked haggard. A man at a food stall told him that several people had fallen ill and some had died of a mysterious sickness.

A large rat scuttled out from under the stall. Coryate shied from it in disgusted surprise. Rats were rarely seen in the full day. It was then that he realized that he could see many dead rats strewn about the ground in this bazaar. He had little medical knowledge, but he knew that the dying of rats was connected with the coming of the dreaded plague. Terror filled him, and he made all haste to leave the place.

Further on, he came to a village where the people had raised a barricade of thorn bushes round the perimeter. One passage had been left open for entry and exit, but armed men guarded it. 'Go on your way,' they said. 'No stranger may enter. The sickness has come to many villages around us.' So Coryate steered a course around the villages he came to. This made the road longer and cut him off from proper food. For villagers often fed him; else, for a few coppers, he could buy victuals from them. He could not eat much anyway now, what with the knot of pain in his bowels and his increased debility. So he ate fruit from the trees along the road, and this made the flux in his belly worse every day.

When Coryate limped into Agra, he went directly to the Jesuits, who were horrified by his condition. They put him to bed and fed him broth, boiled food and whatever medicine they had at hand. He had a strong, resilient body, and slowly started to recuperate. He told the priests that he planned to walk to Kashi and Allahabad. Mateo threw up his hands.

'Tomas, you are not yet a well man,' he said. 'Stay here with us till you are better, and go back to the English, to Sir Roe. The English will not refuse a countryman in such straits. They will care for you, and mayhap send you home on a ship.'

'I shall never return to the English,' said Coryate. 'I came here on my two legs, and I will go home in that fashion.'

'Oh, Tomas!' cried Mateo, and once more threw up his hands, but this time in despair.

16

Diary Eight

October 2002

Haridwar–Rishikesh–Jwalamukhi

'Will you help me pack,' Dom said, his voice weary. We were leaving Pushkar; we had a ten-hour drive ahead of us to Delhi. It was 8 a.m. I checked my bathroom, stuffed my toiletries into a bag, then fastening my hair with a cloth band I went to Dom's room. The door was open. He was sitting on the bed facing it, his eyes on his shoes. He looked not sleepy but sleepless and worn out.

'Did you not sleep well?' I asked impassively, disguising my concern. I pressed crumpled shirts into the suitcase; also slippers and the leather pouch of medicines.

'It's my stomach,' Dom patted his abdomen with two fingers in some sort of delicate ballet sequence. 'I haven't slept the whole night. I took five Imodiums.'

'Five!' I walked into the bathroom. His new pair of pyjamas, fully drenched lay on the floor. 'What, did you bathe in your pyjamas?'

He looked uncomfortable. 'It's only that,' he hesitated,

'they seem to be covered in blood.' He added hastily, 'I washed them, but now they are too wet to pack.'

The thought of blood made me feel sick with worry. I tried not to show my anxiety. 'Dom, we can take a flight from Jodhpur to Mumbai,' I said with all the calm I could muster.

'I am not going to die,' Dom laughed. 'Not yet anyway. It's only my stomach. Let's go to Delhi.'

~

I led Dom to the car; his legs were shaky. I helped him into his seat. I hurried off to settle the bill and organize the luggage to be brought down. The bellboy who had gone to check our minibars—which was stocked with bottles of mineral water and aerated drinks, but not alcohol as it was not permitted in Pushkar—returned, 'No dreenks,' he told the cashier sullenly, 'no cheeps, no peeenuts, no biscoots even.' The cashier said to me. 'No charge.'

I walked back to the car, settled in my seat. Juzer was not down yet. In my anxiety I had forgotten about him. Juzer arrived with his luggage. He got into the front seat. His shirt was disheveled as though he had gotten ready in a hurry; his eyes were red. 'Sorry, sir, sorry ma'am,' he said rubbing his eyes. 'I went to sleep very late. I was watching too many movies on HBO.'

Just as we were ready to move, a bellboy came running to Juzer. 'Sir, sir, minibar bill. You have to pay in cash.'

'What minibar?'

'You've had two packets cheeps, one packet peeenut, and two packets biscoots.'

'What do you think I was going to eat then?' Juzer screamed at him. I had never seen him so angry. 'I said clearly to leave four bread slices, jam, butter and milk last night outside my room. There was only bread. No jam. No butter. And you stupid buggers, you put hot milk in a flask. It was curdled by four in the morning. What was I to eat? Eh?' he said. 'And breakfast is included with the room, no?' The bellboy said, 'Breakfast is. But sir, minibar is not. Minibar pay in cash.' Juzer threw the money at the poor bellboy.

Joginder started the car. 'Meddem, after Jodhpur I am taking Jaipur-Delhi highway,' he said peering at Juzer, 'no other road. Okay?' Juzer was muttering. I didn't know whether he was addressing Joginder, the baffled bellboy or Allah.

~

'What I need is a large Teacher's,' Dom said as we entered Delhi. It was little after seven in the evening and we were in the midst of a traffic jam. Juzer had started to pray.

'What about a doctor? I think ...'

'No. I am all right.'

'But we have to go to Haridwar tomorrow.'

Perhaps the Teacher's did the trick. Dom looked better the next morning. Coming out of Delhi, Dom remarked that the faces of people kept changing. 'It must be because of the migrant population.' But once we were across the Uttar Pradesh border, he said, they looked sullen and violent. 'I wonder if Coryate noticed this.'

We passed fields of sugarcane, wheat and mango orchards. 'But these would have been wooded and full of wild animals in Coryate's time, wouldn't it?' Dom asked Juzer as though he would have known about it. Juzer nodded as if he did. Large pools of water on either side of the road were covered with green slime; buffaloes waded in it, and as though choreographed, white egrets perched on their backs. A young buffalo clambered out of the water. 'Look,' Juzer said pointing to the confused animal that didn't know in which direction to proceed, 'a green buffalo.' He threw back his head and laughed; Joginder gave him a curious look. A family of white egrets flapped their wings and flew into the sky, a series of shapely alphabets strung in the wind.

Fruits and vegetables: red radishes, sweet potatoes, watermelons, oranges, grapefruit were arranged on carts here and there along the road for sale. Some of them were elaborately displayed with a rustic eye for colour and pattern. Along villages, pyramids of straw marked the road like totems. Joginder told me they were used to store dried cowdung cakes. Beyond in the fields, I could see women toiling, sweaty under their clothes, their faces shrivelled in the sun.

When we arrived at the hotel in Haridwar, the manager was in the lobby to welcome us. It was a quarter to four. He enquired courteously about our journey then offered us a welcome drink.

'I would love that,' Dom was the first to speak.

Sir, what will you have? Tea, coffee, lassi, lime? Coke?

'Is there anything harder than those?'

The manager frowned. 'No, no, sir. In Haridwar, no non-veg, no whisky-shiskey.' Dom looked crestfallen. The manager moved to my side, 'But if sir has to have it for medical reasons, okay, I can send the bellboy to fetch a bottle from outside Haridwar. There are many many shops on the way here. But he will have to go in your car. Okay? What does sir want? Peter Scot, MacDowell ...'

'Teacher's.'

'No. Teacher's not there. Only Peter Scot, MacDowell's ...' We settled for MacDowell's. Half an hour later the bellboy came with a bottle of Peter Scot. 'This only,' he said. Dom poured out his revitalizing drink, then we drove to Hari-ki-Pauri to see the evening aarti.

We parked in a large parking area that, some time ago, must have been the riverbed. A variety of vehicles from huge buses to two wheelers filled it. On the other end, close to where we had stopped, the ground was empty of vehicles, but strewn with piles of shit.

The main ghat, Hari-ki-Pauri, that literally means the footsteps of God, is supposed to be the precise spot where the Ganges leaves the mountains and enters the plains. Consequently the river's power to wash away sins at this spot is unmatched and endorsed by a footprint of Lord Vishnu left on a stone.

We stood on a terrace built over the ghat so we could get a good view. People were everywhere: near the temples, on the podium, steps, on man-built islands; most of them were in the water with all their clothes on. Some of the men had taken off their shirts. Older women in the water held on to chains that were fixed to the steps. Except for a few who knew the rituals that were required to be done, most of the others merely bobbed up and down in the water, splashed water on their friends and families, threw fistfuls of coins into the river and generally made immense noise. Juzer pointed out to two old women near the temple below where we stood; they had taken off their sarees, blouses and brassieres and with their petticoats tucked between their legs they stepped into the water, their breasts bobbling about. Juzer watched them, until his attention was captured by a group of Japanese women. I noticed Juzer take out his binoculars. 'You want to see?' Juzer asked Dom who had lit a cigarette and was gazing up at the early stars. 'Chinese women, sir,' he said.

'Japanese,' I corrected him.

'How can you tell?'

I said, 'The colour of their skin is slightly different.'

'Japanese or Chinese,' Dom said, 'you can't use that to ogle women.' Juzer turned around. The Japanese women had taken off their clothes and were in swimming costumes. Juzer focused his binoculars on them as they jumped into the water.

'They are having a great time,' Juzer said; envy tinged his voice. 'Hindu religion seems to be fun. Not like our Islam. If any of these people ever went to Haj they would die. It's so terrible.'

A man selling fake moustaches and beards approached Juzer. He displayed his ware on his own face. 'Arre baba,' Juzer stroked his beard, 'I have my own. So good it is. See.' Another man came to him with dark glasses. 'Go, go. What do we need these for, soon it will be dark. Now go.'

Dom said, 'I think I'll go.' Juzer escorted him to the car. A pujari came to me, pestered me to do the rituals to purify my sins. A woman insisted that I buy a jerry can from her to fill it up with the Ganges water to take home. I turned to look at the crowd. I saw a man standing still in the water. But now and then, he raised his leg and retrieved something from between his toes. It seemed to me like a coin. Not far from him a man scooped water into his palms, lifted them to his mouth, then with his finger he began to clean his teeth. He took the water into his throat, looked up, gargled, then spat the water out.

Closer to me, I saw a man scrubbing his body furiously with a bar of soap. The stream of froth made its way to an old woman who, with her eyes shut, was praying. The foam perambulated around her then dissolved into the holy water as she scooped handfuls of it to wet her hair, then drank it.

I looked away at a group of women nearer the cluster of

temples. They let sail leaves shaped like boats, flowers held in them and lighted candles. Soon the river sparkled with these lights matching the stars above. The bells pealed. The chanting in the temples started.

I woke up at sunrise next morning to the sounds of a thousand bells. It was 5.30. I dressed hastily and went down; I heard chanting of mantras. 'It is the morning aarti,' the bellboy told me, 'you must go.' I woke up Joginder who was fast asleep. Instead of being displeased, he seemed glad to take me.

We drove past the shit ground, which was heavily populated. I hurried up to the terrace where we had stood the previous night. The Ganges appeared self-cleansed, calmer, the people in it tranquil and more pious than those yesterday. People formed queues in front of temples and yogis and sadhus sat on steps close to the water.

A man in khaki uniform walked up to me; he thrust a coupon book under my nose. 'Money please, for the upkeep of Mother Ganges, and poor people.' I said sorry, turned away.

A few minutes later, I went up to him to ask where I could leave my shoes. He asked if I was a tourist, and seemed delighted when I said I was writing a book. Then he became helpful. He pointed to a counter with the notice—'Free.' 'But they will charge when you go to fetch your shoes,' he added. He pointed to another stall. 'That is where ladies leave their clothes. That is also free. But the women attendants there will refuse to give back the clothes unless the ladies pay them ten rupees.'

He pointed to a woman smearing red kumkum on other women's foreheads, 'She will also charge. And the pandas who perform pujas anyway charge a lot. The pujaris in the temples get good money from the trust, but what about the others? They get paid very little by the trust, and there is no guarantee, so they have to take money from the people.'

He told me his name was Rajkumar Goswami. He worked for a private trust on a commission basis; he collected donations from people.

'Will you have tea, meddem?'

He took me through sidelanes and shops into a tea stall roofed with sackcloth. Ten others were sitting in it on benches, almost all of them in khaki uniform. Rajkumar ordered special tea for me, 'with cardamom,' he said, 'for our liberator,' he slapped his neighbour's thigh. 'She has come from Mumbai, she is going to write about our plight. Then the government will know how much we suffer and save us.'

As I sipped tea that tasted like milk pudding, Rajkumar said, 'There are no factories here, so where do common people like us find work. There are road construction jobs, but the police drive us away because they know who we are. At times of festivals, some of us put up stalls in the open grounds to sell cassettes, pictures of film stars and gods, clothes, food, but now some minister's relatives have taken over and converted the grounds into a parking lot. They make all the money.

'It is a mafia. We belong to a private trust, we make forty per cent commission, but the trust makes us pay the ten per cent government tax; they don't pay out of the sixty per cent that we give them. In twenty years, meddem, we are where we were before. There are people amidst us who are BAs and MAs but no job.'

Another man said, 'People think this is a religious place. There is no religion left here. It has become a picnic spot. They say liquor and non-veg is banned but liquor stalls are there on all the roads to Haridwar; also non-veg shops. And in cinema houses, tickets are sold in black. This is a place of lies and cheating.' He slapped his forehead. 'And have you seen those young men, they stand in the river and sneakily pick up coins that people have thrown into the river. See, they steal from Mother Ganges even. *Chi-chi-chi.* If God went looking for sinners, he will find maximum here in Haridwar.'

Rajkumar said, 'All those people who come from cities in air-conditioned cars, they stay here in air-conditioned rooms, sleep on comfortable beds, they donate large sums of money but only to convert their black money into white. That is a big racket here. Through the day there will be announcements, "Please don't brush your teeth in the Ganges, don't use oil in your hair, shampoo or soap." But people don't listen; they pollute our holy river.

'And the government boasts that they are going to make Haridwar like Paris and Japan. They are trying to relocate the flower sellers three kilometres away. They will have to take a rickshaw to the river, which will cost them so many rupees. How will they sell flowers?'

The man with the dark glasses said, 'The Japanese have opened an eye hospital here. They say operation is free. It is. I got my eyes operated there. But they charged me thousand rupees for lenses. In any other shop, it costs only twenty-five rupees. Even foreign people who come here become cheats.'

'Where the fuck have you been?' Dom asked when I arrived back at the hotel. Juzer and he were ready and waiting in the lobby. 'I rang your room, knocked at the door, I was so worried.'

I laughed. 'I thought of running away from the two of you,' I said.

On our way out of Haridwar, we passed an entire village whose huts that faced the road had been turned into shops:

Chicken Point, Chicken Palace, Whisky Paradise, Mutton Palace, Pork Heaven, and so on. Juzer said, 'Last night I didn't eat at the hotel; it has only vegetarian food. So I went out. A man on the street seeing I am a Muslim took me to a restaurant that served meat and all that. He was a Muslim too. You get meat, whisky, everything in Haridwar. I had mutton kadhai. It was very nice. I even took down the recipe. I must try to make it in my canteen.'

We drove along the Ganges to Rishikesh. We stood at a ghat and looked across the river at the row of temples; we were on the wrong side. 'Juzer, why did you insist we must come here?' Dom asked. 'There is nothing to see except the river, the temples, and the same people doing the same thing over and over again.'

We drove back to Haridwar.

Coming out of Haridwar the next morning, I saw the entire wall of a hut facing the road painted with the sign: SPY Massage Cream. Manufactured in Haridwar. KEEP IT UP LOVERS.

The drive back to Delhi was swift.

~

'If you want to go to Jwalamukhi, then you must stay at Judge's Court in Pragpur,' a friend in Delhi told me. 'It is quaint but a comfortable little lodge and Pragpur is a fascinating village. And it's only half an hour from Jwalamukhi.'

Joginder informed me that it would take nearly twelve hours from Delhi to Pragpur. 'We better leave at six in the morning.' We didn't. By the time we reached Chandigarh it was well past 2 p.m. We decided to stop for lunch.

It was dusk when we reached Pragpur and drove into the gravelled driveway of Judge's Court. It was a delightful country manor built for a judge, Justice Sir Jai Lai, in the Indo-European style. The sky was studded with stars but where we had stopped under an awesome tree it was fairly dark. I could make out a swarm of mosquitoes, their translucent wings reflecting the porch lights. Dom opened his door and a humungous dog with skin black and shiny as a panther's leapt at him. It licked his face and neck, pawed at his hands and chest, gasped and drooled in ecstasy.

'Tobby, down, down Tobby,' the watchman shouted. As I opened my door, a giant white Labrador jumped in. 'Tiger, down, down.'

The dogs were overjoyed as we got out of the car and displayed their feelings lavishly. Juzer refused to get out until the dogs had been led away. 'Surprising,' Dom whispered, 'I would have thought he would love dogs. He's a kind person. I can't understand ...'

'I can,' I said. I had been bitten by a mad dog as a schoolgirl. I was afraid of dogs for a long time. 'Perhaps a dog bit him ...'

'If one did, it must have been a brave one.'

The next morning when I came down, Tobby was waiting for me with a rubber ball. He dropped the ball at my feet, tugged at my sleeve. As we reached the lawn, Juzer strolled into the veranda. I threw the ball, but Tobby ignored it. Instead he charged across to welcome the new player. Juzer yelled and locked himself inside the drawing room.

After Pandey, the chief bearer, had been summoned and Juzer had given him strict instructions, Tobby, and even Tiger who had been quietly sleeping all this time, were led into the servant's quarters and locked in it. I could hear a distant howl and scratching against the door. Juzer read my face, which was etched with discontent. 'It's like this ma'am. If the dog's saliva falls on my skin I will have to clean that part of my body seven times. Not just baths, I have to say a lot of prayers also. Dogs are the lowliest of creatures in our religion.'

Pandey who overheard him said, 'Sahib, dogs are far better than humans, okay? Look how Hindus and Muslims fight. They are worse than dogs. I have brought up Tobby and Tiger from the time they were this little.' He indicated a height four inches from the floor. 'They will not harm an ant even.'

'Sir, good morning. Good morning to you, meddem.' A stout old man in a flamboyant striped shirt and flared trousers bowed up and down like an automated see-saw. When he was upright, I noticed he wore three silver rings on one hand and three gold ones on the other. The smile on his face was runny, in that it indicated a persistent enthusiasm to please, something that made me suspicious and wary. He was Mr Kapoor, the local guide. Pandey had informed me when he brought me my cup of tea. The proprietor, Vijay Lai, had explicitly asked Mr Kapoor to take us around the village.

'Very good morning to you, Dom-Morea sir,' Mr Kapoor said as Dom joined us. He bowed lower; his smile turned runnier. Presumably Mr Lai had told him how famous Dom was. 'Especially for you, sir, I make programme for the morning,' he said. He pressed the index finger to the thumb, held them to his nose like some Mogul prince, 'Prag in Sanskrit means pollen. In springtime Pragpur is afire with blossoms smelling very delicious.'

His voice was gravelly, his gestures crafty. 'See, Pragpur is a blessed place, very calm and quiet; it receives all the positive energy for thousands of years from surrounding Shakti temples. You will also get advantage of this positive energy. Yes. Now Pragpur is declared first heritage village in India and fourth heritage village in the world.'

He clapped his hands, then rubbed them together. 'So I see

you not have breakfast yet. So I also have breakfast with you. Then I show you different-different kinds of trees growing here. Mango, lychee, plum, persimmon, citrus and exotic trees like camphor, clove and cardamom. Then I show you village houses and big water tank. Then I take you to my house. Then lunch. My good wife is cooking lunch for me. But to save precious time, it's better to have it with you here, if you do not mind. I am a guide but I am not employed by Judge's Court, see, but this caretaker Badrinath Pandey, he doesn't like it if I eat with guests. So you must inform from first only that I will eat with you. I will eat anything prepared; no fuss, mutton, chicken, but no wine. Wine I take only in the evening. Some guests insist you know. So I take one-two pegs to keep them happy. I tell them lots of stories. They like it very much.'

Dom said, 'I am not very interested in trees and fruits or stories. What I want to see are the different routes by land and by river that lead to Jwalamukhi.'

'Very simple. There is only one route to the temple. By land only. Why you want to go by river? I will make all arrangement.'

Dom looked up at the ceiling, gave a loud snort of impatience. Juzer told Kapoor about Thomas Coryate and the specific purpose of our visit.

'I will tell you truth. Nothing but the truth,' Kapoor slapped his chest twice. 'I am a certified guide and I can show you my license. I will not tell lies even to earn money. People are so happy with me they want to pay me from their hearts, in cash. My duty is to serve people. If I know the route, it is my duty to show you. After lunch, I will take you to old-old people who will tell you.'

In the meantime, Juzer and I trudged behind Kapoor

through narrow cobbled lanes. He pointed to trees, tore off bits of their bark or plucked their leaves or flowers for me to sniff at. He showed us brick houses with metal grilles and wooden and stone arabesques. He showed us the water tank. He took us to his three-room house that was being painted by his two daughters, one as fair as almonds, and the other as brown as freshly baked bread. We met his wife who was, he added with pride, his second.

'But she is a tribal woman. When I married her she was used to eating all kinds of non-veg and daily drinking local whisky. Now no drinks and only vegetables. And that one,' he pointed to the darker girl, 'is really her daughter.'

After lunch we went route-hunting. When we were atop a plateau, Kapoor pointed out three possible land routes that Coryate could have taken before he crossed the river. 'In that direction is the Beas River.'

'Do you not think he would have come straight from Haridwar and Rishikesh?' Dom asked.

Kapoor shook his head furiously, slapped his cheeks with both his hands. 'Dom-Morea sir, how he could? There were too many dacoits in the forests. So your English friend Tom-Corea must have gone back to Delhi, then walked to Hoshiarpur, then to Jwalamukhi. Just the same way you have come. He must have come with a group of pilgrims. He must have walked some bit, then travelled by a cart or on some animal like the local ass.' He laughed. 'Imagine big English fellow on local ass.'

Dom said, 'He was a dwarf really.'

'Ah! But English dwarf is bigger than Indian man. Yes. And if Tom-Corea reached Jwalamukhi temple then I am certain the pandas there have his name in their records. They have old-old records from Akbar's time even.'

'But how would he have crossed the river?'

'No problem for that. There were befello and cow hides. They used to be puffed up like big balloons. Then they hold them and go swimming across. Simple. But only Muslims and Christians. Not Hindus. No baba!' He slapped his cheeks again. 'They not use sacred cow skin. They use goat or ass hides.'

I asked, 'How did they blow air into them?'

'Sister, I don't want to tell lies. I don't know how they filled it with air. But we can find out. It is my duty to serve.'

'And the thieves, did they not attack the villages?'

'Yes. They come. There were only two kinds of people who come. Pilgrims or thieves. So when thieves come, villagers beat drums as signal so that the people in the next village know. In some villages, they have deep holes in the sandstone hill. They put all their money and grains in them. Sometimes they hide their daughters and women even. Some of these holes are still there.'

'What about food? Where did the pilgrims eat? Where would Coryate have eaten?'

'It is like this. The pilgrims carry their rations on mules and carts. So on the way, they share food with Tom-Corea. People here are very hospitable. In the villages, when the pilgrims come during festival time, it is very much like kitty-party! All the people bring food to one house, what it is called—potsluck. They put on the floor all the vessels of food. Everyone eat. Tom-Corea also eat from booffey on floor.'

Lunch at Judge's Court was served under a tree in the front lawn. Juzer wedged himself between the trunk of the tree and the table, looking disgustedly at Tobby who was chasing a bumblebee. Tiger was fast asleep. Pandey offered Juzer the plate of crunchy fried chicken garnished with rounds of carrot and radish. Juzer looked at the dish. 'This is halaal?'

Pandey laughed, 'Pure jhatka.' He drummed his chest. 'We from Kangra Valley don't fuss. We are used to dacoits who cut off men's necks even in one jhatka. Take, it is very tender chicken. Fresh.' Juzer reached out to the chappatis, dal and potato curry laid out on the table. Kapoor clicked his tongue. 'This being Kangra chicken. Tasty. How refuse?' He helped himself.

After lunch, we went with Kapoor to see old temples that he was certain Tom-Corea would have seen. We stopped by a snake temple that consisted of a platform fixed with small idols of men and women on horses or possibly mules, and snakeheads. A heap of salt lay beside the platform. Guarding it was the caretaker: a young delirious man. Dom appeared to be more interested in him than the gods. The caretaker abused Kapoor who shouted back at him. 'He's mad,' he said turning a finger on his temple. Dom asked Kapoor about the heap of salt. Kapoor shook his head, 'I will not tell lies.' He asked the madman. 'He says it is part of the ritual. People come here to pray and leave heaps of salt. As the salt melts the snake poison in the body becoming less and less.'

The Dada Siba temple of Krishna and Radha was very old; its walls and ceiling were beautifully painted in the Kangra miniature style. Kapoor told the pujari about our quest and added self-importantly that he was helping the learned sir. He provided the pujari our names and that of our English hero. The pujari offered prayers on my behalf and to my surprise also on behalf of Dom, Juzer and Tom-Corea. He gave us prasad of sugared gram flour balls.

'What should I do with these?' Dom asked. I ate it. Following my example, Dom ate his portion. But Juzer rolled the balls in his palm, giving them a suspicious look as though he would be turned immediately into a Hindu if he ate them. He held the prasad in a tight fist. He gave some of it to Joginder who touched it to his eyes and ate it. Juzer offered the remainder of the prasad to Raju, a silversmith whose shop Kapoor took us to next. Raju was his nephew.

Kapoor talked to him about old pilgrim routes. Dom wanted to know about the kind of jewellery women would have worn in Coryate's time. He didn't know about either. But he said, 'Also men wore earrings.'

Kapoor stretched his earlobe, bent towards Dom, 'See, that hole? When I was a boy I wear earrings also.'

Juzer said, 'Jehangir did too. He was drinking too much and was very sick. So he takes an oath. That if he gets better he would wear earrings like the Chisti's followers. Within twenty-one days he became well. So he got his ears pierced and put on pearl earrings. It became very fashionable for men to wear earrings after that.'

Meanwhile Kapoor entered into a long and interesting debate with Raju about a boy from the next village who would make a good groom for his daughter. 'But they are asking too much dowry,' Raju said. 'And the boy is not a graduate like he says he is. He is an ordinary cloth merchant only.'

Kapoor looked tired and anxious. 'I have to marry away my second daughter. My older daughter is well married in the next village. She was here a week ago only. She brought me my favourite pickle. Of porcupine.'

'Porcupine!' I was astonished.

'I'd love to taste it,' Dom said.

'I'll give you a small bottle, Dom-Morea sir. Porcupine pickle is old tradition of Kangra peoples. Your friend Tom-

Corea also have it, I think. Come, come, now we must go to another temple,' Kapoor said. 'Chano Siddh is the saint of stolen goods. People go to his temple to offer prayers when their things are stolen. They offer donations of hen, goat, jackal. The pujari family gives them away as prasad. Sometimes even sells them off.'

There was not a single devotee in the temple; it demonstrated the honesty of, the local people. The temple contained a platform mounted with small idols of a man on an elephant flanked on either side by a red man and a black man. Kapoor called out to someone. 'He belongs to the pujari family who has looked after this temple for so many years. But he wants to become a politician. Every year, he sends in his own nomination. He tells us all to vote for him. We say yes-yes. He is mad,' Kapoor turned a finger on his temple. 'We call him politician-saab.'

Juzer said, 'Perhaps Coryate came here to complain about the money that was stolen from him.'

The politician-saab sat with us on a mat and told us a story about the saint. He spoke in the musical local dialect. 'But now I think the temple is losing its power,' he confided in Kapoor. 'Last week, I left my slippers outside the temple and they were stolen. Not found them yet.'

Kapoor patted the old man's shoulder. 'You will find, you will find. Bhaiyya, Diwali is coming soon,' he said, 'my elder daughter and her husband will be coming. I am also having some other guests at that time. There is so much expenses during Diwali. It would be a great help if you can arrange some hens and a goat or two from the donations offered to the saint.'

The old man smiled. He held Kapoor's hand in his. 'Don't worry. I will arrange.' Then he slapped Kapoor's hand, 'But don't you forget to vote for me this time. I am going to win the ticket and stand from this village.'

By the time we returned, Dom was exhausted. 'Enough gods for the day,' he declared, 'it's time for Teacher's.' Kapoor lingered. But he left as soon as we fixed a time to meet the next day.

Dinner was served in the back lawn. As soon as we were seated, an elderly retired colonel blowing into an ancient bagpipe led a military band around the lawn. They were dressed in red coats with brass buttons and white trousers. Pandey told us the colonel was the last one in the village who knew to play the wind instrument. He didn't want money, Pandey informed us, but he loved drinks. With our permission. We watched Pandey pour him half a glass out of Dom's bottle of Teacher's. The colonel put the glass to his lips and in one quick moment he threw his head back. He marched away, playing his bagpipes.

The dogs were tied. The mutton curry, Dom said, was delicious. I had vegetarian food. So did Juzer.

~

Pandey asked me the next morning when he brought me my cup of tea, 'I think I will serve fried fish for dinner. I notice your researcher-saab does not eat our chicken or mutton. He is afraid. But there is no need to fear fish. It is river fish and very sweet. Okay?'

'Okay.'

When Juzer came down I told him about the special dinner plans Pandey had made for him. 'But I can't eat fish which don't have scales or fins! That is not halaal. I can't eat shellfish even. They are all haram.'

I said, trying to be kind, 'Juzer why don't you become a vegetarian. You don't have to worry then.'

'Don't you think I am beautiful, ma'am?' Juzer stroked his beard. 'The prophet has said that at least once in forty days we must eat meat. It keeps our women and men beautiful.' He shook his head in distress. 'At one time all meat in Mumbai was only halaal. It is these Sikhs who have spoilt everything. They introduced this jhatka meat into the country.'

Kapoor arrived an hour early. 'Today is a very special day for our women,' he said. 'It is *kurva chauth*. The day when women fast for the long life of their men. From before sunrise until the time they get to see moon in the night they not eat, not a drop of water even. So my wife and daughters woke me early morning with all their noises. That is why I am here early. We have special dinner tonight. Meddem, you come? I told my missus, I bring you.'

I accepted his invitation, but declined to have dinner with him. It was a family affair and moreover it was our last evening in Pragpur. Kapoor took us to meet the local pradhan, the chief of the village. It was a modest house, clean, uncluttered. In the front room, a woman sat on the bed, her head and face covered with a bright blue duppatta. Several old people ranging from eighty to ninety years of age sat in front of her. She was Leela Devi. The moment we were introduced to her she let her duppata slip, revealing a kind but resolute face. She was the pradhan. After some discussion with the elders about old pilgrim routes, she asked Kapoor to take us to the three old men living by the old banyan tree.

Instead, Kapoor took us to meet Gopal Sharma, the sub-district magistrate. He had fixed a time with him. He begged Dom, 'Sir, if you can only impress him, then he will come with us to Jwalamukhi. Matters will be simple then and we can drive all the way. Otherwise you have to walk sir, like Tom-Corea, which I see you cannot do very well.'

Sharma's office was like a miniature courtroom of an ancient time: rows of chairs were arranged in military fashion in front of his table. They were mostly occupied with people with long drawn faces and an immense repertoire of patience. I sat next to an old man, who, Kapoor informed me, was a wounded colonel. Not of the body, he laughed, but the heart. The bank was reluctant to clear his fixed deposits, hence his presence in the room. The colonel sat as if stunned, clutching a gent's synthetic leather pouch with a small brass lock on its zipper.

Two men rushed to Sharma to report the death of their nephew at the India-Pakistan border. The youth had belonged to the local village. When Sharma had attended to them, he looked up at Dom, an eyebrow arched. But before Dom got into his impressive act, Juzer flourished the British Council letter of support. He said, 'Sir, it is of great importance that we go to the Jwalamukhi temple immediately. We want to find the name of a famous Englishman in the temple records.' His tone matched that of the two men who had brought news of death on the border.

Sharma read the letter offered to him with interest. He yelled out to his secretary to get him the old English Gazetteer. He flipped through the pages. 'My gracious! His name is here. Coryate. In a book in my office. You must write about this. That I find his name in this book.' He held the book in the air for all to see.

He bent towards Juzer with sudden respect. 'So you are their researcher.' He scrutinized Juzer carefully. 'Ah-ha you are a Bohri. I know. I can make out. Tell me, what is the fate of Hindus in Pakistan?' Juzer and Sharma had a detailed conversation. 'You have a lot of information,' he said with a genial nod and a twitch of his jet-black moustache. 'Let us talk on the way to Jwalamukhi.' Sharma signalled to his secretary to ask all the people to leave the room, come tomorrow. 'Let's go, Juzer, we can talk about Pakistan on the way. I've always wanted to go there. Is it easy to get a visa, you think?'

Sharma hopped into the front seat, gave instructions to Joginder. As we turned into the narrow road to the temple, a commercial van overtook us. Sharma shouted out to the driver to stop. 'Do you know who I am? If you don't, then go find out. I'll strip you of our license and put you behind bars.' Pointing at Dom, he added, 'Do you know who is with me? The Ambassador of England. Now get out of the way, you imbecile!'

He turned back, 'This road will take us straight to the temple. There are natural flames in it at many places. The Indian government thought that there was natural gas. They even thought there was river of oil that flowed from here to the Middle East. They thought India would become as rich as Arabia. They drilled many deep holes but they couldn't find anything.'

Kapoor said, 'It has nothing to do with gas or oil. It is Shakti's power. The story is, Shiva's wife Shakti committed suicide. So Shiva carried her body through the different worlds, dancing in anger. He would have destroyed the worlds, so Vishnu sent off his chakra that cut Shakti's body into seven bits which fell here and there. Wherever they fell, there are temples of Shakti. The Jwalamukhi temple is where her tongue fell. So you will see her tongues of flames.'

Sharma took us to the guesthouse next to the temple. He asked for the chief pandits and members of the temple trust to be assembled in the drawing room. We asked them for their old records. They brought us some books dating back to the sixteenth century. They were in tatters.

Dom did not come to the temple. Juzer was curious; he followed close behind Sharma, Kapoor and me, his cap a beacon to announce his faith. Inside, small tongues of blue flame gushed out of crevices in the rock. Sharma performed a puja. 'Can I look?' Juzer asked.

'Why not,' the pujari said. 'Even Akbar prayed here. What is wrong with looking?'

Kapoor said, 'Akbar came here. He built a water channel to drip here to put off flames. Nothing happened, so Akbar became a devotee of the goddess. He presented a *chattra* to goddess; it is like umbrella, made of gold. But when Akbar looked back at his much-valued gift, it had turned to just copper!' Kapoor giggled. 'So much strength Shakti having. Better than a scientist even.'

At seven in the evening, Kapoor came to fetch me. We walked to his house. His daughters had painted the rooms. Pink below the windows and blue above. They were in the kitchen with their mother, helping her to cook the evening meal. When they joined us, we talked as we waited for the moon to be sighted. It was past 8.30 p.m., I was getting restless. The girls, who had been allowed to drink fruit juice in the evening, sang energetically. Their mother waited by the door gazing at the sky, hungry, waiting for the aberrant moon. It did not appear and at 9.15 p.m. I decided it was time to leave.

Twenty minutes later, it was as I was finishing my soup that Pandey came running to the table. 'The moon has been seen, meddem.' He beckoned me to follow him to the rear gate. I saw three old women, each above eighty. They held brass jugs of water that they tilted towards the ground as they turned around, offering water to the earth. From a plate that they held up to the sky they made offerings of flowers, fruit and sweets. The moon shone at them from above. They faced us, blessed both Pandey and me, pressed flowers and sweets into our hands.

~

Next morning before we left Pragpur, Kapoor took us to meet the three old men. They took us to the banyan tree that, they told us, was over five hundred years old. We perambulated around the tree with them as in an ancient rite. They led us down a hill. They pointed to holes in them; they told us they were used to hide women and children from dacoits. We walked down to the cliff over the Beas River that spread like blue ink along the sandy plain.

The three old men pointed to the pathway along the river, 'That is how he would have come, all along the river bank. Then that,' they pointed to the other side where the river's girth widened, 'is where he would have crossed to go to Jwalamukhi.'

17

The Strider's Surrender

Coryate felt much better after he had rested with the priests. They were reluctant to let him leave, and insisted that he would be better off if he stayed with them, or returned to Roe. He nodded but made no answer. He was well aware that he was in worse health than he had ever been in his life. But he had not walked all the way to where he was to accept defeat now. He was more worried by what had happened to the papers he had sent to England than by the future of his body.

So he took leave of them and once he had ascertained the way to Kashi, started on it. Many people had watched Coryate trudge away from them on his unforeseeable road. Few had been more moved by his departure than the Jesuits. They gave him supplies of dried fruit, meat, rice and hard bread, as well as medicines for his belly. At last he turned down a curve of the road and they could no longer see him. They sighed as one and went back to the church, holding hands. For though Coryate had neither known nor surmised it, they were lovers.

They knelt before the altar, hands linked, and prayed for

Coryate's body and soul. 'We should pray for ourselves also,' Mateo said. 'Our brother Tomas spoke of ratfall and plague in the north. If it comes here, we shall have much work among the people. We may also perish, but we should face it with fortitude, like Tomas. As he does, so must we do. At least we two shall perhaps die together. He must face his death alone.'

~

Coryate rediscovered his long stride, though he moved somewhat less quickly and surely than before his sickness. But the road to Kashi was crowded with pilgrims carrying food and the ashes of their dead. Oxcarts and Mogul horsemen also slowed down the traffic. For all these inconveniences, he made good time. He noticed that the pilgrims seemed happy, as though on holiday. They chatted and laughed with one another, and ate a lot of sweetmeats on the road. He did not think this was how they should behave.

As usual, he had picked up a companion to walk with. Ganesh was a tall, serious, pallid Brahmin, his caste written on his forehead. He lived in Kashi and worked as a scribe there. He made copies of the holy books for the temples and worked on the side as a letter writer for illiterate people who wanted to communicate with relatives and friends far away.

'The letters seldom reach the people they were meant for,' he told Coryate sadly. 'And if they do reach them, they often have difficulty in finding someone who can read. But I do my duty, and my clients are contented. You ask me why these pilgrims are so cheerful. Why should they not be? Many have come from distant places to offer puja at the temples of Kashi and bathe in the waters of Mother Ganga, where their sins will be washed away. They have perhaps saved money for this pilgrimage for many years, and now they are on their way.

'But,' he observed somberly, 'they will not be so happy on their way home. They will have lost all their money to the priests in Kashi, who are mostly liars and thieves. They swindle any innocent pilgrim who falls into their hands. But there are some who are worse than they. Dishonesty, yes, one may countenance that, since it is everywhere in this land. But there are also truly evil creatures that live in Benaras, whose evil is beyond anything you can imaging feringhee. They are like demons come to earth. Have you heard of the Agori?'

In earlier and better days, Coryate would have been much inclined to begin a dissertation on demons that referred to classical texts and the Bible. Now, with a dry throat and tired, he forbore. But he was as curious as he had ever been. 'Who are these Agori?' he asked. 'Are they ghosts that come from your ancient legends, or some tribe that lives in Kashi?'

Ganesh made the sign with which Coryate had become familiar, meant to ward off the evil eye. 'Who knows whether they are human or not? Some say they are of the tantric sects, who place much importance on sexual intercourse, but those tantrics I have met deny this. What I know is that they haunt the burning ghats at Kashi, and other places where people are cremated. They steal dead bodies, or take them from the pyres, and eat them. They also eat human excrement. They drink very strong liquor, and brew it themselves. When they want sexual pleasure, they copulate with dead women.'

'Why do they perform these abominable acts?' asked Coryate. Ganesh shrugged and said, 'Who knows, *siyah?* It may be part of their religion, but our religion proscribes these acts. It may be only that they take pleasure in doing as they do. I have never met an Agori, nor do I know anyone who has. For they do not live like other people, and few ever see them.'

'Then it may be,' said Coryate, 'that they are figments of the mind, devils who do not exist at all. For it is impossible that they should do all these things and be never seen by any human eye.' Ganesh only replied, 'Feringhee, they exist.'

They walked on in silence, Ganesh annoyed because the foreigner doubted him, and Coryate slightly frightened by what he had heard. In this way they came into Kashi. Coryate had hoped Ganesh would invite him home, but he did not. They separated in silence, and Coryate found space in a sarai.

~

In Kashi, the Ganges was very wide, and one could see the whorls of the midstream currents. Its shores were lined with ghats and temples, and beyond them were the mansions of wealthy men who had donated money to the temples. Pilgrims often hired boatmen to row or sail them downriver, past the clutter of ghats with temples and splendid houses behind them, so that they could survey the magnificence of the spectacle. Some pilgrims that he met in his sarai had hired a large rowboat for this purpose, and he went with them as a guest. On board, they offered him a share of their frugal meal.

He stared at the ornate, gaudily painted architecture with disapproval as it passed slowly by, but also watched people bathing in the river to be sanctified. He could hardly look down on the practice, for in Palestine he had bathed in the Jordan with the self same intention. Here, as there, the genders bathed from separate ghats. The men wore dhotis, the women sarees. When the women emerged from the water, the wet cloth moulded itself to their occasionally sensuous bodies, and Coryate developed an unusual erection. He thought it indicated an improvement in his health.

The crowded lanes behind the ghats contained smaller temples, and shops that sold a bewildering range of items, from sweetmeats and brocades to containers of Ganges water. A number of touts moved purposefully through the shuffling mass of bodies. Each selected a likely face, then closed in on it and tried to entice its owner into the temple he served to receive blessings (for which he would have to pay). Only one tout approached Coryate. He represented opposed moral interests, for he also offered to take the feringhee to a brothel.

Coryate's sarai lay not far from the two burning ghats, different from the bathing ghats, and that night he walked to one of them. Kashi seemed even more active at this time than by day. Even greater crowds had blocked the narrow lanes. In a mass, they produced a rumbling, menacing sound, like a mob of bees in swarm. But they were essentially peaceful.

The food shops in the holy city bulged with customers. In this Hindu place, they should have been vegetarian, but because the Muslims now ruled, a few—though only a few—were not. Outside these establishments, muscular cooks turned their spits above a fire and cooked mutton kebabs, sparks flying into the darkness beyond, or roasted lamb in clay ovens. The alien smell spread in the hot Hindu air.

Coryate had already been adequately fed once that day, in the rowboat on the river, and would normally not have wanted more, but the smell of the meat as it cooked brought saliva to his mouth. He paused at the door of a kebab house, hopeful that someone would see a siyah and offer to be his host. This happened sometimes, but it didn't this time.

He turned from the door. At that moment the crowd rifted and made way, though it seemed impossible that it could, and groups of mourners came through the gaps in it, noisily weeping and chanting while drums roared in sudden excitation. Four mourners in each group carried biers, each laden with a corpse wrapped in white cloth, except for the face. Each shroud was sprinkled with flower petals: the bodies under them were soon to be burnt on the ghats below.

A Muslim cook shouted as he turned his spit in the fire, 'The Hindus say they don't like the smell of our cooking! Well, now their kitchen downstairs is opening, and we can tell them we don't like the stink of theirs!' The Hindus didn't laugh.

~

Coryate went down the steps to the firelit ghat, where the funerals were about to start. It was densely packed not merely with mourners, but a horde of onlookers, gathered to watch an interesting spectacle. This had always seemed to Coryate a curious aspect of the Indian character. If any small event took place in public, like drunks fighting in the road, a huge crowd would collect within moments to comment and stare. It was as though Indians led lives so dull that a trivial incident became a source of interest, or that they wanted to be voyeurs and commentators upon whatever happened in the lives of others.

After all these months, he didn't understand them, for their minds contained many contradictions. They were in many ways—whether Hindu or Muslim—the gentlest people he had ever encountered. They were also more generous than other people he had met, for he had been mostly helped and fed by common folk all through his journey. But they could be unbelievably brutal, to animals, women, or, in the case of Hindus, those of lower caste, and many had minds without intellect and wanted only to display wealth and possessions.

He also wondered why, in a city where bodies burned every day, so many people came to the ghats. But from the dress and speech of the onlookers, he judged that most of the crowd were visitors, come to see what spectacles the city offered. Had he visited a town in Spain, would he not have gone to see the bullfights? And he himself, why was he here, if not for the same reasons as the gaping crowd around him?

Having settled these questions, of import to him, in his mind which, as he knew, often ran in tortuous and blindfolded circles, Coryate became what (he also knew) he was best at: a watcher and a recorder. He nudged and burrowed his way through the crowd till he was in a position by the pyres where he could watch and settled himself to record. The chants of the priests, the drumbeats, the smell, made his head ache.

The dozen biers that carried corpses had now been laid beside the pyres, which, Coryate calculated, were about six feet apart. Chunks of cheap wood, used as kitchen fuel in Kashi, lay upon them. A whiteclad official who appeared to be in charge of the cremations, dripped a little oil on each pyre, then kindled them one by one with a flaming torch. The wood reddened sullenly. Tongues of flame licked upward from it and entwined, red and with a look and sound of wetness, one with another. The corpse-bearers lifted the stiff swathed bodies, placed them on their pyres for the fire to kiss them more intimately, and drew back as it crackled and leapt up.

Behind Coryate, an angry and querulous old man said to his companion, 'What a stench! The brains and fat of peasants, frying in cheap oil and wood! Why did we come to the poor people's ghat? Had we gone to see the rich people burned, that at least would have been a sight to remember, and the smell would have been pleasant. The rich are burned in brocade, on sandalwood pyres, with perfumed oils. Why did we not go there, having come all this way from our Punjab?'

~

The cremations went on well into the night, and Coryate remained to watch them to the end. When the fire had eaten the bodies on the pyres, the ashes and bones were dumped into the Ganges, while the priests chanted and women wailed. Afterwards, slowly, all the white-clad human figures leaked away into an encirclement of darkness. Coryate stayed. A cold wind now breathed off the surface of the water and dispersed the discoloured smoke above the foreshore. But the heat and stench of the night's burnings were still heavy in the air.

Coryate walked round the ghat and on the foreshore and found much debris: enormous numbers of flower petals, red, orange and white, some partly scorched; deposits of ash and bits of bone; here and there a charred human limb; once, a broken, burnt and empty shell of skull. He peered down into the Ganges. It was covered in an oily film, in which ash and fragile pieces of bone swirled. He had heard that by morning the ghat would be swept and cleansed, ready for new arrivals; more of the debris of the previous night's dead would be fed to the Ganges before dawn. This did not happen; everyone was asleep.

He did not wish to return to his sarai at once, because it would rasp with snores from his dormitory mates. This would affect his concentration and he needed to make notes of what he had seen. He found a rock on the foreshore where he could sit, back braced on the beslimed wall behind. He took Gertrude's blanket from his bundle and wrapped it round him. He also took out his implements of work, paper and pen, ink powder that he mixed with river water, and a new quill.

He started to make notes, writing by the white radiance of an obese moon. He had no other means of light. After about an hour's work, he heard curious scraping sounds near the river. Rats, he thought at first. In such a boneyard, rats would naturally thrive. Then he thought of a hungry crocodile, dragging its scales over the sand towards him. He looked up, blinking into moonlight as strong in these latitudes, in this season, as that of the sun. He became immediately afraid.

Hunched and scurrying towards him from the river was a human figure, carrying something in each hand. As it came nearer it shied away, having apparently seen him, and scampered further downshore. Coryate had recovered from his initial terror and curiosity, the core of his nature, made his eye follow its course, till it hid itself in the niche of a temple.

Coryate tramped down the shore till he reached the place. Meanwhile, he had been thinking. Was this one of those weird folk Ganesh had mentioned: the corpse-eaters, the Agoris? He had heard secretive mentions of them from others in Kashi and he had become very inquisitive about these people. He shouted into the shadows, 'I would speak with you. Come out!' Silence followed, except for a rat-like scurrying.

'Come out and speak to me!' Coryate cried. When his call was unanswered, he plunged into semi-darkness, feeling no fear. Amidst the seething shadows, he identified one as possibly human and, at this moment, the clouds above parted, and the bone-white moon illuminated the place where he was.

In a corner of the temple wall, he saw a creature that glared at him with crimson and bulbous eyes. It was naked, but for a rag that barely covered its gross, hairy genitals. Its body was burnt black by the sun, save where pink sores, encrusted it. All its bones showed through the flesh. Its face was so covered in long white hair, discoloured with dirt, that Coryate could not discern its features. It was not tall, but had huge hands, with filthy talons. It had come from a nightmare.

'What are you?' asked Coryate, panting as though after a long run. 'Are you beast or man?' In all his travels, he had never before seen such a creature. The wall behind it held an alcove, in which two objects lay that he had seen it carrying in its hands: a clay flask of the kind used to carry liquor, and to Coryate's horror, a charred human calf and foot, partly eaten.

In a guttural and thick voice, unaccustomed to much use, the creature said, 'Why do you harass me? Have I ever done you harm?' He stared at it, amazed to hear such words.

'I live as I may,' it said. 'My masters taught me how I should live to obtain peace with God and to be reborn into a better life. It is a very hard life, and I have lived beyond my time. You are feringhee. How have I ever harmed you? Why do you pursue me thus, crying out loudly, in this dark place?'

'Are you what they call a corpse-eater, an Agori?'

The creature backed to the alcove where its prizes lay. 'Does it matter what I am, siyah?' Its voice was still guttural, but now pitched lower. 'Do you know how many faiths there are in this land? More than a thousand, I think.' It took the gnawed leg and the flask from the alcove, and cradled each in a meditative fashion in its long-clawed hands. 'Mine is only one. There are others like me, but we live in the dark and harm no other living person. Why do you shout at me so?'

The voice of the devil, Coryate thought, come to cozen me. What sorrow there is in those terrible eyes, that voice out of hell. But I will not look in its eyes, nor listen to that voice.

The creature in the alcove unstoppered the clay vessel, and a raw reek of liquor came to Coryate's nostrils. It threw its hairy head back and swigged. When it had finished, the coarse white hair round its lips was glisteningly wet. It said. 'Once I met your Nazrani priests in Agra, siyah. They said that every day they ate the body of your god, and drank his blood.'

It held the vessel of liquor out to the Englishman, and with its other, taloned hand offered him the gnawed human limb. 'There are a thousand sects here. Do not disdain mine.'

Coryate fled from it till he reached steps, leapt up them, and arrived in the bazaar. It was only a short distance from there to his sarai, but he ran all the way till he reached it.

~

When he awoke the next day, his limbs ached as they had never ever done; the rest of his body itched and burnt, and his head felt like a melon ready to burst. Once he had gone outside, squatted beside companions from his dormitory and excreted, he knew the flux had come back, but worse than before. He lay down once more, wrapped in Gertrude's blanket, and thought. The encounter with the terrible creature last night, had it been real, or had it happened inside his head?

Had the creature been terrible in itself, or a sad and wounded human person, trying to reach out to others, unable to alter what it had become? Coryate began to wonder, as he had often done before, who he was. He also wondered what this land had turned him into. He had seen it change many people, few of them for the better.

He left the Hindu city and walked towards a place of which he had been told, Sarnath. This was a small town, and there, where the grass had yellowed because it had been much trodden by bare or sandaled feet for many years, he saw domes and temples in reddish brick and tonsured monks with peaceful Mongol faces and yellow robes. The absence of large numbers of human bodies, as compared with the rest of the country, was the most striking quality of the place. It had acquired quietness, like parts of Coryate's own country, Somerset. He lay down in the grass and fell asleep in its smell.

A clacking sound awakened him. A young monk had settled himself nearby on the grassy slope and was busily sending messages to heaven with a midget prayer wheel.

'Ah,' said the monk. 'You are awake at last. I have watched you. Why are you here, feringhee? You have been asleep here for many hours, as though you craved death.'

Coryate said thickly, 'Only God knows, for I do not. Who are you, child? You are young enough to have wisdom.'

'I am a monk, a devotee of the Lord Gautama, the Buddha. Do you not know who he is?' The priest started to tell him. Coryate lay back in the thick grass and listened as the quiet ruminative young voice went on. 'So,' he said at last, 'the Brahmins drove your sect from India, many moons since, and yet in the end it returned to its old places?'

'Something like that,' the boy priest said.

'Here even the grass smells of kindness,' Coryate said.

~

He went on walking. The country was always the same, and so was the condition of his body. He lurched and staggered over the dry red clods. The little monk had given him a necklace of large brown beads, and he trickled them through his fingers as he went, counting them: seven hundred and one, and two, and three, and four ... For some reason this soothed his mind and helped him walk, for he could no longer remember Greek or Latin words; the roll of the hexameters had abandoned him after he had met the Agori in the dark.

He came to Allahabad, which some said was called Illahabad. No matter: it existed, a place of white houses, temples and mosques, like everywhere else, trees scattered between the dwelling places, fertile fields around its boundaries. He walked down from a tilt of hills to the conjunction of two rivers; one of brown water, one of blue; where the currents met and churned, the water became white.

'The brown water is the Jamuna,' a passerby told him. 'The blue water is Mother Ganga, always pure.' He laughed to himself. He had seen both rivers as they flowed through other places, degraded and defiled by the dead, by decomposed flowers and the bodies of diseased people, by human and animal excrement and a constant rain of ashes. How could they purify themselves, or each other? But he saw in a flat place on either side of the water, thousands of tents pitched and huts hastily erected, and the ant-like swarms of devotees. They were sometimes wealthy and had retainers to look after them, but mostly poor.

But they plunged into the holy water, rich or poor, to bathe in it and raise their arms afterwards to the large and indifferent sun overhead. 'Whom do they pray to?' Coryate wondered. 'What do they pray to? The thing that has the power to make them rich or keep them poor?' Yet there were so many human bodies present, all praying, that it seemed to make the place sacrosanct.

In the huge encampment by the river he watched different kinds of priests. Some were clad in aromatic white silks from head to foot, some filthy, hirsute and completely naked. All seemed in a state of delirium or ecstasy; they chanted and rocked to and fro where they stood or squatted. The common people also bathed in the river, their eyes closed in mindless ecstasy, and a few chanted or clapped cymbals.

Coryate looked out over the crowded water to the low hills on the farther shore. He wished he had not left Sarnath, for there he had felt some kind of contentment, and here he was fully conscious of his body and of the illness that had now devastated it. He must now get back to Agra and the Jesuits to seek shelter and healing. The question now was whether he could walk so far. He had never doubted his abilities in this, but his body had betrayed him and he no longer trusted it.

He started back towards Agra. Because of the bloody flux in his belly, he had to walk very slowly and with frequent stops to ease it. He could not eat, and the green, slimy water he drank from wayside pools and wells made his bowels worse.

But, mile after mile, he plodded on, and put one foot down in front of the other, like a machine that could not stop. His flesh now burned with fever, but he went on only because there was nothing else for him to do. His head was cluttered with too many thoughts, too many memories: of Gertrude and Odcombe, Jonson's oratory in the Mermaid, and the smooth body of Anne Harcourt. Fewer people walked on the road with him; from them he heard that the plague had come to Agra.

When he reached the church, a new priest was there, a stranger. 'My fellows are dead of disease. It comes, it goes, and next time it comes, I doubt not that I shall perish also, and you too, it may be. Mateo and Mario told me of you, and you are welcome to lodge with me as you did with them. But an Englishman has also been here seeking you; and I will send him word now, to say you have come. Meanwhile, lie down and rest; from your looks, you are in sore need of rest.'

~

Coryate woke from an absorbed and desperate slumber to find two men talking to him: the Portuguese priest and an Englishman whom he slowly realized to be Richard Steele. They had last met in the mountains by Multan, and he had given Steele whatever part of his manuscript he had written at that time, to be conveyed by him to England. Surely this was good news. He sat up and looked into Steele's glaucous eyes.

'Have you returned from England, Master Richard? And while there, did you deliver my writings to Master Jonson?' The eyes shifted; the bearded lips smiled. 'Yes, Tom, yes,' they said. 'Those are safe. But I have word for you from Sir Thomas. He is anxious for you and wishes you to return safely home. He is with Salim in a place called Mandu, where the court now lies. If you come there, he will send word to our ships in Surat and find some captain to bring you to England.'

'But what did Master Jonson say when you delivered my writings into his hands? Did he not read them, Richard? They are the best work of my life.' Coryate's voice trailed away. The wasted face that looked into his, and the vile breath it exhaled, irritated Steele; also he felt guilt that he had burnt the man's papers and never taken them anywhere near London.

It was out of guilt and vexation that he said, 'Go to Mandu, Master Coryate, and let Sir Thomas send you homeward thence. For nobody else of our countrymen cares a fig for you or your writings. I had not wished to say this to you, but I was much at court when I returned, informing our King about the Indies, and know you what he asked when I told him I had encountered you there in the hills by Multan?'

Coryate said eagerly, 'No, Master Steele. Pray tell me what he said. The exact words, if you will.'

Steele, looking into the ruined but still hopeful face that stared up at his, replied, 'Why, he laughed much and loudly, slapped his thigh, and cried, "What, is that fool still living?"'

~

Coryate had hardly any options left. His great plans had all failed. He knew now that he would never reach Tartary, much less Cathay. He had no idea what had become of the many words he had already written about the Indies. He was too weak and ill to walk much farther. If he accepted Roe's offer, he might with good fortune come back to England and Odcombe and recuperate under his mother's care, though he did not even know if she was still alive. He might be able to complete his book, for the material was all in his head.

So he started to walk towards Mandu, his body and belly aflame with fever and the flux, and his mind with all that Steele had said. Other travellers directed him, but there were few on this road, and it was a lonely way. His legs bore him onward, as they had long been accustomed to do. His mind no longer recorded impressions as such, only blurred reverberations of what he saw and heard, but he went on.

~

Roe sat in his rooms in Mandu. They were in a goodly palace, with courts and pavilions, which perched on a hilltop and overlooked the plains beneath. Smoke drifted peacefully from the cooking fires of the small town on the slopes. It was pleasant weather, cool and breezy after the September rains.

His new chaplain came in to him. Edward Terry was a small, cheerful young man, but seemed unusually agitated. 'Sir Thomas,' he said, 'the man Coryate, of whom you wrote to our people in Agra, he is here below, and craves audience.'

'Bring him here,' Roe said, but Terry hesitated. 'He is in very poor health, Sir Thomas, both in mind and body. Might it not be better if I called our apothecary first, to see to his ailments?' Roe stared, and repeated, 'Bring him here.'

When he saw Coryate, he was horrified. The man had lost an incredible amount of flesh since they had last met in Ajmer. The skin hung loosely on his skeletal body, made yellow by the sun, but with a feverish flush under it. He was even more ragged and filthy than he had been before. He swayed to and fro, and muttered to himself as though demented. Terry had placed a protective arm around his shoulders, partly to hold him up, and partly perhaps to reassure him that he was with friends. Coryate seemed to recognize Roe. 'Sir Thomas ...'

Then he pitched forward and fell in a heap at Roe's feet.

'God's teeth!' cried Roe. 'Edward, bring water and a strong cordial to revive him. Summon the apothecary, for I think the poor wretch is likely to die.' But it was a long time before Coryate came back to his senses. Terry, solicitous as a woman, fed him brandy, and some life returned to his eyes.

'Send me to Surat and the ships,' he muttered. 'Sir Thomas, I am for home.' The apothecary said, 'He needs food, Sir Thomas, and sleep.' Coryate looked up and said, 'Yes.' Then he swooned once more. They carried him to a pallet in Terry's room, and there he lay like a corpse, but one that mumbled gibberish to itself, and cried out now and then.

18

Diary Nine

December 2002–Febuary 2003

Varanasi–Allahabad–Mandu

All the way back to Delhi, I kept thinking of the three wise men. Dressed in white with large white turbans on their heads, their faces had been burnt to the colour of honey by the sun.

'Ma'am, today is Shab-e-Baraat,' Juzer said as we entered Delhi. 'I will go to the Nizamuddin mosque.'

'What's this Shabe-thing?' I asked.

'It is the time when Muslims believe that Allah looks at his account books. He decides what sort of fortune or misfortune to give to people in the coming days. It's also the day when people remember their dead relatives. They go to the cemetery to offer prayers. They remain awake the whole night. Many go to the mosque.'

'I'll go with you.'

'It will be very crowded.'

It was. All varieties of fluorescent lights illuminated the narrow street crammed with people. Stalls selling food, cosmetics, toys and childrens' clothes lined either sides of the lane. Juzer stopped a candyfloss seller and bought himself a large shocking pink tuft of sugar. He offered to buy me one. I declined.

We passed a roadside kitchen. Juzer pulled out some bank notes from his pocket and gave them to an old man. A number of poor people sat on their haunches outside the shop in rows. They glanced at two men inside the makeshift room; one of them slapped dough into large rotis; the other dropped ladlefuls of curry into leaf bowls. 'They feed the poor here, free,' Juzer said as we pushed our way through the crowd towards a narrow alley.

Beggars sat at its mouth like a symptom laying bare the malady of the street ahead: there were more beggars and flower-sellers, people selling caps, rosaries, religious posters, and more beggars; stalls hawking kebabs, sweets; shops selling chadars to be offered at the dargahs of Nizamuddin Aulia and Amir Khusrau. And more beggars.

We took off our shoes at the entrance. 'Better cover your head, ma'am,' Juzer said. I wrapped the duppata around my head. Using our elbows, a trick I learnt from Juzer, we pushed through the swarm of people outside the tomb of Amir Khusrau. A board said: 'Ladies not allowed.' I halted. No more elbows.

A large number of tubelights cast a heaven-like blue glow. I peeped into the doorway: the entire room was painted and the tombstone was covered with roses; fans and a huge chandelier hung from the roof. People with scarves on their heads touched them to the tomb. Now and then as I pushed my head into the doorway, the attendant waved a hand at me to move away, so that, possibly, the tomb couldn't see me. I pulled my head back into my neck like a snail.

People along the jali or trellis on either side of the tomb prayed. Some women tied colourful threads to the jali. Others sat around it reading the Koran, or simply praying in silence. I had never before seen such a crowd. The large quadrangle in front of Nizamuddin Aulia's tomb was crammed with believers and but for the small arc in front of the *qawwal* singers, even the floor couldn't be seen. Juzer told an attendant that we were journalists and he led us behind the qawwals to the marble jali of the tomb of Jehanara, the daughter of Shah Jehan. We sat down against it.

A tall Afghan *khadeem,* a keeper of the mausoleum, walked to each of us, fanned our faces with a large cloth fan that smelled of the Delhi heat and of collective sweat. He was dressed in a grey Pathani suit and a bright pink scarf.

The man next to Juzer whispered, 'From Afghanistan he is. Came here seven years ago. Father has a bakery. Came for mother's operation with his wife and four children. Lives here only, in Nizamuddin. He likes India like anything. Doesn't want to go back to Afghanistan. Muslim religion is too pious here, he says, and all Muslims are safe to practise their customs. But he has to go. His visa become over year end. Poor fellow. May Amir Khusrau's blessings be with him.'

A number of torchbearers rushed from the tomb of Amir Khusrau carrying *roshini* or light. The prayers began. After it was over, a qawwal let out a fierce holler almost like a war cry. He was handsome in a youthful way; his eyes were like almonds, a lustrous brown. His companions joined him. They began to sing to the drumbeats and the whine of a harmonium.

Juzer pointed out a man in a white kurta pyjama sitting with the priests near the tomb. He faced the qawwals. Now and then he raised his hand. 'He is the chief priest,' Juzer said, 'he controls the pace of the singing.' I saw him raise a hand and turn it to the sky. The qawwals sang louder. Faster. People clapped, swayed to the repetitive beat.

A woman not far from where we were seated suddenly stood up. She was fat, old and dressed in a burkha; her face was clearly visible. It was crisscrossed with mystifying agony. Her eyes were fixed but the facial muscles twitched and contorted. Her hands and body moved in sudden uncontrolled movements. She began to weep.

The qawwals, on instructions from the chief priest, increased the tempo of their song. Faster. The drummer thumped hard on his drum. Harder. The woman raised her arms above her head; she shrieked. Groups of people started to stand up. The chief priest raised a hand; the qawwals clapped frenetically wailing in droning voices. This went on for a while, then slowly the chief priest brought his hand down and signalled the qawwals to stop.

The woman, one hand raised, turned around. A number of women rushed to her side and pulled her into the enclosure of Jahanara's tomb. I peeped through the jali; I could see the woman pirouette. She wobbled, her head hit the wall. 'Why don't they stop her?' I asked Juzer.

'No-no-no! It is religious ecstasy. She is in a trance because of mystical love. It is not right to stop her.' Juzer said. 'That is why the chief priest urged the qawwals to sing faster. Sometimes, if they stop suddenly, I have heard, the sufferer chokes and dies.'

The woman had stopped turning now. She sat down and seemed to roll about. A few minutes later, as though nothing had happened, she walked to the chief priest. She prostrated in front of him, and then taking some folded bank notes out of her blouse, offered it to him.

I stood up to watch her. 'Why is she giving him money?'

Juzer said, 'It is a custom. Had she been a man, the chief priest would have made the qawwals continue till he danced round and round like a madcap and he fell to the ground and rolled and rolled. Then that man would have to give a large sum to the chief priest. The chief priest controls everything. If he realizes it is a rich man who is in a trance, the performance would last for a very long time.'

The Afghan was standing next to us. He said, 'Poor woman. Her son died in a road accident a month ago. She hasn't cried for all these days. Good she got to cry.'

~

In the months after our return to Mumbai, Dom grew easily tired. He was feverish all the time and could not eat. He had become half his size. His stomach ached, and he passed blood in his stools. The doctor I took him to said after he examined him that his liver was enlarged and he was certain he had felt a lump in it. I was concerned about Dom, and he, about Coryate. 'We have only two more trips to make,' he said, his lips dry and broken.

I took him to a specialist at the hospital. After a thorough investigation, he told me that the pain in his stomach had no link to the cancer in his neck. He said Dom could continue on the trip in a week by which time he was certain the pain would have subsided and the bleeding would have stopped. 'But let him take it easy,' he warned.

Ten days later, we flew to Benaras. Juzer had arrived there a few days before us. I left Dom resting in his room as Juzer and I went to the Manikaran Ghat. It was late evening and the street and shop lights illuminated the dust that clouded the old city. We hurried through the narrow lanes winding this way and that with some sort of urgency. As I turned a corner, I got hit on the back of my head. A man dressed only in a loincloth passed by me carrying a large log of wood. Following him were a number of men chanting *Ram naam satya hai.* Two of them carried the corpse of a woman.

We stood on the higher steps of the ghat from where we could see the Ganges undulating salubriously in the moonlight like a large full-fed python. Pyres burnt alongside it. I counted them; there were seven. 'I can smell roasted flesh,' Juzer said inhaling the air. He pointed to the pyre closest to us. The head, arms and feet of the corpse stuck out of it. The fire enveloped the torso, burnt it completely. A man plucked out an arm, threw it in the adjoining pyre, then the other limbs one by one, then with a stick he shoved the skull into the flames.

An old man next to us said, 'Poor people can't afford a lot of firewood, so after the middle is burnt they throw the rest of the corpse into other pyres. Everything becomes equated in death,' he raised his head, 'rich-poor, all castes. Everything equal.' The first pyre had burnt itself out. A dog sniffed the ash for any remains of the corpse.

Juzer looked up at the sky as though in prayer. 'Ma'am, this is a good omen for me. Watching the dead. Today is night of thirtieth. Every Ramzan night, dead bodies are liberated by Allah to enter heaven. Thousands of souls are liberated each night, and on the last night, that is, the thirtieth, as many are liberated as in the whole month.' He raised his head to the stars. 'I am sure Coryate came here.'

A fat man who had been tending to the pyres walked up the steps towards us. His eyes were red and his black skin was streaked with ash and sweat. Juzer stopped him, 'You are the Domm?' Domms were the traditional tribe of cremators.

'Yes,' he replied. 'Now only my family left. All others have died or gone away. This is our business.'

Adopting an accountant's air, Juzer asked him how much he charged. 'Whatever people want to give, I take.'

Juzer said, 'I have been an auditor of a Muslim *kabrasthan* where we bury our dead. There are charges. I will tell you how much if you tell me your charges.'

'Five hundred to a thousand rupees,' the Domm said.

Juzer asked him about the ritual of skull-breaking. 'Hindus tap the skull five times,' the Domm said, 'to liberate the soul to the five elements.'

The old man next to us laughed. '*Ja re baba,* some of you hit so hard as though the dead one was your personal enemy.'

'Tell me about the Agoris,' Juzer whispered. The Domm shook his head. 'Are there any of them still around? Have you seen them?

The Domm said, 'I have seen one or two.'

'That's great! I am told they come to the pyres to eat human flesh.'

'Some people throw the dead woman's waist and the man's chest into the river to feed the fish. It is a ritual. The Agoris pluck these parts out of the river, eat them.'

'How horrible. Why?'

'They believe that it gives them tantric power and strength.'

Juzer bent closer to the Domm. 'I've also heard that these Agoris eat faeces?'

The Domm shook his head in several directions, which could mean both yes, and no.

'And sex? I've heard they have sex with dead women's bodies?'

'No.' The Domm rushed away into the lane.

The old man made a sour face. 'These Domms search the

ash of burnt women's corpses for jewellery. If they find any, they give it to their wives and daughters. And firewood that has not burnt in the pyre is also taken away by them. They sell it to others. Only sometimes they give it to the poor, free.' He coughed. 'I bought some firewood from him.' He pointed to the pyre in the distance, still burning. 'My son,' he said. 'He was twenty. TB.'

Juzer said to me, 'Ma'am one minute, I promised my mummy I would dip my feet at least in the holy river.' He ran down the steps.

'Careful,' I shouted after him. 'The water may turn you into a Hindu.' I saw him testing the water with his toes. He immersed his feet one by one into the river.

Not far from him, a sadhu took a fistful of ash from the pyre; he rubbed his body with the ash, then washed his feet thoroughly in the holy river. He scooped the water in his hands and took it to his mouth. He rinsed his mouth and teeth thoroughly, threw his head back, gargled, then spat the water into the river.

~

Juzer was jubilant next morning as he had located an Agori centre. If we had expected to walk into a room full of naked, ash-bodied, drugged Agoris with blood red eyes, skulls and corpses strewn about, we were wrong. The room was neat and bare. A man dressed in a starched kurta pyjama sat behind a low desk. He had a podgy face, cleanly shaved, and bright brown eyes.

'We want to ask about Agoris,' Juzer said.

'Ask.'

'We want to talk to an Agori.'

'Talk.'

We looked perplexed. The man said, 'What is it you want to know. I am an Agori.' He smiled at Juzer's expression. 'The trouble is that a lot of media people are spreading wrong rumours about us,' he said. 'Not all of us wander about naked.'

Agora, he explained, literally meant a path that was not fierce. It was a mental state of being. 'In the beginning of time, people lived the Agora way and led a simple life. There was no social bias and they followed the path of supreme non-discrimination. Because discrimination led to material and carnal indulgence. We believe by reversing values ascribed to things we would be enlightened speedily. So we willingly disregard all ascetic and Hindu taboos; we become indifferent to normal ways of dressing, eating and social behaviour.'

'And practise abnormal methods as *shavasadana*?' Juzer asked.

'That is the spiritual exercise we perform with a corpse. I am not going to deny that such practices do not take place. We have to go through various stages to obtain the Agori state of being. Suppose you want to go to America, you will pass though many countries. And if they appear tempting, you will stop to enjoy. It is the same. Some Agoris have weak will power. So they resort to all kinds of practices. So they drink wine, use addictive substances, have sex. A repulsive environment is deliberately adopted by the Agoris. So they wear torn clothes, live near ruins and crematoriums and carry human skulls and bones. The skull and the skeleton is our actual beauty. Our life breath is in it. The skin and flesh only make us beautiful. And they will rot and smell foul. That is why we drink from the skull cup. And when we perform exercise with a corpse we are breathing our breath into it. So we become corpse-like and attain a state of necrosis.'

Before he got to horrific particulars of the state of the dead, I asked, 'Why do you live near cremation grounds?'

'What's wrong? The Domm and his family cook their food there. They are healthy. The dogs eat the flesh of corpses, and give birth to pups, which are all right. No place is important or unimportant. It is all in your mind. But all this is not needed to follow the Agori path. All one needs is to control one's tongue and genitalia. These are the two pleasures we have to do without. Eventually.'

~

'It was my goodluck stars that I located the astrologer Guddu Sharma in Delhi,' Juzer remarked. We were on the road to Allahabad. 'I went to his house to find out if the Kumbh Mela happened in 1617 when Coryate must have gone to Allahabad. Mr Sharma is very good; he has software to find out if the correct constellation of stars occurred over Allahabad in 1617. He's so sure it did and our Coryate must have seen the Kumbh Mela.'

He looked back at me. 'If goodluck stars are following us we might even bump into a Naga in Allahabad.' He laughed.

The Nagas were ascetics who smeared their bodies with ash and renounced clothing as a sign of giving up everything, including shame. Juzer had provided me newspaper clippings of the Kumbh Mela in 2001 and it was in these that I had read about the Nagas who wore silver rings and other similar ornaments on their penises. There was an account of the Naga sadhu on his Japanese motorcycle that was presented to him by the manufacturer to help him preach, and other Nagas who carried cellular phones and hand-held movie cameras.

One Naga had become popular as he had for many years remained seated in the lotus position, with his right arm stretched out. So had Keiko Aikawa, the middle-aged Japanese woman, an ascetic who spent four days and nights buried under the ground, without food, water or fresh air.

When we were in Haridwar, Juzer had combed the streets and the banks of the Ganges to look for Nagas. When he obtained an address for them, he rushed me to the Daksha Prajpati temple next to which, he was told, was the Naga akhara.

At the temple I found an old pujari squatting on the steps along the Ganges. His name was Misra, he told me, and he was by tradition a pandit. Ten years ago, he had become discontented with life and had come to Haridwar from Benaras. He never returned. He was a Sanskrit scholar and a school teacher. He performed prayers on the banks of the Ganges.

Juzer asked him about the Nagas. The Naga sadhus, he told us, were ascetics who were militant. They were divided into akharas or regiments. They carried weapons—sticks, knives and spears, especially the trident. They smoked chillum, a clay pipe filled with tobacco and hashish, and smoked through cupped hands. 'It is smoked by many sadhus,' Misra told us, 'like Lord Shiva; he being Lord of Hashish, and himself is like the Nagas only.'

Juzer asked him whether they indulged in sexual activity. 'Do they? These Naga sadhus?' The Nagas were required to inhibit their sexual ache, Misra explained, and retain its energy so that it could be transformed into psychic and spiritual power.

Misra told us that some of the Nagas performed the yogic exercise called *chabi*—the key, which required the linga or organ to be pulled down, so that the energy from it rose up to the mind. So they wore large chains on their lingas.

Sometimes, he said, they attached to their organ a heavy weight of more than 10 kilos that they dragged about until the power of muscles and nerves was completely destroyed. They wore chastity belts made of wood shaped like a *langoti*.

He told us the way to the Naga akhara. 'You may find a Naga at the Devi temple,' he added as he waved to us.

The akhara was around the corner from the temple. Several Nagas sat on mattresses, and to my surprise and perhaps Juzer's disappointment, they were fully clad in white kurtas and pyjamas. No naked skin, no ash. We were introduced to the head. The guru Shankaracharya, he told us, wanted the Hindu religion to be protected by a militant force so strong that it would shun all worldly ambitions and aspirations and resist all temptation. This was possible, he realized, through the rawness of nudity.

The Naga sadhu, he explained, was one who had no desire for clothing, sex, or money. He was ready to die any time for the cause of religion. The sky was his clothing, the ground his bed. And the ash on his body symbolized his readiness to destruct any time. The order was rigorous, he told us, so were its expectations.

I asked him how he had become a Naga. 'I was in school,' he said, 'once I went to the Kumbh Mela with my family. There I saw the Naga sadhus by a smoking pit of ash and coal, a cloud of chillum hanging around them. One of them talked to me. I was very impressed with what he told me. I told him I wanted to become like him.'

Recruits were ordained as Nagas, he explained, at the Kumbh Melas at Allahabad and Haridwar. At a ceremony a day before the big bathing day, the new recruit's heads were tonsured. They discarded their sacred threads, if any, since they were now above caste. A mantra was whispered into their ears by the senior head priests in the akhara hierarchy. They were now ready to start their lives as Naga sadhus. They performed duties at the akhara to which they are attached. The more rigorous among them retreat to the Himalayas, only to emerge for events like the Kumbh.

I was surprised to see Juzer hesitate over a question that he wanted to ask. The head meanwhile joined his hands and our meeting concluded. Later, Juzer told me he had wanted to ask about *sakhis*. 'They are transvestite sadhus,' he told me. 'They choose Rama or Krishna as their deity and regard him as their lover. Since the deity is a male, they become the mistress of the Lord. They imagine having an erotic love relationship with him. Some sakhis pretend to have regular sexual intercourse with their Lord.' Juzer had laughed as he said, 'Except on the days when they're having their period.'

The next day in Haridwar, Juzer and I continued our search for a proper Naga. We took the ropeway to the Devi temples. The idols of the two goddesses were bits of shapeless stone or bark painted a greasy orange with oozy black eyes looking at us in terror. The pujari at the Anjana Devi temple told Juzer the story of Anjana that amused him to the tips of his ears.

One day Shiva asked Lord Vishnu to dress up like a beautiful woman. When he did, Shiva became excited and released his semen that was hot and could burn the universe. The rishis took the semen on a special insulated leaf, and with the help of the wind-god, Vayu, released it through a windy whisper into Anjana's ear. She gave birth to the monkey god, Hanuman.

Juzer's remark that followed the story had made me smile. 'Sounds like propaganda for heat insulation and artificial insemination.'

I think it must have been the heat of the day that prompted me to reply unthinkingly. 'It is possible such things existed,' I said, 'in those times. It's possible that the world recreates itself each time and people go through the same discoveries and inventions and wars and ultimate destruction.'

Juzer had a strange look in his eyes. I remember this clearly. He said to me, 'Ma'am, you have said something that is tremendously accurate. But that's all I can tell you. My religion does not permit me to tell you more. You have arrived at the edge of realization. I have a friend in Canada who said those same words as you. He too was at the edge of knowing about it all. But I am sorry my lips are sealed.'

He had turned away. But I am certain that the look in his eyes was one of awe and respect. For little me, as Christopher MacLehose would have said.

In the other Devi temple, the pujari smeared red marks on my forehead and to my surprise blessed Juzer from a distance with a raised hand. The pujari also gave me a red and gold scarf that had been offered to the deity and blessed by her.

Juzer asked the pujari whether they performed sacrifices in the temple. The pujari talked about hens and goats that used to be sacrificed in the Devi temples. I remember being equally amused and alarmed when Juzer said, 'That I know. I am asking about humans.'

It was beside this temple, under a tree that we saw our first proper Naga. He sat cross-legged smoking a chillum. His hair was matted, his body was covered with ash, his eyes were red. A tall, hefty man was talking to him. We walked to them.

'So, this is not just tobacco you are smoking?' the man asked the Naga.

'Tobacco, tobacco,' the Naga replied waving a hand in the air, which seemed to say 'get lost!'

'You can't fool me,' Juzer said in a sing-song way. 'I know that is full of hashish.'

The Naga looked up at him but did not reply. Juzer said, waving a finger about, 'You Nagas are hooked to it. That is why you are able to bear all this hardship.' He beat his chest, 'But us Bohri Muslims we can bear anything without any sort of help.' He threw back his head and laughed in his trademark style.

The Naga seemed to shift his position. I glanced at the trishul with pointed spears near his leg. The Naga took a deep drag at his chillum, and then with a twitch of the corner of his lips and a look through the corner of his eyes he dismissed Juzer on the spot. We walked away.

The tall man walked up to Juzer. He had shifty eyes under unruly eyebrows. Hair sprouted like twin fountains out of his earlobes. 'I've heard a lot about you Bohri Muslims. I'm Devprakash.' He shook Juzer's hand. 'You're right, these buggers smoke hashish. I was trying to get him to give me some. Need some peace. That's why I've come to Haridwar.' He waved a hand, which seemed like an awkward salute, 'I'm Chief of Crime Branch, Mumbai.'

~

Through Guddu Sharma's help, Juzer had made an appointment with Mohan Das, an astrologer practising in Allahabad. We picked him up from his house. He was frail, fully grey and walked with a limp. He was eighty-nine. We drove to the bank of the Rivers Ganga and Jamuna where the Kumbh Mela took place.

Mythological legends say that at the beginning of creation, all the gods were under a curse that made them weak and cowardly. Brahma, the creator, advised them to retrieve the *kumbh*, the pot containing *amrit*—the nectar of immortality. The gods sought help from the demons, and together they churned the primordial ocean to bring up the nectar. The gods carried the kumbh containing nectar, the demons tried to wrest the pot from the gods. A few drops of nectar fell in four different places: Allahabad, Haridwar, Nasik and Ujjain. Since then, when the planets are aligned in the same position, pilgrims and devotees converge to commemorate this divine event.

Mohan Das limped closer to the waters and said, 'See, that is the brown Ganga and over there, that is the blue Jamuna river. And that is where they meet. Of course you are not being able to see the mythical subterranean Saraswati. This place is called *triveni* or triple braid. It is such a power-spot, a crossover point between heaven and earth. The water here is so powerful that even a small portion is enough to cleanse a lot of sin.' He flung his hands away from him.

The Kumbh, he told us, dated back to 464 BC, when a naked astronomer, possibly the forerunner of the modern naked saints, first observed the winter solstice in Allahabad.

He added, 'At the Kumbh Mela this time, there were many Naga sadhus. Many came from the Juna akhara. They are being very feared and also very respected. Someone had to defend Hinduism from Muslim invaders; it is why they were formed. They carry long snaking swords and sharp tridents. They know martial arts like experts and they attack anyone who gets in their way.

'But, see, the trouble is,' he said pinching his nose, 'the Kumbh Mela now has become a circus. Like a tourist thing. This time so many foreigners come here and a lot of peoples trying to make money from them only. There was a Naga riding a big elephant. A woman was sitting in a cage of snakes. Another one was buried in sand. There was also a sadhu sitting on a bed of knives over an open fire. And yes, an Agori sadhu who openly practised tantric magic. He was telling people that he would eat their flesh. People think he was making joke. But it is true, they eat flesh. Dog flesh, man, woman flesh, yes. They eat even number 2.' He raised two fingers. '*Chi-chi-chi*! What is all this? Before, at Kumbh Mela time, people want to liberate their souls. Do you know, until British people's time, some sadhus practised religious suicide here?'

It was believed, he explained, that those who killed themselves at the confluence of the Ganga and Jamuna became free from the cycle of birth and death. Five different methods of religious suicide were practised. Suicide by drowning, by jumping off the holy banyan tree, by self-cremation, by breathing smoke or by cutting off flesh to feed birds and bleeding to death.

'Huien Tsang, the Chinese man, has written about religious suicides. "A man who commits suicide like this, goes to heaven where he enjoys lots and lots of women." And no peoples or rules are there to stop him.'

Dom grunted. He muttered incoherently although I heard him. He said, 'I'd rather stay here on earth for a bit longer and enjoy the company of beautiful women.'

~

We returned to Mumbai. Our travels were over except for the last one that followed Coryate's final walk from Mandu to Surat. 'Let us finish this as soon as possible,' Dom said to me wearily, stroking his neck. 'We must finish this book.'

But I didn't make any plans to travel yet. Dom could hardly move. Both his feet were swollen. I pestered him to consult a doctor. He refused. I fixed an appointment with a homeopath; he agreed to go to him. The homeopath gave him packets of sugar pills and powders, a tube of ointment for his feet. He also asked Dom to soak his feet in rice-water and brine. Dom started to write his book on Coryate, one finger poised over the keyboard, his feet immersed in a bucket.

Two months later, towards the end of February, we set off in the direction of Mandu.

~

I saw his face in the flicker of the candle flame. His lips were unhappily compressed before they parted to utter dire words. 'Power gone, meddem.'

'Will it be long ...'

'Yes long. Four a.m. it coming back.'

'What has happened?'

'Nothing. In Mandu power-cut always.'

I filled the register, then hurried back to the front lawn where I had left Dom standing in the dark. Crickets in the trees trilled in chorus. Frogs croaked in the lake nearby. Stray birds chirped, and a noisy man came rushing after me with a pencil torch. 'Careful meddem, walk only on stones. Insects, frogs and sometimes snakes even is coming in grass.'

We sat at a table swathed in candlelight. 'I wonder if there is any beer in this godforsaken place,' Dom muttered. It had been a long and rough drive.

'Yes-yes,' the attendant who was standing behind him replied. 'I bring very cold beer.' He brought two bottles. 'Sorry sir, beer not very cold. Power cut for six hours in day also.'

Juzer went out with a candle to pray.

~

I slept badly that night. Besides the mosquitoes that whined in my ears, when I woke up in between I saw a large healthy lizard curled on the windowsill gaping at the moon. I turned to the other side but couldn't sleep. Dom had also had a bad night. By the time we reached the dining room, Juzer was eating a large breakfast of half a dozen parathas, a bowl of potato curry, curds and pickle. The young man next to him sipped tea.

He was Rajender, Juzer told us; he was the local school teacher. He had bumped into him in the morning in the market. He was doing his doctoral thesis on Mandu. He had made a map with locations of all the buildings, tombs and mosques. 'Now we can know Thomas Roe's residence here,' Juzer said gulping down a large piece of paratha, then suppressing a burp.

This was the one important bit of information that we needed in Mandu. Therefore, map in hand, Juzer and I went with Rajender to inspect every single structure. Dom stayed behind to read his crime fiction. 'After all, I won't be able to read in the night,' he said.

Juzer had seen a picture of Roe's residence in Forster's book. It was a mausoleum with three domes. Roe was an important man to Jehangir, Juzer said, adopting the tone of a detective and, therefore, his residence would have been large and not too far away from the Emperor's. It would also have had a water tank, perhaps a caravansarai, and, maybe, a large garden. A private pool, even.

Juzer had also read somewhere that Roe's and Terry's names had been scratched on one of the walls of his residence. So he spent the afternoon inspecting the walls of the selected structures with a magnifying glass. We found the names of several lovers, and hearts drawn in varied shapes. But we did not find Roe and Terry's names. This didn't deter Juzer.

Rajender talked to me about his thesis while Juzer was screening the walls. His research was about the only tomb in the country built for a eunuch. 'She was known as the queen of eunuchs. Jehangir's harem had many eunuchs. Maybe she was a part of that. I don't know.'

I said, 'Eunuchs in the Mogul court were men who were castrated. They were not really women.'

'Not correct. In Sanskrit, *napumsaka* means eunuchs, hijras, those born with neither male nor female sexual organs. *Kamasutra* called them people of the third sex. But this is not to be mixed up with homosexuals or castrated males. Although, today, it is all mixed up. Every eunuch is a homosexual, and every swami is a cigarette-addict. They have become evil men who engage in all forms of sexual intercourse without a female womb, forcing themselves upon other men. It is because of such sinful activity they are engaging in that they are reborn in next life without their sexual organ, as a hijra.'

We found ourselves that evening in front of Hijdo ka Mahal. The sky had changed its colour; a cool breeze blew from the hills around us. Though it didn't have three domes, and it was far away from the centre of Mandu, Juzer plucked out the magnifying glass from his shirt pocket, and as he went towards a column, we heard loud claps from behind it. Two eunuchs emerged from the shadows; the bigger one looked like an animal. Her face was bloated and dark and her nostrils widened like a snout. She clapped in Juzer's face. He let out a curse and as he turned to avoid her, she held him by his arm. Rajender intervened. 'Mausi, let him go,' he said, 'he's a friend. They're here to write a book. Tell me, do you know anything about this tomb?'

The big one sat down; she signaled to her paler, daintier

friend to sit next to her. She clapped her hands. Rajender said pointing to her, 'She is Sheila, and this is her sister, Ila.'

'My brother,' Sheila said patting Ila's back. I raised an eyebrow. Sheila smiled at me. 'Our idea of love is different from you people,' she said. 'We don't have love like man-woman kind. We have deep affection. So she is my sister, brother, mother, father, everything.' She said to Rajender, 'This tomb is very old.'

Juzer, more composed now, asked, 'Mausi, do you think she would have been in Jehangir's court?'

Sheila clapped her hands. 'Arre, how should I know that? It was such a long time ago. And I am just a few years older than you.' She consulted Ila, then said, 'Yes, in those times we eunuchs had an important place in the king's court. We looked after his women. We were invited to all big ceremonies—weddings, children's birth, big-big dinners. Nothing happened without our blessings. Now time has changed. No one respects us. We live like beggars. We have become outcasts.' Ila winked at Juzer, then burst into giggles.

Sheila added, twirling a lock of hair in her fingers, 'In cities it is all right. Our sisters dress up in shiny sarees; wear lipstick, rouge, kohl, flowers in their hair. Then they go out in the streets, wriggling their hips, strutting their breasts and earn two, three hundred rupees. But here, it is a hellhole.'

Sheila blew her nose and wiped her fingers on the column. 'I was taken away from my parents when I was twelve. My foster mother took me to Bhopal where I lived for many years. Then she handed me over to the old woman here. She died last year, but she gave me a terrible time. She made me walk four-five kos to collect money. Who wants such a life?'

She looked down sadly at her large feet. But when she looked up, her eyes shone. 'Last month we had gone to Indore.

There was a big wedding. We went to see a film, old one, *Mughal-e-Azam.* Dilip Kumar was Jehangir and Madhubala was Anarkali. How beautifully she dances and sings. I wish we were back in those times.' Sheila clapped. In a hoarse, broken voice she sang the song from *Mughal- e-Azam:*

'Jab pyar kiya to darna kya ...'

Once you have loved why should you fear?

19

Road's End

Edward Terry, though he was a chaplain and was, therefore, expected to be of calm disposition, was a congenitally flustered young man. But his general fussiness was not his only resemblance to a mother hen. One of his missions in life was to look after helpless and distressed creatures. He took Coryate, a battered bundle of stresses and diseases, under his wing. He shared a room with him so that he could medicate him, feed him and administer to his needs.

Coryate treated Terry as, in the Old Church, he might have done a confessor. He told him about Odcombe and his parents, about his father's corpse in the cave, and his guilt over Gertrude. He told him about his great walks in Europe and the Near East, and his coming at last to India. He also spoke of Anne Harcourt. Terry listened in silence, but with almost palpable empathy.

The compound allotted to the English in Mandu lay between a mosque and a tomb. The main building, where Roe had his apartments and offices, had three domes. Terry had his room here, which Coryate shared. Other houses, less elevated in stature and without domes, flanked it. All were of brick and mortar and like most of the other edifices in Mandu, painted a pale rose. Small rooms were slotted into their walls. In these, the rest of the English were quartered. In the centre of the compound was a tank, a man-made stone container for muddy water. Steps led down to the water, and Coryate liked to sit on them and look downward. His gaunt, ruined reflection stared up at him, and he would study it ruefully for hours on end.

The call of the muezzins troubled and irritated him. Terry, a Christian priest, did not react to these incessant cries, but accepted them as one of the many sounds of this country. But Coryate reacted, though he had walked through many Islamic nations, and did so violently, with a stream of baroque obloquy in English. Sometimes he shouted Hindustani obscenities at the priests, and Terry thanked god that they were too far off to hear him. He often wondered how Coryate had managed to pass through so many Muslim lands without having had his throat cut. By his own account he had often blasphemed against Allah and the Prophet in public, and he seemed proud of it.

Partly to prevent trouble and partly for Coryate's health as it improved, Terry went for long walks with his friend. Mandu was full of palaces with terraces and fountains, ornate mosques and large elaborate tombs. Several tanks provided water. The Englishmen often found groups of musicians by the tanks. They sat and played their instruments, sonorous or shrill, while court ladies sang romantic ballads. Mogul horsemen patrolled the street, and nobles and veiled women passed by in palanquins, their retinues around them. Some distance from this aristocratic area was a town where poor people, mostly Hindus, lived: a squalid, thinly populated place, with no future.

As Coryate grew stronger, he walked in the hills around Mandu, mainly alone, since Terry was much occupied with Sir Thomas's work. An unusually heavy monsoon had left the countryside emerald: a colour punctuated at intervals by trees that flowered brutally red, or orange, or purple, or virginally white. Yellow and blue flowers showed themselves in the thick grass, under which the earth, after the long rains, smelt rancid and raw, as though it exuded its own blood. Often Coryate glimpsed the delicate deer that Jehangir shot by the score when he hunted, and birds surrounded him, throats full of music.

All this succoured and reassured him. He became certain that he would finish his book on India and be knighted for it; come home to Somerset once more; and at last die and be buried in Odcombe, in a tomb magnificent in marble, the showplace of the county. There he would lie in splendour, peace and fame, his travels and travails done.

When he returned from these walks, Terry thought he had never seen him look so hale, and that gladdened him, for in spite of Coryate's innumerable quiddities and oddities, Terry had come to love this ragged dwarf who was different from other men.

~

The pleasant weather that had immediately followed the rains ended. Some weeks of intense heat followed and generated an ochre dust that crept into houses and clothes and scarified the skin. Jehangir had always prized his comfort; he announced that the court would move northward to cooler weather. Wherever the Emperor went, the English envoy had to follow. So one day Roe announced to his people that they must make ready to leave, but nobody grumbled. The English had grown tired of Mandu: the absence of women and liquor, the boredom, now the heat; they were glad to go.

For them it was relatively easy to move. But the shifting of the court was as difficult and cumbersome as the shifting of a city. The preparations took weeks during which Mandu was in uproar with the movement of soldiers, baggage, elephants, ministers and flunkeys. They were to precede Jehangir's retinue and make all ready in advance of its arrival at each halting place before it reached its final, still unstated, destination. In the middle of October, the court left Mandu while drums beat and musicians played. The little group of Englishmen, with its baggage animals and servants, trailed in its wake. So much dust filled the air that it was hard for the travellers to breathe, leave alone see more than a few feet ahead.

Progress was unbelievably slow, only a handful of kos a day. When, on the second evening, the whole immense snake of people and animals ceased to drag itself through the dust and coiled in upon itself for a night halt, Coryate said to Terry in the tent they shared, 'Edward, I fear that the flux is upon me once more.'

Terry looked closely at his friend and discerned that he was truly very sick. His bulbous eyes were scarlet and his skin crinkled as old parchment. He touched Coryate's forehead. It burned with fever. Terry could smell and see that the flux had indeed returned. Coryate's loose Indian pajamas were sticky with mucus and blood.

For two days more, the mobile city slithered, slowly down the road. The cloud of dust above it was visible for miles around. Coryate lay swaddled in straw, naked from the waist down, in the bed of an oxcart. Terry sat by him. Dust and sound moved through the air around them. The rumble of wheels on the packed dirt, the cries of baggage animals and their drivers, were two identifiable parts of the sound. But all was blurred into one by the underlying and unabated drone of human conversation. It ran down the disorderly train, more than two miles in length, until nightfall, when camp was made, lamps lit and fires kindled. Coryate knew little of all this.

When he could, Terry changed the straw around him, for it was continuously defiled by his bloody excretions, and threw water over his body in an attempt to cleanse him and cool his fever. He also gave him whatever medicines he had. He was touched because the people in and around their small part of the procession—cart drivers, camp followers and even soldiers—tried in their own ways to help. So did the peasants who stood in their fields to watch the Emperor pass. Many of these people came to look at Coryate in his cart. They shook their heads, clucked and murmured in sympathy. Some seemed to suggest remedies, but Terry could not understand a word they said.

But the procession moved very slowly. An old peasant woman who had emerged from the fields to cluck her tongue over Coryate repeated some words several times to Terry. When he spread his hands and shook his head in incomprehension, she made an impatient sound, took an armful of straw from the cart, and ran back to her hut. Terry shouted in protest, for he assumed this to be some form of petty theft, but the cart driver tried to reassure him. He smoothed the air over Terry's head with his hand, as he might have gentled one of his own oxen, and tried to soothe the angry Englishman with his voice.

An hour passed, but they had not moved far from where they had encountered the woman when she came back. Terry now had a proper look at her, and he shrank away. She had a long nose and obsidian eyes, a witch's face framed in wild white hair. The sun had blackened her skin, and through her torn blouse he could see her sad, slack udders. Between her hands she carried a piece of burlap and piled on it were flat stones she had heated to redness in a fire. Each one was wrapped in the straw he had at first thought she had stolen.

With the terrifying abruptness and the same movement, as a hoptoad, she leapt into the cart and squatted beside Coryate, who was barely conscious. For Terry she was the embodiment of evil, she was all his parents and tutors had warned him to flee, but, in spite of his dread, he tried to intervene, to save Coryate from her spells, because he loved his friend. The cart driver caught him by the arm and calmed him down, as he would have done a recalcitrant bullock.

The witch heaped the hot stones, each in its straw case, around Coryate's feet and hands, and on either side of his body. When she had finished she picked up her ragged piece of burlap and looked down at her patient for a few moments. Her face was impassive. She hopped, toad-like, off the cart and once more disappeared into the fields. An unpleasant medicinal aroma rose from the bricks. She has packed herbs with them, Terry thought. Should I take them from his body? This may be black magic. Then something in him, not English, something that denied all he had ever been taught, said, No. It is only kindness.

At nightfall, as they made camp around the small and squalid town of Dhar, Coryate broke into a profuse sweat. Then he opened his very blue eyes and seemed to recognize Terry, who touched his cheek and found the fever had broken. The cart driver came up with a clay bowl of what seemed to be vegetable soup. Together they fed Coryate, who accepted it all gratefully and then fell into a deep and peaceful sleep, under a sky that glittered with more than a million stars.

~

Two hours later, Roe summoned Terry to his tent, a palatial structure a hundred yards from Coryate's cart. He had been told that day that the Emperor had at last decided on his destination. The court was bound for the town of Amdavad, in the province of Gujarat. Roe had now been able to make his plans. Coryate, sick once more, was a constant burden, and had to be sent home as soon as possible.

Roe planned to despatch him to Surat at once. Two East Indiamen were to leave for England in December, and he wanted Coryate on one of them. He had intended to send him with Steele, but had remembered the bad blood between them and decided to entrust him to Terry's care instead.

'Amdavad is not a great distance from Surat,' he told the young chaplain. 'I need you with me there. Leave Coryate in Surat and come to me at once in Amdavad. I will give Coryate two letters, one to the factors, the other to the captains. I have instructed whichever captain sails first to take him as a passenger.' Roe drew a deep breath and glared at Terry.

'The court leaves for Amdavad tomorrow, and I do also. Coryate has become your friend, Terry. Fetch him to me before I leave, that I may bid him Godspeed. But I am glad to see the back of him. No twenty other men have caused such a pother here,' said Roe bitterly, 'as this one crazed dwarf has done.'

~

Two days later, after an enfeebled Coryate bade Roe farewell and the Emperor's procession, like a gargantuan snail, moved on, Terry and his charge started on the road to Surat. Coryate had aroused feelings of infinite tenderness and pity in the younger man. Terry felt an urge to shield and protect him. What tore at his heart now was that while Coryate needed time to recuperate, none was available. They had to push on; December neared, as did the departure of the ships.

Roe had provided Terry with enough money for them to travel in small ponycarts. But the roads were bumpy, and the food available in the villages where they lodged was not suitable to an invalid. The flux remained upon Coryate, though he was better than before. But in a village one day Terry, coming back to the hut where they had spent the night, was horrified to find Coryate in tears, and even more horrified to see that he had opened one of Roe's letters to the captains, entrusted to him in Dhar.

'Am I come to this?' Coryate asked brokenly, showing him the letter. Terry felt he should not look at a confidential document, but he did. It contained lengthy lists of instructions to the shipmasters. A single sentence commanded that one of them should take Tom Coryate back to London. Roe laconically described the passenger as 'an honest poor wretch.'

'I am no poor wretch,' Coryate sobbed like a child, his face buried in Terry's chest. 'I am Coryate. I am Thomas Coryate, and I have walked through the world.' He wanted to tear up the letter, but Terry would not allow this. He took charge of the two documents: one with Roe's seal still unbroken upon the envelope, the other opened. He tried to think of plausible explanations to offer the people in Surat for the one with the broken seal, and finally decided not to attempt any.

On a cool December day, their last ponycart reached a large village. Smoke rose from cooking fires outside the thatched huts. The air smelt of it, of the broad river they could see not far off, and, pungently, of the sea beyond. Coryate's Hindustani had not been of much use in the past few days. The people here spoke a language of their own and dressed differently from those farther east. But their driver turned to them, nodded, and said, 'Surat.' Then he pointed northward and said, 'Angrez.' He turned the pony's head northward.

The gilded bells on its harness tinkled as it moved into a trot. This was a sound they had heard constantly on this trip and it had horripilated Coryate's delicate nerves. Now the bells seemed to remind him of other matters. 'It must be Yule at home,' he said to Terry. 'Is it not the season?' Terry nodded. 'It is the season of Yule,' he said, 'though truly I do not know whether the day itself is past, or yet to come.'

They came into an area of roughly whitewashed one-storeyed brick edifices. Redfaced men stood outside, squinting as the sun swelled overhead. 'Angrez,' said the driver, and pulled up. Terry and Coryate climbed stiffly out of the cart and Terry said to one of the men, 'We are English, and come to see Master Duke or Master Holman with papers from Sir Thomas Roe.' A tall man with cold eyes said, 'I am Matthew Duke. I am first factor here.' He eyed Coryate curiously. 'Come in, sirs, out of this God-cursed sun.'

The ground floor of the factory was piled with bales of cloth and smelt of it. The English had their quarters on the upper floor. Here they met the other factor, Holman, who was grossly fat and smelt of rum. The factors offered them tea and bread. The commander of the fleet, Pring, and the captains of the ships in the harbour were summoned. All this took time and during it Coryate, as was now his wont, did not say much. Terry talked and handed over the letters, which were duly perused. No mention was made of the one with the broken seal.

A tall captain with an equine face said to Coryate, 'I am Nathaniel Salmon, master of *The New Year's Gift*. We sail in two weeks and I can take you, sir.' Coryate nodded, and so it was decided. 'I am for Amdavad,' Terry said. 'Sir Thomas requires that I come there soon.' The factors offered him a pony. 'Someone will need to ride here from Amdavad,' Duke said, 'soon enough, and he'll bring it back.'

'Then I must leave at once,' Terry said, and flinched from the look in Coryate's eyes. The pony was saddled, and they went outside. It was still early afternoon. Terry drew Coryate away from the others and put his arms around the little man. 'May you have a fair voyage to England, dear Tom,' he said. 'My devoirs to your good mother. One of these days you will be astonished, for you shall find me at your doorstep in Odcombe. Sir Thomas will be pleased to hear that you have found passage on a ship so swift and safe.' He hugged Coryate's wasted body and kissed his cheek.

'I hope that I may conduct myself in proper manner, once I am come to England,' said Coryate softly, 'for now I am no more a man.' Tears suddenly filled Terry's eyes. He kissed Coryate's cheek once more, very hard, then turned away and mounted his pony. Halfway down the track he turned for a last look at the shrunken figure that stood quite still and bereft amidst the tall shapes of the factors and the captains, with their red faces and cold eyes.

~

In the few hours available to him, Terry had told the Surat factors and also Salmon, the captain of *The New Year's Gift,* a little about Coryate. Else, he feared, they would have taken him at the worth of Roe's brief and contemptuous introduction, and treated him as a misshapen human parcel to be taken from one shore and dumped on another, part of the other English debris that was annually shipped home from the Indies.

So the factors, though they were coarse commercial men, understood that Coryate, for all his peculiar appearance and ways, was a person of some consequence at home and treated him with more respect that they might otherwise have shown. The shipmaster Salmon was a fairly lettered man, with a small store of books in his cabin. The recent translation of the Bible occupied the place of honour. The other books were equally divided between religious tracts and nautical almanacs.

Already, in England, much before Terry told him of Coryate's travels and books, Salmon had heard the name well spoken of. So he went out of his way to cultivate the company of the dwarf. He even lent him his precious copy of the Bible. Glancing through the new translation gave Coryate pleasure, though he told Salmon he thought the English was too simple.

Salmon persuaded Coryate to dress in European clothes once more. At first he proposed to furnish him with a proper English suit, but none could be found on ship or shore that would fit. There was no time, nor were there any tailors, to make one. Coryate was eventually dressed in the baggy canvas pantaloons and tunic of an ordinary seaman; Salmon promised him warmer attire once they entered European waters. But Coryate knew he looked clownish in his new clothes and he also felt that he had somehow lost part of himself.

~

Though still a long way from good health, he knew himself fortunate to be alive at all. He was much improved since his relapse at Dhar, but now he saw the world through the abnormally sensitive eyes of a convalescent. When he was not reading Salmon's Bible, he walked abroad. His weakness limited him to a small area in the village around the factory, but his reawakened eyes made up for the unsteadiness of his step. He could see things as though he had never seen them before: as though they had never existed before and this was all Eden.

It was now winter in India, as it was in England. Snow was unimaginable here, but in the relatively prosperous area around the English factory, the village women were dressed for cold weather, in longsleeved blouses made of thick cotton, scarves and full skirts. The rich primary colours of their clothes dazzled Coryate's eye. Sunlight flashed from the many silver ornaments they wore: necklaces, bracelets, anklets. Some of the young ones were beautiful, with delicately etched features.

They delighted Coryate, a flock of brilliantly feathered birds descended from the sky to settle around wells and under trees. When the women noticed him staring at them, the young ones drew their scarves over their faces as veils, but after a while let them fall. He still stared, but they had decided that he was harmless. And I am, he realized with surprise. It is nothing to do with my sorry state now; I always was.

His eyes moved around him, slowly absorbed what they saw: women, pulling children, trees, birds, flowers, cattle with garlands round their necks, their horns painted blue: all had been dipped into deep sunlight, purified and renewed to remake the world. This is a beautiful country, he thought. I am glad that I came to see it. Now I must go home and write about all I saw. He had watched similar scenes before, he recalled, but never been so moved, nor rendered so full of wonder.

Early one morning, as he left the warehouse on his walk, hopeful of more wonders, he met the fat factor, Holman. Holman was usually drunk. It was too early for him to be drunk yet. But he was taking his first draught of the day, and as he tilted his flask to his mouth Coryate smelt rum. Holman lowered the flask and met disapproving blue eyes. He said defensively, 'Christ's blood, Master Coryate, how can you blame a man if he needs a tipple now and then? I have been in this Godbeshitten chamberpot of a spot three years now, and I swear no man can live here without liquor. But there will be plenty this night.' He laughed. 'We shall celebrate Yuletide.'

'I had forgotten about that,' said Coryate. 'Is it the day?'

'Near enough,' Holman answered. 'Where do you go, sir, on your dawn walks? There is nothing worth the seeing here but wenches with big bubbies, and they will not fuck.'

'Around the village,' said Coryate, 'where daily I see God's marvels and wonders.' Holman, startled, eyed him closely for some moments. 'Why do you not walk by the river?' he suggested at last. 'It is pleasant enough there, though a fair way. The cool air may clear your head somewhat. I can send one of my boys with you, for you seem not fully … ah …'

He saved himself further words and called to a dark, slender youth who had come out of the factory and stood yawning in the early sunlight. He introduced him to Coryate. 'This is Cardozo. He has Portugee blood, but he is a good boy. He knows the gibberish spoken hereabouts. Cardozo, take Master Coryate to walk by the river, so to improve his health.'

Coryate and the boy walked through clumps of palm trees that clattered above their heads like swarms of birds. Nettles caught at their feet, thorn trees at their clothes. Neither spoke. Coryate had once found it hard to keep silent more than a minute, but now silence was his familiar; and the boy could clearly not think of anything to say. Then they saw the glimmer of water ahead and heard its indistinct lisps and whispers.

The Tapti was a broad river, blue in this season. Trees lined its banks and birds chirped and twittered in the trees. On the far side Coryate saw a small herd of roe deer come down to the water to drink. The white sails of fishing boats swelled in a wind from the south, and he heard the calls of the crews. He was glad that Holman, for whatever reason, had sent him here.

Cardozo and he walked down the banks for some time. Then under a large tree with tortured branches, they came on a golden girl, very pretty. Ample breasts quivered under her blouse like heavy doves. She was eating something from a leaf wrapper and a cylindrical basket, full of vegetables, lay beside her. She gaped fearfully at Coryate, but quickly recovered her poise and smiled, mostly at Cardozo, with very white teeth.

'Wild tribes live here,' Cardozo said in accented English. 'She is from one of them.' Liquid dialect rippled through Coryate's ear. 'She came to collect tamarind.' He indicated the tree overhead. 'This is a tamarind tree. They say ghosts haunt it. She says you look like a ghost come from the tree.'

The girl giggled and asked a question. Cardozo was reluctant to translate it until Coryate pressed him. 'Sir, these people have no manners. She asks if you are a ghost. She says you look more like a ghost than a man.' Coryate felt a hurt in his chest. Then the girl leant forward and offered him her food.

Coryate took two small green chillies from the leaf container, but his hand started to shake, for as she leant forward her blouse gaped open and, standing above her, he could see her plump young breasts and her dark nipples, erect.

'Sir, don't eat those ...' Cardozo started to say, but Coryate had already bitten into them. Liquid fire scarified his lips and tongue and as he swallowed them it spread into his bowels. He gasped in agony. Cardozo fetched him water from the river and at last, though his belly and the inside of his mouth felt scalded, he was able to wipe his nose and eyes. The girl spoke. She had a mischievous smile on her face.

'What is she saying?'

'Sir, I think I should not tell you.'

'Tell me!' said Coryate with all the force he could muster.

'These people have no shame. She says you are no ghost, because of the way you looked at her breasts. She says an old man like you should not look at young girls' breasts.'

The hurt in Coryate's chest increased. 'Let us go hence, Cardozo.' They walked away, followed by the girl's laughter.

'I am not an old man, Cardozo,' Coryate said at last, and felt foolish as he spoke the words. Cardozo did not reply. 'I am only forty years old,' Coryate insisted. Still no response came. He said almost pleadingly, 'What is my age, you think?'

'I know not, sir,' Cardozo replied at last. 'But to my eye you will be upward of sixty years. Seventy, mayhap.'

The hurt in Coryate's heart increased. At the same time a familiar and dreaded claw hooked into his belly. Whether because of the chillies or the river water or both, the flux had come back strongly. He said, 'Walk on ahead, boy. I must ease my bowels, so leave me. I will follow and catch you up soon.'

'I will go slowly, then,' said Cardozo, and disappeared among the trees and shadows.

Coryate lowered his pantaloons and squatted on the bank of the Tapti river. By the waters of Tapti he squatted and wept.

~

Once darkness had fallen, in the open land outside the factory, the Yuletide party took place. The weather was cool. The sailors from the English ships at Swalley Hole had excavated a deep firepit and built stone walls around it. It exuded flames and smoke, like some minor enclave of hell.

Three Englishwomen were at present in Surat, a Company widow and two Company wives. They had come from their sequestered quarters, dressed in whatever finery they had with them. Through an interpreter, they directed a team of native cooks. They themselves did not approach the fire, for they needed to preserve their best clothes from smutch and smirch.

But their presence put the male guests on their mettle. Besides the employees of the Company, the naval commanders and the shipmasters from Swalley were present, as well as the masters' mates. Crewmen had been called to perform whatever manual tasks might be necessary. Casks of beer, wine and rum had been fetched from the ships and broached.

When Nathaniel Salmon arrived, he noticed Coryate's absence and inquired from Holman, who was already too drunk to speak, where he was. Matthew Duke enlightened the captain. 'He has fever and the flux. He lies abed upstairs.'

Salmon went upstairs. Coryate was lying on a pallet in his room, a brimming chamberpot beside him. Salmon tried unsuccessfully to avert his eyes and nose from it, and at last called a reluctant sailor and ordered him to empty and wash the vessel. Coryate's eyes were wide and childlike with pain, shame and distress, and he shuddered spasmodically with fever.

'How now, Thomas!' cried Salmon. 'What has come upon you? It is Yuletide, man, a time to be festive! Come down to the rest of us and we will chase all your megrims away.

There are beautiful English ladies below, and I'll warrant you have not seen one for years. Come down and your state will improve. You can only worsen, lying here alone in the dark.'

Coryate's body, like an animal's, understood itself. It knew it was dying, and accepted this. But his mind, as yet, could not, or not entirely. It did not want his body to die in the dark but, while it lived, to be amongst other, living bodies.

'Did you not tell me once that you like to drink sack?' Salmon continued. 'I have a cask of it below. It is the best, new from Spain. Come, help us drink it. It is Yuletide, Thomas.'

Clearly as in a picture, Coryate saw himself in the Mermaid, fire burning in the hearth, orange flames tinctured with blue. He sat by Jonson's side, a mug of sack in his hand.

With an effort he sat up. 'Sack!' he muttered, 'Sack! I have not tasted sack these many months. Give me some sack.'

Salmon's arm round his waist, he tottered downstairs, into the warmth, the firelight, and the roisterous noise of the party. His spirits rose suddenly. He could hear his own language spoken all round him and the band of the *Anne Royal* playing 'Greensleeves'. He was introduced to three Englishwomen, and dimly realized that one of them was his enemy Steele's wife. All that was irrelevant now. He was unaware that the women were looking at him with profound pity. He felt sorry for them, coarse of face and body, mare-like; but that was irrelevant too. Salmon pressed a mug into his shaking hand.

'Drink, Thomas, drink! There is a cask of it entire!'

He smelt sack and started to remember, and then tasted it and took a deep draught, and then it all came back, perfect as it used to be. The idea of his death, became irrelevant.

~

At one end of the compound, Holman sprawled face down, snoring as though concussed. Others were in the same case, and their slumped bodies, under the incandescent light from the firepit, resembled casualties of war. But *Anne Royal's* band still played, raggedly and out of tune, and some people were still drinking. All the food had been devoured long since.

Salmon came out of the factory and surveyed the scene. He was very sober. The factor Duke came up, still not quite drunk. 'How is he?' he asked. Salmon shook his head.

'Truly I do not know,' he said. 'Now I shall carry guilt for the rest of my days, that I made Coryate drink. I thought it would cheer his sad heart. When he so bepuked and beshat himself that none would come near him, and then collapsed, I thought him a dead man. But Mistress Steele aided me to bring him upstairs, and it was she cleansed his body and revived him. Then he seemed better, but now he is singing, or trying to sing, and, God's wounds, but I like it not.'

'He drank more than even a well man could carry,' Duke grunted. 'Oftentimes, in their cups, I have heard men sing.'

'He is sober now,' Salmon said. 'And drunkards do not sing like this. This is like a ghost weeping. Come and hear.'

~

Where he was, it was cold and wet, and smelt of garbage and a tidal river. Coryate swam through vortices of darkness, sank and then rose once more. In the distance he could hear a thin, unmusical voice that wailed forth broken words. He could make out what the words were, and it seemed to him that he had heard them before.

'I leant my back against an oak,
Thinking it was a tru-usty tree.

But first it bent and syne it broke.
Sae my true love hath forsaken me ...'

So much pain in his body, so many different pains. In his mind he saw individual faces, each one plainly etched. He knew each face well, every feature of each face. He knew that he knew these faces, and they belonged to people he loved, but was terrified because he could not put a name to any of them.

Then he saw his own face, and knew it was his; but he did not know his name. He saw his own body and knew he was leaving it. The thin, faraway voice continued to wail in his ear.

'Martinmas wind, when wilt thou blow,
Shaking the green leaf from the tree?
O gentle death, when wilt thou come?
For of this life I am we-e-ary.'

He saw his body slide away into a black river, and reached a hand down to assist it. Its hand took his firmly and drew him downward. Darkness filled him utterly. He ceased to feel. He knew with relief that in a moment he would cease to think.

~

'Is he dead?' Duke asked in a whisper.

'Yes,' Salmon said. He looked down into the twisted face, the beard wet with vomit and blood. 'Yes. Yes, he is dead.'

'It must have been painful,' Duke said, 'from his looks.'

'Yes.'

'We should be thankful then, for him, that it is over,' Duke murmured. He rose from where he had knelt by the pallet, pulling the coarse blanket over Coryate's face. 'And we should think where to bury the body. Soon it will start to stink.'

'Yes,' said Salmon. After a pause, he added indistinctly, 'He told me once that he dreamt of having a marble tomb in his own village in the county of Somerset.'

'We all dream,' said Duke. They went downstairs. The compound was empty. Embers smouldered in the firepit. As they came out of the factory, the eastern sky reddened.

'He knew more of the Indies than any other Englishman,' Salmon said. 'But the book he dreamt he would write is lost on the roads, and no man will ever read it.'

'Poor little sod,' Duke said. 'By noon we should find somewhere to put him.'

20

Diary Ten

March 2003

Surat

The route from Mandu to Surat that we followed was in part the road that Coryate would have taken. It detoured here and there running parallel to the old road. As we left the fertile plains of Maharashtra and drove into the interior of Gujarat, the landscape changed. Trees gave way to short thorny brambles. The soil was darker, harder, and punctured with the deep hoof-marks of cattle.

Dom had never been to Surat. Juzer had been there a few months earlier to meet the head priest. His community was well represented in the city and his second cousin, Abaas, lived here. But the last time I was in Surat was thirty-nine years ago. I had been twelve. I remembered it as a village newly grown into a small town, at odds with its own shape and extremities. Amidst alternating tracts of swamp and thicket it contained mud huts, market squares, brick houses, ruinous parts of the old warehouses of the English and the Dutch.

In an ancient square, my father told me, African slaves were once sold to wealthy nawabs. But what I had liked were the old English and Dutch cemeteries. The tombs seemed to me then like life-size dolls' houses where weary people could sleep for a long time.

Like a purring animal, our car slipped through the new streets of Surat. It was almost midnight. Dom said that he could imagine Coryate's aggrieved ghost, slouching about in the shadows of the modern apartment houses. I tried desperately to fit them to the old images stored in my mind, and failed. As we reached the guest house, fireworks started to explode in the town behind us. India had just beaten England in a World Cup cricket match.

~

Dom did not want to be awakened before ten. It was 8 a.m. and I had just woken up when Juzer called. His voice squeaked like a schoolboy's. 'We found the tomb, ma'am.'

He gushed over the telephone. 'I had given instructions to Abaas a month ago. I had given him the exact longitude and latitude of the tomb that was mentioned in Strachan's book. I had also given him notes on the entire history of the East India Factory in Surat and the names of the key English factors. Now Abaas has located the tomb and contacted two people who know about it. Meghnani and Jolly Christie.'

I accepted what he said with a bewilderment of mind. After a long journey etched with purpose and impatience, the end couldn't be so simple. Was it not, I asked myself, merely a collusion of coincidences? I got ready in a hurry. Juzer was dressed for an African safari: khaki jeans, heavy-duty shoes and dark glasses. He told me in voluble gasps that the tomb was not far from our guesthouse. It was in Rajaggri village in the Suwali area, which the English had called Swalley Hole. He also told me, rather unnecessarily, that the archaeological department of the Government of Gujarat had declared the tomb to be Coryate's. Then he proceeded to give me a detailed description of the tomb, though he had not yet seen it.

I felt vaguely dispirited. With so much information readily available not much remained to be discovered. But Juzer's high spirits were unabated. 'I am going now to see. You want to come?'

Prickly trees curtained the commemoration of an old scene. Coryate's tomb perched on a carbuncle of a hill was raised on a platform, crowned by a dome held by four sets of columns. A circle of thorny branches surrounded the monument. We walked around to the rear. A frail old man swept the ground. On seeing us, he jumped, then dipping a rag in a bucket of water began furiously to clean a rickety black board with a message in Gujarati. He pointed to it. The tomb had suffered damage during the earthquake, it said, it was unsafe. Juzer asked him nonetheless if we could go inside it.

The old man cleared away some of the thorny branches. As we stood on the platform he told us he was Dhirubhai and had been appointed to look after the tomb. A salary had been fixed for this two years ago, he said, but he had not received any yet. We asked what he knew about the tomb. It was an Englishman's, he told us.

'But this one looks like a Muslim tomb,' Juzer said, firmly.

'It is an Englishman's.'

'Is there another tomb?' Juzer persisted. 'A Muslim tomb?'

'Only this one. An Englishman's.'

'Is there a Muslim cemetery nearby? Was there one?' Dhirubhai shook his head. Juzer said, 'It's like this ma'am, Foster writes in his account that the Persian Ambassador

Nagd Ali Beg committed suicide on board an English ship. When it docked in Swally Point, the sailors buried him a stone's throw away from Coryate's grave, which was marked but with two stones. There is one problem here. See, Ali Beg was an important official and he was a Muslim. So they would have definitely buried him in a Muslim cemetery. I think there must have been a Muslim cemetery here and perhaps Coryate was buried next to it.'

Dhirubhai shook his head violently although I was certain he couldn't understand a word of what Juzer had said. He held his stand, 'This one is Englishman's, not Muslim.' He gave us his employer's name and phone number. Somabhai would be able to tell us more; he lived in Vasu village.

I inspected the tomb, which was a curious combination of styles, part European and part Mogul. It was made of brick and plaster and once painted a salmon pink. It had red motifs over the pointed arches and a blue floral pattern at the springing of the dome. Outside, on top of the dome, a four-point star extended its tentacles in four directions.

Dhirubhai pointed to two metal strips jutting out of the ground. They had held a marble plaque declaring the tomb to be Coryate's, he told us. He had not seen it himself, but this is what he had heard. I told him how important it had been for us to find Coryate's tomb and expressed a desire to take back with us to England a bit of brick or mud from it. The people in Coryate's village were waiting for our return, I added dramatically.

He disappeared, then returned with a brick. 'Take,' he said, 'this will make them happy.' I turned the brick in my hand. It was like a tile, thinner than normal bricks, and although its edges were broken it was apparent that it had once been a square of adobe.

I made Dhirubhai hold the brick in his hand and stand before the tomb; I took photographs of him. Juzer stood nearby, his face sullen. He brightened up considerably when I asked him to stand next to Dhirubhai. I shot pictures of them and of the damaged columns in the back whose bricks were clearly, visible. They were square tiles like the one now in my hands.

I took out some bank notes from my purse and pressed them into Dhirubhai's palm. He pulled back his hand as if I had injured him. I put the money into his shirt pocket. Dhirubhai turned his head away; his brown eyes were muddy. He whispered, 'I have heard there is a mad fakir's tomb in Mora village. It is not far from here. That may be your English fakir's tomb. I don't know. There could be a Muslim cemetery there. I've heard Muslims lived in that village.'

Juzer retorted, 'You said this was the Englishman's tomb. Is it or isn't it?'

'It was a long time ago. How can I know?' Dhirubhai raised a hand in the air; it shook. 'Don't take my name, sahib,' he said to Juzer, 'I will not get my salary.'

Juzer laughed. 'You haven't in any case.'

'At least I can have hope,' the old man said.

~

We returned to the guesthouse to pick up Dom. Juzer's excitement was contagious. In unyoked enthusiasm, I poured out the events of the morning to Dom. He was neither curious nor impressed. He sat on his bed, motionless and drained. 'I can't get my fucking feet into these shoes,' he said. When he removed his socks I noticed his feet were badly swollen. Then as his trousers lifted slightly I saw that the skin on his ankles and legs was lacerated and bleeding. 'It hurts terribly,' he looked dismally at his feet. 'I think I'll stay in the room today and work.' His face brightened. 'England is playing Australia in the World Cup today. I can watch it on telly after lunch.'

Juzer and I went to Vasu village in search of Somabhai. We found him in Madhuban Stores which he owned. He told us that the archaeological department of Gujarat, which had now shifted its office from Surat to Vadodara, had appointed him as the watchman of Coryate's tomb. At that time, he had lived in Rajaggri village for fourteen years. But when he moved out, he had appointed Dhirubhai to look after it. The government paid him a monthly salary of Rs 1350, he told us. I was tempted to ask him why he hadn't paid Dhirubhai. But Juzer stopped me.

Somabhai took us to the local office and arranged for us to speak to his boss Trivedi in Vadodara. 'Of course it's Coryate s tomb', Trivedi hollered into a crackling line, 'whose tomb it is if not his?' It was noted in the survey record of the area, he said, as well as in the Surat Gazetteer. The marble plaque on it was taken to Surat by Sarabhai Nawab, a politician who ran a side-business in stealing gravestones.

Juzer asked for his address and Trivedi laughed. He died a few years ago, he said.

Somabhai walked us to the car. 'You must go to Mora village,' he said. 'I've heard that there is a grave of a mad fakir there. Some of them say he was a white man.' He swirled a finger into his mouth, dug out a morsel from between his teeth, studied it, then wiped his finger on his trousers. 'Don't tell anyone I told you.'

~

Dom appeared to be better next morning. The rest and the cricket match seemed to have done him some good despite the fact that England had played miserably against Australia. Juzer told him about Meghnani and Jolly Christie. Meghnani was a retired college professor. He had written books on Surat. Christie was a talkative fellow, Juzer said, and added, 'Abaas says he has insatiable passion for dead people.'

Jolly Christie's house was a modest building on a narrow quiet street near the church. The kitchen on the ground floor was the hub of the house; it contained the living, dining and sleeping areas besides a cage for a loquacious parrot that spoke each time Jolly stopped. Mounted on two opposite walls were two large clocks showing different times. There were bedrooms upstairs but they were full of books. Jolly's own bedroom had books everywhere, including the space under his bed.

Jolly was a robust, healthy man. Dressed in a black shirt and jeans, his hair was curiously cut in thick layers of black and grey; it resembled the terraced tea-gardens of Assam. He talked from the moment we met. 'Surat is a glorious city of history. Its river Tapti has witnessed many historical ships and events. It changes its course,' he said, 'like our women do their minds, seven-eight times. Our poor Coryate, the one-barefoot man also buried here under the waters of the river and the sea together. No money, no clothes, just one shoe.'

He slapped his chest, said to Dom, 'I am a poor mill worker, sir. I have no education; only love for history and dead peoples. I am self-learnt. I have 8000 books, xeroxes of rare volumes. Every time we fight, my wife throws them all out. "What use these," she screams, "they bring no money, no name." But each time I bring all the books back.' He looked solemn. 'I call myself naked fakir because I have only my books and my hobby—making biographies of graves.'

He took us to the English cemetery and pointing to

each grave, told us who was buried in them and when and how they had died, and why. He behaved as though he was acquainted with them. Many graves were of women who had died young, and children. I noticed some of the tombs were built of square brick tiles similar to those on Coryate's tomb. Juzer was more specific. He told me that all the tombs before 1750 were built of square bricks.

We walked through a narrow lane to the back to the Dutch and Armenian cemeteries. Dom did not come with us. His feet were still swollen, he said, and painful; he could not walk. Facing the cemeteries was a row of buildings that appeared to have been old warehouses. They had no windows except ventilators fixed high on the top of the walls. Parts of these walls were built of old square brick tiles.

The largest tomb in the Dutch cemetery caught my attention. It was elaborate in structure and embellishment but in many ways it resembled Tom Coryate's modest tomb in Rajaggri—the circular columns, the dome, the pediment, red and blue motifs, pink hues still visible in the plaster, the old square brick tiles. I noticed a smaller tomb behind it. On its dome was a four-pointed star identical to the one we had seen in Rajaggri.

Walking back to the car, I thanked Jolly for his time. As I started to tell him that we planned to go to Mora village, Juzer put up a hand in some sort of a signal which I couldn't understand, so I completed what I had started to say. Jolly risked a sidelong look at Juzer then insisted that he come with us. 'I also want to spend time with sir,' he said. 'I am so honoured to be with a learned man.'

When we were on our way, Jolly turned around and asked Dom, 'Sir, you must be seventy? Eighty?' Dom only smiled. I told Jolly he was sixty-four.

'Arre! I am same-same. Sixty-four. I am very sturdy. But you look so old. That's wonderful. I am being so happy to meet you.' Dom later remarked that he believed Jolly was trying to pay him some kind of compliment.

Jolly talked all the way. 'I know what you're up to,' he shook a finger at Juzer. 'But I am your friend so I am telling you. You are making terrific mistake.' He slapped Juzer's shoulder. 'That fakir grave in Mora village is not Coryate baba's, okay. You are going there for that reason only, no?' He slapped his chest. 'Ask Jolly Christie. Expert authority on graves.'

He made squelchy sounds with his tongue. 'I will give you biography of this grave. It is called Fakir-ki-Tekdi. Means small rounded hill of a poor fakir. Fakir meaning holy man. Old man. Now when women die of pregnancy, people offer prayers at this fakir's tomb. Who he was, nobody is knowing. He was some madman. Now you don't go and say it is our Tommy's tomb. Na-na-na-na,' he shook his head, 'that misguiding history.'

Just as I started to say something, Juzer put up a hand. Jolly looked puzzled. He rubbed his hands together. 'Very clever. Ah! Very clever. I know now what you are thinking. You are thinking Nagd Ali Begh's tomb is in Mora.' He laughed out aloud. 'Wrong. From beginning to end wrong.'

The city road gave way to a narrow track that wound its way to the twin villages: Mor and Bhagua. As we turned into a narrow lane to go to Bhagua I heard the sound of a bird. I wasn't sure it was one.

'Is that a bird?' Jolly said it was. *Ghoot ghoot,* he mimicked its cry. All along the lane, thorny bushes on either side reached high, like walls, as in Somerset lanes. The sun was setting in front of us, an orange disc that sunk lower as we drove towards its flaming centre.

At the start of the village, Juzer asked a tailor if there was a Muslim cemetery or an Englishman's grave in the locality. Jolly stood close behind him, a hand perched over his ear. 'See, I told you sister,' he said to me. 'Your juice-man is asking for Muslim and English. I can read minds like anything. Even dead people's minds.' He laughed and walked away to the car saying, 'I will sit with my learned sahib. More better than looking for graves. Be careful of snakes. One bite and dead.'

The tailor pointed to a low mound of thorny trees. 'A mad fakir's grave is there.' He looked at the car, then at Dom and Jolly. In a greedy tone he asked, 'Is this going to be a tourist place? Will lots of people be coming? Good bijjiness?'

Juzer and I walked to the back of the hill; it was littered with shit and used condoms. Juzer held the thorny branches as I crawled up the hump. On top of it was what appeared to be a tomb that had been built of bricks and mud.

When we returned, Jolly was talking to Dom. He sniffed, wiped his eyes, said, 'Sir, every time I think of how our Coryate was robbed in Tehran by Muslim cheats I feel like crying. See how these Muslims killed our poor Coryate in the end.'

He sniffed. 'Only some people know this story. When Coryate walked to Swally he heard the call for prayer from a nearby mosque. Coryate climbed the minaret to offer prayers and the Muslim people beat him so hard he died on that high spot. Then they buried him somewhere. Now he is lying dead, alone, and we don't know where even.' He sniffed.

~

After breakfast next morning, utilizing the cutlery on the table, Juzer revealed his strategy; He put a fork down at the edge of the table. 'Say this is the old Swally Point. If we go there and find some remains of the English port, then we can work backwards and find out where Ali Beg could have been buried. It must be nearby. If we find his grave, then throw a stone, we will find Coryate's.'

'But what about the Muslim cemetery?'

'I've abandoned that idea.' He clicked his fingers. 'Also ma'am, one thing, if we dig up the two graves we can say which is Muslim and Christian. The Muslim one will be perpendicular to the Kibla direction. I have my Kibla-finder, with me.'

We walked along the sandy shore of Swally beach, but we found no remains of the old port. We found a Sikh with a bicycle. Next to him were a number of utensils and crates of eggs. He ran a mobile canteen, he told Juzer, and he had to organize dinner for seventeen people on the beach that night.

Juzer asked him about the old port. He shook his head. He knew the stretch of the beach well, he said, and there were no remains. Juzer asked him if he had seen a Muslim or Christian grave near the sea. The Sikh pointed to the distance. 'Ask in lighthouse. An old tomb be there.'

We drove to the lighthouse. Next to it was a mound of debris. I wasn't sure whether it was half-fallen or half-up. It was two stories high, and had flopped in like an eggless soufflé.

'We don't really know whose tomb this is,' the caretaker of the lighthouse told us. 'There is a story about Mr Woxon, the assistant secretary of Bombay. Mr Woxon and his Mrs went for a boat ride. Boat capsized and they both drowned. So they were buried here,' he pointed to the tomb, 'in Hajira. That is why it is called Hajira; it is meaning tomb or grave. There was a cemetery here one time. But this is not certain.'

He talked about the old lighthouse that was completely

wrecked and about the English ships that sailed to the creek. I told him about our stroll in the blazing sun looking for remains of the port.

He laughed holding his belly. 'Everything is changed,' he said continuing to laugh. 'The entire region was subdivided into a number of villages with new names, for revenue collection purposes. Old Swally was very big before. It contained Rajaggri, Hajira, Suwali, Mora, and many other villages. Swally Point, where the ships docked, is not now in Suwali,' he said, 'but in Junagaon.'

We set out on our expedition with renewed enthusiasm. We drove through the narrow lane beyond the village Junagaon, all the way to the Hanuman Temple where it ended. The lane opened into a vast field. At some distance from us several young boys were playing cricket.

We got out of the car. The soil was black under our feet, like clay, parched with deep hoof-marks on it. I noticed that the vegetation was different from what I had seen so far in this area. The tiny tentacled pink and yellow plants were like seaweed. We walked towards a point in the distance that shimmered in the sun. It was moist earth. The area had once been a creek and had been silted up. 'This is it!' Juzer clapped his hands in the air. He threw his head back and like a Red Indian gave his symbolic yelp: Ha. Ha. Ha. He turned round and round in precise madness.

He stopped his revolutions abruptly. He looked crushed. He said, 'We have located the old creek. But it is so far from the Rajaggri tomb. Assuming that to be Coryate's tomb, why should the sailors carry the Persian Ambassador's corpse all that distance?'

~

We decided to go back to what was Coryate's tomb. 'It took us thirty-two minutes to reach here,' Juzer said tapping his watch. He sat still for a moment, contemplating the distance, then hopped out of the car, to look for Dhirubhai. Shortly, he returned with him and another old man. He was Nanubhai; he had lived in the village for over sixty years.

Nanubhai lit a beedi. He sucked at it several times, then with the air of a deft performer he told us the old story about king Mordhwaj. 'Once upon a time, all this land belonged to the king. The sea was his closest friend. But one day, because of his nephew, there was a misunderstanding between him and the sea. So the sea washed away all his land. The king was so miserable, he died. He was cremated and his ashes were buried under seven tombs with all his riches. Years passed. Then when some people heard about the treasure in his tombs they dug them up. Many of the tombs were broken. Except this one.' Nanubhai pointed to Coryate's tomb.

'But this is built for an Englishman,' Juzer said looking at Dhirubhai. Dhirubhai shook his head furiously.

'Look at these square bricks,' Nanubhai said with aplomb. 'They are very old and were in use before the Europeans came.' He surveyed Juzer carefully, then looked at me. 'Come with me,' he said walking away, 'I'll show you something. I've not told anyone about it.'

We followed him across fields and through bramble and cactus fences. He stopped under a thorny tree. 'Two brothers owned this plot. They had a fight so they divided it into two. A similar tomb was here. I've seen it with my own eyes when I was a boy. It was already broken. When this plot was to be levelled I helped to break it down and clear the rubble. We dug up a grave here. We found bones in it.'

Juzer said urgently, 'Tell me, which direction was the grave?'

'It was under this tree. This way or that way, I don't remember.'

Juzer clicked with his tongue. 'We could have made out if it was a Muslim grave or English.'

I asked, 'Where are the bones?'

'We threw them away. What to do with bones?' He pointed to a pile of bricks, 'See, those are parts of the tomb.'

As we walked to the edge-of the field, Juzer said sternly to Nanubhai, 'Next time you find a grave always check the direction. And one more thing, remember to always keep a little bone.' He laughed, patted Nanubhai's back, 'You could have become a rich man.'

I inspected the discarded rubble. Some of it had been putts of a round column made of square bricks. Others had pink motif on them. Without any doubt I could say these were similar to Coryate's tomb. Juzer selected a piece of rubble, held it up like an important scientific specimen. 'We were looking for two tombs within a stone's throw. We have found it. This could be Coryate's and the other Muslim looking one, Ali Beg's.' He hissed through his teeth, 'If only he had kept the bone.' He put the specimen in his bag and wandered away.

Nanubhai pointed to another tree in the next field. 'The third tomb was there. It was destroyed many years ago. And two more are still around in the outgrowth behind this field. There are too many thorny trees; you can't go there now. But I've seen all these five tombs when I was a boy. They belong to Mordhwaj.'

'Have you not told the officers from the archeological department about all this?' I asked.

Nanubhai shrugged his shoulders. 'They never asked us. They won't believe us villagers if we told them,' he said as he walked out of the field. I followed him. But instead of going back to Coryate's tomb, he walked in the opposite direction. I called out to Juzer. The path opened into a vast open ground.

Juzer's hand went to his mouth. 'Oh! Ma'am, it is the same place we came to this morning. The same place where the boys were playing cricket.'

Nanubhai pointed to the moist tract not far from us. 'That was where the English ships came,' he said to me, 'My grandfather told me this.'

~

Juzer had fixed up a time with the old professor, Meghnani. We drove to Surat to meet him. He was finishing lunch when we arrived. It was a few minutes before noon. It gave me some time to look around the living room where we waited.

A showcase fitted into a wall displayed an assortment of curios, plates, bowls, cups and saucers. Two ice-cream bowls caught my attention. They contained scoops of ice-cream, made of cotton, crowned with pink plastic wafers. A solitary Siamese Fighter swished its tail about in an aquarium. Then Professor Meghnani appeared, an old man, his round face made rounder by the twin circles of his spectacles.

He started to speak after apologizing for his bad English. 'Suwali was founded by English in about 1608. It was called Swalley Hole and the English ships of the East India Company landed there. At that time there were only fifteen or twenty families living around the castle of Surat near Chowk Bazaar. By the seventeenth century, the European traders, their agents and brokers lived in Surat. During the Mogul time they couldn't buy property here, they could only rent premises. The old English Factory was taken on rent in the Mughal Serai area. The English Factory was having residences, godowns below them and chapel. Later they bought property from a Parsee and set up the proper English Factory.'

Meghnani held his cheeks in both his hands and rolled his head about in dismay. 'Poor Coryate. He was very sick when Roe send him here with his chaplain Terry. Roe give letter for the Company ship's captain to issue him one-way ticket to London.'

Juzer said, 'Sir, I don't think Terry went with Coryate. I think Richard Steele and Herbert did. There is an account of a Bill of Entry ...'

'Forget any bill-will,' Meghnani said, 'think psychology of human. Roe would not send Coryate with Steele. Steele lost Coryate's manuscript, I think so, and he told Coryate the King didn't like him. Even if Roe didn't want to send Terry, Terry would have suggested to Roe. Terry loving Coryate a lot.' Meghnani nodded.

'Terry go to Ahmedabad to join Roe. Coryate stay in the English Factory in Surat for six days. It was Christmas time, and English men and women are having good fun.'

'Were there many English women here?' I asked.

'Of course. Women everywhere near men. Women here also. Marriages took place even. Steele's Mrs was here also. So in a drinking party Coryate took the wine of Sec—you are knowing what is Sec? Spanish wine. Fine wine. Coryate get dysentery. Very bad dysentery. Much much bleeding and shitting, and throwing up like anything,' the professor made a foul face and held his nose with two fingers. 'So he died.'

Juzer said, 'I am sorry, sir, he died on his way to Swally.'

'Not just you my son, we're all very very sorry. Yes, he died in the Factory. He was so sick. Think psychology of human. How can he walk all the way to the ship? You tell me? He died and the factors buried him in the old cemetery.'

'Where was that?'

'In Swally. But now it is washed away by the sea.'

'And the tomb in Rajaggri?'

'We don't even know who built this monument. It is like Mogul structure. Maybe English peoples want to build something in memory of Tom. They give plan for tomb and the local Muslim artisans build it in a style they know. For a long time no one knew it was a Christian tomb. Now the archaeological department of Gujarat has notified it as Coryate's tomb. But is it?'

'What about the marble plaque?'

He thumped his thigh with a fist. 'Who knows it was there? Many marble slabs from tombs have been robbed. All the houses around the English Cemetery are encroachments and if you were going into each of these houses with a gun you will find the marble slabs stolen from the tombs and used either as kitchen platforms, shelves or counters to store water pots. But I don't think you can find Coryate's.'

He scratched his head. 'For years, scholars believed that Coryate's tomb was in the English Cemetery in Surat. Not possible. At Coryate's time there was no cemetery in Surat. Dead bodies were sometimes taken back to England on ships. It was built much later.' He clutched his hair in a fist. 'So much confusing. But personally, I think Coryate's grave is now under sea.'

~

Muharrum had started. Juzer left by the morning train for Mumbai. Dom decided to take to bed for the day. I ordered sandwiches for him for lunch and two bars of his favourite fruit and nut chocolate. I returned to Coryate's tomb. I cleared away the thorny branches, I walked up the steps to the pavilion. Cool winds blew from the sea, perceptibly cooler than the previous day. I sat on the masonry bench that ran along the columns. I could see far away.

I heard footsteps on dry branches. It was Dhirubhai. He sat down on the bench facing me. 'It's so pleasant here,' he said, 'and look you can see the sea from here.' He scratched his foot. 'I think King Mordhwaj built these seven pavilions when he was living. Who would build them after his death? I think he built them to come and sit here; also to keep watch.'

He started to giggle. 'Nanubhai told you he found bones in the grave in the field. If the king's ashes were buried in it, how he find bones?'

I stood up, looked towards the creek. I could see long stretches of soil that glittered in the sun. I asked Dhirubhai what it was.

'Salt,' he said. I walked with him to the creek. The moist tracts of earth that I had seen were now dried and covered with a white substance: salt. Dhirubai said. 'During *poonam* when the moon is full, the sea tide comes all the way up to the edge of this village. It takes four hours to reach here and another four hours to recede. If you come here on the eighteenth March, about 2 p.m., you will find the sea here where you stand.'

~

It was our last morning in Surat. Dom had yet to see what had been designated to be Coryate's tomb. We drove to Rajaggri village. He looked at the tomb with disinterest. He did not speak. He lit a cigarette. I went to find Dhirubhai. When we returned, Dom joined his hands and said hello. He offered him a cigarette, which he first declined then accepted.

He plucked a matchbox from his pocket, lit Dom's cigarette first, then his own.

Dom asked him about his crops. 'Not good soil here,' he said with a frown, 'only stringy beans and millet.' I smiled to myself. Dom was trying to chat him up, I thought.

'Why don't you grow other plants?' Dom asked.

Dhirubhai shook his head. 'Not enough mud.' He pinched his fingers together. 'Sand.'

'There is sand here?'

Dhirubhai brightened. 'You don't know, sahib? When we dug for a bore-well in the field, at forty feet, all sand. Just like sea-bed it is.'

'Do you think, a long time ago, the sea came all over this land.'

'I don't know sir. But this I have heard. That some three hundred-four hundred years ago, the sea submerged all this land. Except this one,' he pointed to Coryate s tomb, all other pavilions were under water. That is why they broke down. They are not made of cement mortar. Only mud and lime. Only this one remained because it is on a hill.'

I led Dom down the path to the creek. He stumbled over the deep hoof-marks on the soil as he walked away, alone, limping, dragging his right foot behind him. He walked to the edge of the old creek. He stood there for some time, staring out over the muddy water. His mind, I was certain, chronicled the apprehended imagery; Coryate's private history intact in it. Dom limped back to the car, but was silent after he had reached it. I did not invade his silence.

Later, at the guesthouse, I said, 'What did you think?'

He shook his head. 'It's impossible to think. If there's anything left of Coryate now, it might be in any of the places we saw, or none of them. I think the English buried him in Swalley Hole. There were mariners with them, don't forget. They charted the longitude and latitude of the tomb. According to those he would have been buried there. Other Englishmen were buried there.' He hesitated. When the Tapti changed course and the sea came in, his tomb would have been washed away. Whatever's left of him would be part of the earth in that field by the creek.'

'It seems so sad,' I said. 'All those people in Odcombe, hoping we would find his grave ... the old Vicar and everyone else ... and it was such an ugly, gloomy field.'

'All over the world,' Dom said, in his most irritating way, 'famous people are buried in famous tombs, which you have to pay an entrance fee to look at. Nobody worries about what happened to them; the guidebooks explain it. But people in England and India are still worrying about Tom Coryate.

'He may not have a magnificent tomb. But he has more than that. People in Odcombe still want to know where he's buried. Meghnani and Jolly nearly cried when they thought of all that he'd suffered. If Coryate knew how important he's become to many people now,' Dom said, 'I think at last he'd be happy.'

Epilogue

It is a bright and sunny morning in Odcombe, a splendid respite after the rain that had persisted most of the week I was in London. I walk up the hill to the old church, holding a bunch of wild daisies I had picked on the way. From the gate I see an old woman tidying a flowerbed. She looks towards me, and when I reach her she smiles. 'Are you here in connection with Dom Moraes?'

'Yes, that's right,' I reply, surprised that she should ask me this.

She hurries over to edge of the lawn and pulling off her plastic gloves she wipes away bits of grass and dust from the gravestone. I stand beside it, read once more the inscription on the slab of Jaisalmer stone:

Dom Moraes who followed Thomas Coryate's footsteps and returned home. July 1938 – June 2004.

I had it put there over a year ago. I lay the flowers over the stone.

'The church is closed. I will get someone to open it for you,' the woman says rushing off. She shortly reappears with an elderly woman who seems splendidly dressed for the morning; her face is heavily made up.

She holds my hand in both hers. 'Thank you for coming,' she says. She opens the church door and leads me inside.

'Spend as much time as you need to, dear,' she says, 'and if you want to ask me anything,' she looks around her, 'oh dear, I am sorry the flowers have all dried up. A woman comes in every week to do the arrangements. Had I know you were coming I would have asked her to change the flowers.'

I look around the church, then ask, 'I don't see the old brick we got back from Coryate's tomb.'

The old woman clasps her hands in front of her. 'That's in the church safe, dear. Don't want anybody to steal it. You brought it all the way. It must have been difficult following Coryate's journey through India.'

It hadn't been easy. Dom and I had started our travels two years ago and completed writing the book the year after. The book was to be launched in Odcombe. We left for London with copies of the book but unfortunately without the brick; we hadn't received permission to carry organic material with us. The brick was couriered to us by the British Council in Mumbai. It was packed in a special yellow bubble-wrap cover marked: *Limestone Sample. Of No Commercial Value.* When I tore open the cover, to my horror, ants, spiders and bugs sprung out of it. 'Now look at what you have done!' Dom chuckled.

The Odcombe Village Hall was filled to capacity with people who had driven from nearby villages. The vicar, then ninety-eight, launched the book. The older people of the village had tremendous pride in their local hero. In the front row four old women aged between 101-103 years wiped away the tears as Coryate's letter to his mother was read. His various letters from India appeared in Samuel Purchas' *Pilgrimes*. In this particular letter Coryate boasted of his audience with the Mogul Emperor, Jehangir, at which he claimed to have delivered an oration in Persian, the official language of the Mogul court:

> I might both procure unto my selfe accesse unto the King, and be able to expresse my mind unto him about the matter for the which I should have occasion to discourse with him. These were the reasons that moved me so long to tarry at the Mogols Court, during which time, I abode in the house of the English Merchants, my deare Countrimen, not spending one little piece of money either for dyet, washing, lodging, or any other thing. And as for the Persian tongue, which I studyed very earnestly, I attayned to that reasonable skill, and that in a few moneths, that I made an Oration unto the King before many of his Nobles, in that language, and after I had ended the same, discoursed with his Majestie also in that tongue very readily and familiarly.

Sir Thomas Roe's chaplain, Edward Terry who had shared both a tent and a room with Coryate in India wrote on the 'itch of Fame which engaged this man to the undertakings of those very hard, and long, and dangerous Travels'. He added that Coryate was 'so covetous, so ambitious of praise, that he would hear and endure more of it than he could in any measure deserve.'

It was, therefore, not entirely inconceivable that Coryate, despite the long and ardous journey and terrible illhealth, believed that he would finish his book on India and return home to his mother. He was certain his book would bring him fame; he would die in Odcombe and be buried in a splendid tomb made of marble. The air was pure in Odcombe, Thomas Coryate had proudly proclaimed, as was its water. People here lived to be very old. Only Coryate had died young in Surat.

~

On our first trip to Somerset, Coryate's Odcombe stirred Dom enough to write this poem:

ODCOMBE

Sunlight leapt up in summer; each bird alive
was calling you in welcome to the combes
and brought you to my England as it once
was: Sunday bells and smells, pink villagers
smiling from stiles to ask us how we were.
The rabbits ran where Coryate had once been.
and planes left trails over the last long men
and the stone circles and hawthorn hedges.

This was temporary, I knew. I wasn't well,
trapped between proffered pity and the pain.
I would have shown you Somerset if I could
but stayed indoors in a deep leather chair.
Still, not a bad day; down the flowered lane,
Coryate awaited me; and you were there.

Dom wasn't well. The oncologist had given him three months to live but he had survived for over four years. I remembered the day we had gone to the doctor. 'Two months at most, perhaps three, the cancer had metastasized,' he said candidly. 'We will have to surgically remove the tumor; it will sour and ulcerate soon.'

At a bar nearby Dom said to the waiter, 'The doctor just told me that I am dying. Get me a stiff vodka.' He raised his glass to toast the lump in his neck. 'Here's to Gorky,' he said and gulped down the entire contents of the glass. Some weeks later as we drove to the hospital Dom touched Gorky. 'He's been living with me all these days. I feel sad to let him go.'

~

In the coming months Dom grew weak and wistful. For what was left of his time depression cramped his mind; ghosts of friends lost and the memory of his dead mother unsettled him. Guilt and regret troubled his mind. On his behest, I took Dom to an astrologer. We had interviewed her for a book we wrote together some years ago. He asked her if his death would be painful. He was one of the few blessed with *ichamaran*, she told him—*the wish of death*. He would feel pain only to the extent he could bear, and whenever he wished to be gone death would hurry to him.

'I have to go,' he said to me next morning. His eyes were forlorn as he spoke aloud words from a poem he had written a long time ago:

How many years? I do not care to count.
Time is no longer generous and free.
Soon he and I will settle our account,
For, to be honest, it is he who's won.

~

I got Dom a large fish tank and filled it with a variety of fish. He liked a pair of rare blue spotted gold fish most of all. One of them died. In grief, the widowed gold fish lost her colour, and this saddened Dom. He said, 'I have thought of a name for her. I am going to call her Gorky.' He got a can of Chinese bloodworms for Gorky that evening. 'This is high protein. Now, she's going to live longer than me,' he said.

How long? Neither of us knew. So I planned the remnants of his life and he planned his dying.

One morning he took me to his family grave. He was deep in thought. 'No, not here,' he said shaking his head woefully. 'Don't bury me here.' Then he took me to some of the churches in Bandra. He made enquires, said, 'None of these will do. After six months of rest in my grave, they will move me to a hole in the wall.'

I told him about the old cemetery in Sewri. I had gone there with a friend sometime back. Trees grew tall there and it was peaceful. 'Besides, there are some very old English graves,' I said.

'Splendid. I will have some English corpses for company.' Dom smiled and then he added with a gleam in his eye, 'If you ask me, I would like to be buried in Odcombe. Its air and waters will bring me the rest I need.'

Dom chuckled. 'Do you remember in Pragpur, that local guide, Kapoor, he called Coryate, Tom-Corea, and he called me, Dom-Morea. There's a connection between Tom and me! Can't you see?'

~

One morning Dom wanted the fish tank moved to his bedroom. 'When I wake up tomorrow I want to see Gorky.' The tank was too large, I explained. I promised to get him a smaller one. 'Goody. And get a partner for Gorky,' he added.

He called late the next morning. 'Gorky is floating on the top. I think she's dead.' He moaned as though he had lost a dear friend. 'Not long now for me to follow Gorky.'

I tried to quell his gloom. 'We can go out for dinner. I will call some of your friends.

'Super,' he said cheering up. 'I am tired. I think I will take a nap. I will call you in an hour and then we can decide.' He slumbered into a sleep that knew no margins of time.

Dom lay in a rosewood coffin, too small, not for his body, but for the man he grew to be. His face was death-pale, yet peaceful and perhaps even thankful for the final journey. His hands were crossed over his chest. They were porcelain pale and glowing as though the moon had lent them its sheen for the day. I remember staring at his face as he lay there. It had acquired a surreal sort of beauty that comes with the absence of memory. It was creaseless, painless, rid of all guilt and regret.

Dom was buried in the ground in an old cemetery in Sewri. Inscribed on his gravestone were the lines from his poem:

Is there ever an end to this?
I have seen maybe a quarter
of what is suffered by losers,
by winners by those between
I was not intended to rest, but I did.

~

I had written to the vicar of Odcombe and asked if he would bury the earth from Dom's grave in the cemetery at the back of the old church. It was Dom's last wish, I wrote. I had packed fistfuls of earth from his grave in the casing of a chocolate box. This time I wasn't even going to seek permission to smuggle the soil into the UK.

On reaching Odcombe I went to visit the vicar, handed over the box of earth to him. I remembered only too clearly when Dom and I were last here. The vicar had invited us to tea. Dom had pictured that afternoon in a poem:

TEA WITH THE VICAR

The vicar is 96; his wife died last year
in a traffic accident. We met her once.
Now his daughter tells us the tragedies
in her own life, smiles, offers us all tea
and after this chaste liquid's been imbibed,
smoked trout, plum cake, and Cheddar cheese:
the fattening victuals of the local tribe.
But before this, everyone else says grace

for us, that we shall be happy in all ways.
Very curiously, all of them seem to mean it.

You wander like Alice in the garden, the flowers
fill it with delicate English colours, their slight
fragrances reach the nostrils, the light is about
right for a photograph and a kind of ecstasy
enters and fills me as your heartshaped face is
etched forever by a Nikon lens on Somerset.

Perched on Ham Hill, Coryate's cadaver eyes me.

On 19 July 2004, Dom's friends drove down from London to Mason's Arms, the only pub in Odcombe. Dom had drunk here only a year ago in memory of Thomas Coryate. With glasses raised we drank to Dom's memory.

The memorial service was held in the church. The ancient organ had been dusted and an old organist who had been located in East Coker played Dom's favorite pieces of music. The vicar performed the service interspersed with psalms, which we sang. In the front lawn just outside the main door to the church, he sprinkled the earth from Dom's grave. 'This earth smells of chocolate,' he remarked with a chuckle. On top of the earth we placed the Jaisalmer memorial stone, which I had brought with me from Mumbai.

The vicar blessed the resting place. 'He came here to write about our Thomas Coryate, whom we had forgotten,' he said with a hand raised to the exuberant July sky, 'and now through Dom may we remember our Tom always.'

It was Dom's birthday that day. It was a good party. I wished he had been there.

—*Sarayu Srivatsa*
April, 2023

Acknowledgements

We spent three years researching and writing this book in various parts of India where Thomas Coryate travelled, as well as in London and Somerset where he lived many years of his life. We wouldn't have been able to do it if we hadn't received the continual help and support of the British Council and the Taj Mahal Group of Hotels. We are grateful to them, and in particular to our friends Ratan Tata and Paul Smith in Mumbai, and Edmund Marsden in Delhi.

We would also like to thank Standard Chartered Bank, IDFC, the Reliance Group of companies and Air India for their assistance, and our friends Vasant Raj Pandit and Jaithirth Rao for encouragement and timely help.

Many people helped us in many ways, and we owe them more than we can repay. We thank the Holiday Inn, Agra, Judge's Court, Pragpur, Jagat Singh Palace, Pushkar, Marriott Welcom Hotel, Delhi, the Madhya Pradesh Tourism Development Corporation as well as Professor Irfan Habib, Professor Simon Digby, Mukesh Ambani, Ravi Dubey, Farhat Jamal and Rabindra Seth.

ALSO IN SPEAKING TIGER BY DOM MORAES

GONE AWAY
AN INDIAN JOURNAL

'Entertaining, intelligent, irreverent [and] unexpected.'
—E.M. Forster

One of the most unconventional travelogues ever written, *Gone Away* covers three months of Dom Moraes' life spent in the subcontinent at the time of the Chinese incursions on the Tibetan border in 1959. In that short time, a remarkable number of memorable things happened to him, some of them the sort of fantastic situations that could only enmesh a poet, perhaps only a young poet—a visit to a speak-easy in Bombay; an interview with Nehru and an hour spent closeted with the Dalai Lama in Delhi; and a meeting with the great Nepalese poet, Devkota, whom he found already laid out to die by the side of the holy river Basumati. After a short stay in Calcutta, where he tried, with limited success, to investigate the lives of prostitutes, he went up to Sikkim, the north-eastern border state into which no visiting writer had been allowed for almost a year. Having made his way by jeep right up to the frontier, he ran into a Chinese detachment and was shot at, but escaped to safety.

Full of humour, felicity of phrase and oddity of behaviour, *Gone Away* communicates the special excitement of the traveller on every page. Unforgettably funny is the account of the Sikkimese soccer match played in an impenetrable mist and involving the loss of several footballs kicked over an adjoining cliff. Yet, though humour and irreverence prevail through the pages, this is a book which catches and holds the mood of modern India and illuminates as much as it entertains.

MY SON'S FATHER
AN AUTOBIOGRAPHY

'A minor classic.'
—Stephen Spender

The first in Dom Moraes' trilogy of autobiographies, *My Son's Father* is a coming of age account of growing up in Bombay and Oxbridge of the 1950s, by a man who has been called the poet of his generation.

Dom Moraes' childhood in Bombay was as privileged as it was lonely—peopled by his father's frequent absences. As he says in the opening lines, 'Missing my father is my first real memory of him.' It was also a time of conflicted emotions and, frequently, terror. As Moraes' beautiful mother, Beryl, sank gradually from neurosis to madness, she swung between smothering the young Dom with love, and subjecting him to a variety of bizarre and sometimes violent punishments—a relationship that left him deeply scarred for life.

Travelling with his father, the legendary editor, Frank Moraes, opened up a world of rich experiences for Dom. As editor of *The Times of India*, the elder Moraes introduced his young son to a range of famous and fascinating personalities—from the anthropologist Verrier Elwin and poet Nissim Ezekiel, to Dom's hero, the iconic Stephen Spender—the first person to tell him he was a poet.

London in the mid-fifties introduced Moraes to Soho and its Bohemian ways, to his first love, and to a doomed relationship. Oxford in 1956 was the turning point. Another boyhood hero, W.H. Auden, came to Oxford as visiting professor of poetry, read and liked his poems. With this as inspiration, Moraes finished his first book, *A Beginning—Poems*. He found another love in Judith. With the birth of their son, Francis, Moraes' life seemed at last to be set on an even keel.

With humour, wit and irony, Dom Moraes chronicles the early part of his life in prose that is a sheer delight to read.

NEVER AT HOME
AN AUTOBIOGRAPHY

'A remarkable book... Dom Moraes is a superb writer.'
—S. Krishnan, *The Hindu*

A sequel to *My Son's Father*, *Never at Home* resumes the story of Dom Moraes' extraordinary life.

Beginning with the death of his mother, an abiding, if destructive influence in his life, and ending with his success as a man of letters, *Never at Home* recounts the most significant events in the later life of Dom Moraes. It includes his greatest triumph: winning the Hawthornden Prize as a nineteen-year-old poet at Oxford, and becoming the toast of literary England.

Looking back at the years that follow, Moraes tells of his marriage to the beautiful actress Leela Naidu, of his son's childhood, his increasing fame as a writer and his experiences as a journalist that took him to places as far-flung as Bhutan, Chile, Vietnam, Israel and Zaire. Every place he visited and every relationship he entered into left a deep impression on him, but none ever held him. Neither at home in the West he had left behind nor the East to which he returned. We leave Dom Moraes as a figure waiting for peace, and a place he can call home.